MW00571794

My name is

Lola

ALBERTA

"When Ted moved us all
to Canada for 'one year,'
we never knew what a
difference it would make."
— LOLA, APRIL 2012

TEXAS

THE WEST SERIES

Aritha van Herk, Series Editor

ISSN 1922-6519 (Print) ISSN 1925-587X (Online)

This series focuses on creative non-fiction that explores our sense of place in the West - how we define ourselves as Westerners and what impact we have on the world around us. Essays, biographies, memoirs, and insights into Western Canadian life and experience are highlighted.

No. 1 · **Looking Back: Canadian Women's Prairie Memoirs and Intersections of Culture, History, and Identity** S. Leigh Matthews

No. 2 · **Catch the Gleam: Mount Royal, From College to University, 1910–2009** Donald N. Baker

No. 3 · **Always an Adventure: An Autobiography** Hugh A. Dempsey

No. 4 · **Promoters, Planters, and Pioneers: The Course and Context of Belgian Settlement in Western Canada** Cornelius J. Jaenen

No. 5 · **Happyland: A History of the "Dirty Thirties" in Saskatchewan, 1914–1937** Curtis R. McManus

No. 6 · **My Name is Lola** Lola Rozsa, as told to and written by Susie Sparks

My name is

Lola

For Joan,

As Lola always said, "the value of my life is measured by the richness of my friendships,"

Susie Sparks

UNIVERSITY OF
CALGARY
PRESS

BY LOLA ROZSA

AS TOLD TO AND WRITTEN BY SUSIE SPARKS

THE WEST SERIES
ISSN 1922-6519 (Print) ISSN 1925-587X (Online)

University of Calgary Press
2500 University Drive NW
Calgary, Alberta
Canada T2N 1N4
www.uofcpress.com

LIBRARY AND ARCHIVES CANADA CATALOGUING IN PUBLICATION

Rozsa, Lola, 1920-2012, author
       My name is Lola / by Lola Rozsa ; as told to and written by Susie Sparks.

(The west, ISSN 1922-6519 ; 6)
Includes index.
Issued in print and electronic formats.
ISBN 978-1-55238-719-1 (bound).—ISBN 978-1-55238-735-1 (open access pdf).—
ISBN 978-1-55238-736-8 (distributor pdf).—ISBN 978-1-55238-737-5 (epub).—
ISBN 978-1-55238-738-2 (mobi)

       1. Rozsa, Lola, 1920-2012. 2. Rozsa, Lola, 1920-2012 —Family. 3.
Philanthropists—Alberta—Calgary—Biography. 4. Calgary (Alta.)—Biography. I.
Sparks, Susie, author II. Title. III. Series: West series (Calgary, Alta.) ; 6

FC3697.26.R69A3 2013   971.23'3803092   C2013-906103-7
                                                             C2013-906104-5

The University of Calgary Press acknowledges the support of the Government of Alberta through the Alberta Multimedia Development Fund for our publications. We acknowledge the financial support of the Government of Canada through the Canada Book Fund for our publishing activities. We acknowledge the financial support of the Canada Council for the Arts for our publishing program.

This book has been published with the support of the Rozsa Foundation.

Printed and bound in Canada by Friesens
♻ This book is printed on Sterling Premium paper

Front Cover Image by Lawrence De Pape
Cover design, page design, and typesetting by Melina Cusano

TABLE OF CONTENTS

PREFACE

They said we'd be here a year.

We were living in sub-tropical Baton Rouge, Louisiana, when the call came from Shell's head office. Ted was to relocate to Calgary, Alberta, as Chief Geophysicist. My job was to pack up the kids and the household for yet another move in what had become our no-madic exploration of every promising oilfield across the southwest. Neither of us expected what an amazing adventure would lay ahead.

That was April of 1949. They said we'd be here a year. Fortunately they were wrong.

This is our story. It is written in loving memory of my hus-band, Ted Rozsa, and dedicated to our children, grandchildren, and great-grandchildren, each of whom have been so much a part of the life he built for all of us. He would be proud and grateful to know they are extending his generosity and honouring his legacy.

Lola May (Estes) Rozsa
2012

CHAPTER ONE

The Fabric of Our Lives

The taste of ripe summer strawberries still warm from the rich black earth transports me back to the screened porch of my childhood where I impatiently wait for my turn to crank the ice cream freezer. Fat rain drops hesitantly plopping into the dry dust of late summer reminds me of oncoming gully washers – grateful relief from the dust storms of north Texas. And each time the scent of hot biscuits fresh from the oven wafts over me I'm enveloped once again in Mama's love. I wonder why it is that I can bring back those little distant memories with such pleasure and yet scarcely recall the real hardships we had to endure during those Depression years.

But from the long perspective of my tenth decade, I've decided that it's like looking at a pointillist painting. Stand too close and all I can see is the minutia. Stand back and I understand how the warp and woof of learning and experience have constructed the much-layered and multi-coloured fabric of my years. I see now how the unbroken thread that runs through my life has been a longing to return to those memories of home – a longing for my children and grandchildren to have the opportunity to store up those perfect moments. I see now how those family gatherings around the huge oak table that once belonged to my parents so strongly influenced my own life and shaped the way I would raise my own children. I've always wanted them to experience what seemed like an idyllic childhood and to see how they too have been enveloped in the love of the family that raised me. So I begin this story with a time long before I was born because, as we like to say in Texas, the fruit never falls far from the tree.

We never knew most of our ancestors, of course, but around that big oak table their stories were passed down and became ours, and their values formed the character of those who came after them. And now, because I've just celebrated my ninety-second birthday and have the privilege of the *very* long view of our family's history, I've realized how so much of who we have become was determined by those who came before us.

My mother, Nannie (Morris) Estes, was among the progeny of intrepid English immigrants who arrived in North America long before the Revolutionary War and whose descendants pushed south into Virginia and became tobacco planters. Their descendants, in turn, worked their inherited lands until they were leached out and became worthless, and then they were forced to make decisions that would ultimately determine their futures in tragic times.

Most antebellum Virginians chose to stay in the South, so their children packed up their slaves and household goods and made their way in successive emigrations through the Carolinas into Tennessee and on to Georgia, Alabama, or Mississippi. But *my* two maternal great-grandfathers in Virginia, twenty years prior to the Civil War, freed their slaves and gave them what little land they still owned. And then they loaded their own families into covered wagons and made their way west across the Blue Ridge to Ohio and then to Illinois.

Historians have named this trek out of the Old South the oil-slick migration because extended families travelled together and, as the adult children inevitably married, their spouses and extended families joined them and oozed west and south along with them. But by the time the South seceded in 1860 and the first shots of the Civil War were fired, my formerly Southern ancestors were putting down roots in Illinois, learning to farm corn and to raise horses. And by the time I was old enough to go visit them, there were Alexander,

Morris, Zink, Pinell, and Bennet cousins all living close by. The extended family had, for the most part, stayed together.

My father's forebears, two brothers who emigrated from Italy to the United States in the early nineteenth century, were apparently descended from the notorious d'Este family who were famous for fifteenth-century political intrigue. It's said they were patrons of poets, artists, and scholars, and one of them, Alfanso d'Este, the Duke of Ferrera, was the husband of Lucrezia Borgia.

The brothers settled first in Tennessee, changing their name to Estes. However, by the time their American descendants started their trek to the western frontier, all pretence at aristocracy was lost to the harsh reality of survival in a wild and unforgiving environment. While trying to cross the Missouri River in a wagon train, my great uncle's wagon was swamped, all their possessions were lost, and tragically one of their children was drowned. Nothing remained except to continue, so he and his wife buried their child and kept on.

Grandfather James Estes and his wife Anna (Baron) Estes finally settled in the small prairie community of Grandview, Texas, where he took up farming and she birthed their first child in 1874. That boy, Charles William Estes, would become my father. Three additional children followed in rapid succession, but in 1885 their mother died, leaving eleven-year-old Charles to help his father care for his younger siblings. Undoubtedly this loss was catastrophic for the young family, but Charles had been raised with a strong religious faith and even stronger work ethic so, despite their real poverty, he was still able to attend school sporadically. To help support his family, young Charles packed water, served as a janitor, built fires at the schoolhouse and the church, and served as a clerk and delivery boy and as a day labourer working on farms and ranches. Eventually he was invited to live with relatives residing in Meridian, Texas, and Uncle Jim Robinson, a judge, encouraged him to study using his extensive law library as a lure, and for about six months Charles gave serious consideration to becoming a lawyer.

In the end though, he turned away from the law and attended summer normal school and then taught in the county for three years. My mother loved to tell about what happened when the teenaged teacher took two of his students aside as they arrived at the school obviously not presentable enough to join the rest of the students. Their clothes were dirty, their faces grimy, and their hair uncombed. Charles led them to a washbasin, handed them a bar of soap and a comb, and told them to join the class as soon as they had cleaned up.

However, at the end of the day when these children returned home, their father took exception, and the next morning he rode his mule to the school to confront the young teacher. Belligerently, he shouted toward the school's door, "I sent these chil'ren to school to git larnin,' not to git baths and their hair combed and parted!" But Charles had heard the bully was on his way so he came out to the schoolyard to meet him armed with the axe he used to chop wood for the school's stove. The confrontation was short. From that time on, *every* student arrived at school with face shining and head neatly combed.

When he was twenty-one, Charles resigned his position as school teacher and accepted his true calling. Before his mother died, he had been part of a devout Christian home where the Christian principles lived and taught by their mother formed the character of each of the children. Family lore has it that at the age of six Charles led his younger siblings in a game of camp meeting, insisting that he be the preacher. And by fourteen, he had joined the Cumberland Presbyterians at Old Rock Church near Valley Mills, Texas.

The Cumberland Presbyterians were a break-away sect of the rigidly Calvinist Presbyterians who preached a doctrinaire theology largely incomprehensible to the uneducated people of the frontier. The division, which had started even before the Revolutionary War, culminated with the Second Awakening in about 1800 when unschooled itinerant preachers travelled the sparsely settled frontier collecting people for revivalist camp meetings and river baptisms.

No longer would the Presbyterians be all head and no heart, at least in the South.

Word of mouth spread the news that a preacher would be holding a religious revival meeting and people would start to assemble, some from very far distances, which meant they needed to camp overnight if they were to participate throughout the several days of the revival. In truth, camp meetings were often the best entertainment going. The people on the frontier worked hard to make a barely subsistence living, so if there was any diversion to be had, these farmers jumped at the chance. Some undoubtedly came out of sincere religious devotion; others came out of curiosity. It was the preacher's job to make sure the latter left as born-again believers.

Through the several days of the revival, emotions ran high. Once one speaker exhausted his message, the next would jump up on the stage to take his place so there was virtually non-stop preaching and gospel singing from morning until late at night. People expected to be emotionally overwrought; they sang, they cried, they went into trances and shouted exaltations. It was all about casting out sin and welcoming the Lord into a changed life.

At twenty-one, my father was licensed to preach in the Cumberland Presbyterian Church at Waco, Texas, and immediately began leading revival meetings and gospel-singing, pausing only in August when he was needed to help pick cotton with his brothers and sister. But within a year, the church sent him to Indian Territory, (which became the state of Oklahoma in 1907), and he became the full-time pastor of the Cumberland Church at Davis. He made $25 a month. A hardship pay supplement wouldn't have been out of line, but unfortunately no one seems to have thought of that at the time.

Indian Territory was a dangerous place to be in those days. It was to have been a sanctuary created for all the displaced tribes that President Andrew Jackson had driven off their ancestral lands in the southeast, but that plan was short-lived as wave after wave of white settlers encroached. In the spring of 1899, a United States marshal was murdered, and my father, by then known as Preacher Estes, was assigned to officiate at his funeral. He stood on a tree stump in the Davis Cemetery and quietly delivered a message on law and order. Then, following the service, he enlisted several others to help him patrol the town because he fully expected retaliation. On the following Sunday, Preacher conducted his regular morning worship service with his rifle leaning against the pulpit.

Shortly after, he accepted a call to Indiana to assist with the gospel-singing at revival meetings and stayed to marry Jesse Gayle Morgan, a young music teacher whose home was in Washington. Almost immediately they each decided to enrol at Cumberland University in Tennessee to complete the necessary training to be ordained for the full work of the ministry, and their subsequent adventures in the small parishes of rural Indiana affirmed their calling.

In 1903, their first child, Barron Morgan, was born, and the following summer they brought him home to Texas where Preacher was to lead camp meetings near Meridian. It was a wonderful opportunity to introduce his young wife and son to his family, but tragedy struck a few months later when they returned to Indiana. Their second child, Mary Evangeline, lived less than three weeks after her birth. Then Preacher became very ill with the flu and his fifteen-month-old son developed pneumonia and died within a few days.

It's hard to imagine from our perspective today that such a tragedy could occur, but this was still the medical middle-ages, long before antibiotics and long before we learned to appreciate the necessity of sterile medical instruments. Three years later, when Preacher's wife delivered their third child, she never recovered from the delivery and died when baby John Dillon was only a few months old.

Preacher was left alone to raise his newborn. His own family was far away in Texas and Oklahoma. The ladies of his congregation helped out as they could with the cooking and housekeeping, but that very difficult time forever changed my father. From that point forward, he never permitted any family member to go through any health crisis alone. It was an ethic that would be indelibly imprinted in all of us.

CHAPTER TWO

Building a Gospel of Works

Preacher was a big man with a big personality. Hugely charismatic with a wonderful tenor voice, Preacher loved to sing, whether he was leading a gospel service, singing in a men's quartet or glee club, or simply singing with his family around the table. People of all ages flocked to him and his enthusiasm was so infectious he was a natural-born builder – both literally and figuratively. His boundlessly optimistic attitude toward the future made him the one that churches sought out to refresh the spirit of lagging congregations, and whenever an evangelical revival was proposed, Preacher was the one they called upon.

It so happened that a little church in Grandview, Illinois, proposed a revival to be held in October, 1908. The town was so tiny that its two churches, the Presbyterians and the Methodists, had only half-time pastors and shared the town's choir in services held every other Sunday. Fortunately, Miss Nannie Eleanor Morris had been taught to play the pump organ, so she served as the Methodist organist and alto voice. She was equally at home as a Presbyterian though and was quite willing to fill in at the Presbyterian revival when Preacher arrived for the autumn revival meeting. Even though Nannie was also teaching school in Dudley, she made herself available during the evenings for the services and, as the week progressed, a romance blossomed.

After the revival, Preacher returned to Indiana and commenced a letter-writing campaign that, by February, finally persuaded Nannie to become his wife. They married at the Presbyterian church in Grandview and then boarded the train to Fort Branch, Indiana, where Nannie had to learn to run a manse and be a preacher's wife — as well as mother to two-year-old John Dillon. In the next ten years, she would give birth to another son and five daughters, including me, the youngest. But that was the easy part. It was much more difficult to learn to adjust to the constant change as new congregations came calling.

It was a hard lesson to learn. Nannie was terribly homesick and had bound herself to the Fort Branch congregation in a kindred tie, making the congregation her surrogate family. In fact, they *were* like family. Preachers didn't make much money so congregants were expected to contribute not only their tithe for the preacher's salary but also a portion of their produce, whether from farms or kitchen gardens, not to mention their occasional spare chickens and maybe a lamb or two come spring. They would donate their own children's outgrown clothing and shoes and, in times of illness or childbirth, women from the congregation would make themselves available to help.

But preachers were expected to move along to new, and hopefully more prosperous, congregations every few years. It would keep the message fresh and provide new professional challenges for the preachers. Nonetheless, it created painful separations for their wives and families as they had to make new friends in new schools and towns.

Barely six months into their marriage, Preacher announced that he had accepted a call to a badly neglected church in Newton, Illinois. He and Nannie and little John Dillon arrived to find a small frame church desperately in need of repair, with a tiny manse tucked under the windows of the church, equally decrepit. Worse, there were fewer than three dozen people left in the congregation, most of them women. But, to their credit, these women had already announced a reawakening and had had preliminary plans drawn up for the construction of a new church building. It was Preacher's job to sell the idea to potential new congregants, and he set to his task each Sunday morning with compelling messages wrapped in his sermons and supported by scripture.

Miraculously, in less than two years he was able to hand the keys to the new church to the trustees and, during the dedication service, an additional $5,000 was raised to help defray most of the indebtedness against the new building. *The Newton Monitor* for November 22, 1911, reported, "Much credit must be given the pastor, Rev. Charles W. Estes, who first proposed the erection of a modern church … and who, since the first shovel of dirt was thrown, has been constantly 'on the job.' His optimistic view of conditions encouraged the membership, and if any became blue or despondent, a short conference with the pastor would at once shorten the length of the discouraged one's face."

The Newton church was the first of many. Preacher discovered he genuinely enjoyed the challenge and seemed to be a builder at heart, and his success story spread rapidly to other congregations in Illinois. Nannie learned to pack up the household and move to a new location pretty efficiently, but she never really got over the painful separations from her church families. However, it was at one of their early postings in Illinois that they discovered the old oak table, forgotten by its owners and left in a dusty attic. It would become the focal point of our family, the place where all of us convened for breakfast and family worship, the table where the children did their homework, it was the site of our family sing-alongs, a place for story-telling and, best of all, a table big enough and with enough extra leaves to feed thirty people. It was the table that grew with our family, the table that gathered the family back together when there were inevitable separations. And even now, even though that table has long since disappeared, it remains in my memory as the heart of my family.

Today, most preachers are paid living wages and are expected to rent or buy their own homes, but a hundred years ago that wasn't the case. In those days, the manse was customarily owned by the church. And it was usually within walking distance of the church, if not, indeed, cheek-by-jowl. Life, for a preacher's family, was lived very much in a fish bowl.

For the Estes family of six children, it was a very busy fish bowl indeed. Preacher had already built several new churches in Indiana and Illinois, and along the way he had acquired a Jersey cow that accompanied the family with every move, so it was quite a contingent that arrived at their posting in Hobart, Oklahoma in 1918. The little town in southwestern Oklahoma had once been part of the Indian Reservation, and Preacher was to organize Sunday afternoon services for the Kiowa communities on the outskirts of town, as well.

The assignment in Hobart included a large modern church with a tiny six-room cottage hardly more than a holler from the church door, but the people were friendly and enthusiastically welcoming. There was an active Ladies' Aid Society, and the relatively prosperous congregation had even assembled a fine orchestra composed of the young people of the church. But 1918 and 1919 were unfortunately the flu years in the southwest.

The Spanish flu epidemic had taken hold during the final years of World War I. The war didn't cause the flu, but it spread like wildfire in the close confines of the soldiers' quarters. The massive troop movements across Europe accelerated its contagion, and it was lethal to the young men whose immune systems were already weakened by battle fatigue. It was first diagnosed in the United States in January of 1918 at Fort Riley, Kansas, just north of Oklahoma, and it had a strange affinity for young adults. Unlike most other strains of the flu that attack babies and weakened old people, the Spanish flu went after young healthy adults, so Preacher, along with many others in Hobart, worked tirelessly locating and isolating the sick, organizing soup kitchens, and nursing those who didn't die outright. Before it was finally over in 1919, the Spanish flu had affected 28 per cent of the population of the United States and had killed more than 500,000 people.

If there was any good to come out of that terrible time, Preacher always said that it at least offered him the opportunity to meet everyone in Hobart and to offer them his service.

It wasn't long after that he and five other professional men organized the first Rotary Club in southwestern Oklahoma, and he became such an enthusiastic Rotarian that he once stopped the train in Mt. Carmel, Illinois when he was on his way to Indiana to conduct a funeral so that he wouldn't miss his obligatory Thursday Rotary meeting. The secretary of the Mt. Carmel Rotary Club met him at the depot, rushed him to the meeting place so he could register his attendance, and then hurried him back to the waiting train.

However, the ladies of the congregation evidently prevailed upon him to attend more closely to his wife than to his fellow Rotarians the evening I came into the world. Not only did they insist that my mother should have his seventh child delivered in an actual hospital, rather than at home where the others had been born, they also suggested that my father's place should be with her, not at his Rotary meeting. It was the only Rotary meeting he ever missed.

The ladies continued to watch over my mother as she recovered, and they presented her with a beautiful, handcrafted Tennessee cedar chest as a baby gift. I kept it until I was able to give it to my oldest daughter, and I hope that she, one day, will hand it along to hers.

I came along in 1920 and don't really remember very much about Hobart, but my mother often spoke fondly of her Oklahoma church family. She described how the congregation eventually purchased a new manse, a larger two-storey frame house across the alley from the church with a lovely garden and a chicken house. It had huge maple and locust trees shading the lawn where she and Preacher hosted garden parties and outdoor revivals on the hot summer evenings.

The new manse wasn't quite as close to the church as the other had been, but it was definitely close enough for the congregation to know what the seven Estes children were up to at any time of the day or night. In truth, Preacher didn't really need any congregational monitoring because we all knew his rules and knew not to expect there would be any relaxation at any time. No child of his would play cards, use tobacco in any form, drink alcohol, go to dances, or blaspheme or use profane or rough language. Nor, by the way, would his daughters bob their hair.

One of my brothers, however, stepped out of line just one time – in extremely trying circumstances – and regretted it immediately. One very cold January night, the furnace in the church overheated and the sparks from the chimney set fire to the roof of the church just as the worshipers were arriving to attend an evening service. As the fire quickly leaped out of control, my brother was heard to exclaim, "Golly!" My father hauled him into the house and washed his mouth out with soap.

My brother never forgot that lesson, and the rest of us were forever respectful – not only of my father's cure for rough language – but also for how quickly a fire could devour a huge building. Sadly, it wouldn't be long before we would learn that lesson again, with far more tragic results.

Both Mama and Papa lived their faith and understood their Christian calling to minister to *all* those in need, not just to their own church family, so my father's ministry to the Kiowa people in the surrounding county was important to them both. He at first held Sunday evening church services in the Kiowa County Court House, but his congregation quickly outgrew the courtroom and he started a new building campaign in 1924, which his congregation back in Hobart enthusiastically supported, and they did what they could to help.

On Christmas Eve, the young people of the Hobart Church went out to the little Kiowa school in Babbs Switch bringing gifts for all the children wrapped in cotton batting to look as though they were covered in snow. Then they hauled in a huge cedar tree and decorated it with Christmas ornaments and tipped each branch with tiny candles. Santa was to appear later in the evening with Christmas treats for everyone so, as that time drew near, the building filled with families excited to sing carols and celebrate the joy of the season.

My mother later told the story. As the program got underway, Santa entered on cue but as he began lifting the gifts from the Christmas tree one of the tiny candles came in contact with the cotton trim on his costume and caught fire. Then, in an attempt to smother the flame, someone accidentally upset the tree spreading the blaze to the gifts and decorations and in panic the more than two hundred assembled people raced to the exit.

There was no other escape. The windows were permanently screened with heavy hail-screen wire nailed to the outside, and the only exit was at the rear of the building. Its door opened *into* the room. Very few were able to get out in time; bodies were piled like cordwood near that door.

Word reached my father just as he was leaving the Christmas Eve service at the Hobart church to go out to Babbs Switch to join the Christmas celebration. The fire whistle blew along with all the church bells in town summoning help. But when he arrived, it was all over.

Thirty-six bodies burned almost beyond recognition were re-covered from the smouldering ashes. The still-living victims of the fire were rushed to the hospitals in the area and were lined up in the corridors awaiting treatment. Preacher, along with many other volunteers, worked through the night and throughout Christmas Day trying to identify the dead. The women of Hobart turned their Christmas feasts into meals for the volunteers and the turkey car-casses into soup for the injured. And finally, the women organized to work in shifts at the hospitals and to help the families broken by the tragedy.

My father directed the mass funeral service for the twenty-one victims who were never able to be positively identified. Among them were members of the Babbs Christian Endeavor Society, the youth group that had been organized by the school teacher from

Hobart, a member of my father's church. She died with them that terrible night.

As a result of that tragedy new legislation was passed regarding the construction of public buildings that would in the future require numerous well-marked exits with doors opening to the outside and windows unimpeded by permanent barriers of any kind. Preacher led the building of a new, fireproof brick school to replace the little frame one that had burned and, at its dedication, he spoke with tears streaming, still grieving.

It's hard to imagine now, but in those days life was heartbreakingly precarious. Just as there were no building regulations to protect the citizens of those little towns, public health wasn't an issue for most town councils until much later in the twentieth century.

One summer afternoon when I was about five, it was decided that the Junior Christian Endeavor Society in the church, along with their adult leaders, would have a picnic in the town park and, much to my delight, I was taken along by my two older sisters. By evening, thirteen of the fifteen children who had been present at the picnic became ill, apparently from drinking contaminated water from the public fountain.

The next day, my sisters and I complained of headaches, and from that time forward we got progressively sicker. By the second week, all three of us were delirious and running dangerously high temperatures. We were diagnosed with typhoid fever — an often-fatal illness in the era before antibiotics — and my mother was nursing the three of us round the clock.

The women of the congregation realized she couldn't handle it alone, so they organized a twenty-four-hour-a-day rotating army of nursing care. They dragged our beds out to the screened sleeping porch where we could catch a breeze through those sweltering summer nights. I have no memory of it now, but we were told that these good women stationed themselves at our beds, wrapping us in cold wet sheets to bring down the fevers, trading them for fresh sheets as our hot little bodies dried them out. But despite their unrelenting care, our temperatures kept rising until finally, after six or seven weeks, the fevers broke and we slowly began to recover. Fortunately, none of us developed encephalitis or septicaemia, but I remember that my hair all fell out and I was so weak that I had to learn to walk all over again.

When I think back on those times, I mostly remember my mother as the one who affirmed her faith each day with her work in the church and with her family. In her mind, the family was the core of civil society. The family's values defined the individual and the individual transmitted those values to the extended family and then to his larger community. There were no social safety nets; the family was critical to survival, literally and figuratively. In hard times the extended family would step in to help in a crisis, and when family wasn't enough the church or community family would take over – just as it had during the typhoid fever episode. To choose to step away from the family unit was unthinkable.

Nannie and Preacher were truly a team in a time and a place where most Southerners would have said that a woman's place is in her home and, like her children, better seen than heard. But in my mother's case, her role was to organize the women of the church who, in all honesty, kept it going. She would step up to serve in his place when Preacher was ill or was called out of town on church business. She not only sang in the choir but could fill in for the organist if necessary, and very frequently she attended church conferences as a delegate. The Cumberland Church, far ahead of other denominations, gave women meaningful roles in its administration allowing them to study for the ministry as well as to lead congregations, and Nannie was never reluctant to take any role that would be helpful to Preacher's flock.

My older brothers and sisters, of course, all sang in the choir and were expected to be active in their schools' sports teams, the band, and drama and glee clubs as well, and Preacher and Nannie were very present in the parent teacher associations. We were all expected to be self-sufficient, and the older ones were trained to fill in for Nannie if she was called away for any reason, so there wasn't much time for any of us to whine, "I'm sooo bored!"

No, there was no radio or TV or Internet, but we always had a cow that needed milking. And my brother Charlie and I discovered we could make a little spending money if we'd bottle the milk our family didn't need. We'd load up the wagon with that surplus and could make five cents a bottle selling milk to our neighbours. Of course, Mama wasn't at all sure that our first attempts at commerce were made out of the goodness of our hearts. We seemed to be leaning dangerously close to a decidedly unchristian greed to satisfy our appetite for sweet treats. "But," as she often said, "sometimes you just have to let the milk settle a little before the cream will rise to the top."

Mama kept us busy. In the unlikely event that any of us had any spare time, there were undoubtedly people in the congregation who could use our help. And, even as a very little girl, I was expected to help Papa at his revivals and camp meetings, so I learned to climb up on the stage to help him lead the gospel-singing.

Preacher may have been the disciplinarian, but my mother knew how to temper his rules by telling us stories and indulging our silly pranks and the playful tricks we played on one another. She always had faith that the cream would eventually rise and that sooner or later we'd all turn out just fine. I often wonder if she ever really knew what an important role model she was for all of us, particularly for the five girls in our family.

Women's liberation? It would never have crossed my mother's mind. She was free to do exactly as she chose, and she chose to be my father's partner in life and to lead God's work in the church.

Women's suffrage? Well, that was a contentious issue. Generally in the South of her youth, men and women both were reluctant to expose the gentler sex to the ugly political arena. But yes, she would support it if the female vote would help to make necessary change in public policy. She had seen what alcohol could do to good men. Too much of the trouble that many families had to suffer was caused by strong drink. Prohibiting its manufacture and sale, she reasoned, could only be good for society as a whole and for individual well-being. She would support both female suffrage and Prohibition, as would my father.

In Oklahoma, the road to Prohibition had been pretty clearly paved by the women of the National American Woman Suffrage Association. They had established chapters in the little towns across the state to encourage women to lobby for the vote to ensure that the dry laws instituted in Indian Territory prior to 1907 remained. And, when they joined forces with the Women's Christian Temperance Union, they were a formidable force for wholesale reform. Singing "Lips that touch liquor will never touch mine," Oklahoma women mobilized. They pasted posters on farm wagons, they picketed in parades and shouted from soap boxes at county fairs and even at revival meetings. And they made it happen; in 1918, Oklahoma extended the vote to women.

Thanks to voters like Preacher and Nannie, Oklahoma did, indeed, stay dry, at least under the law. But ironically, the resulting boom in illegal moonshine caused plenty of upstanding citizens to support the bootleggers, who were at least bringing them good Canadian whiskey so they wouldn't have to drink homemade moonshine. As Will Rogers famously predicted, "Oklahomans will vote dry as long as they can stagger to the polls." And they did — until 1984.

Nannie and Preacher, however, were lifelong prohibitionists. They stayed in Hobart for eight years. Their church family was always welcome at the manse along with anyone else who happened by. Everyone was invited to take a place at the big oak table where the food was warm and ample, and, if they were asked to sing with the family after supper, it was a small price to pay for the hospitality offered to them.

Preacher was invited to give the commencement sermon at the Hobart High School seven of the eight years they were there and, after they moved away, he was called back to officiate at the funerals of fifty people – those from that congregation and others who had simply been friends of the family.

In 1926, though, another congregation came calling. A new church needed building. I was to become a Texan.

CHAPTER THREE

Growing Up in Texas

Papa always said that it was healthy for a congregation to move along to a new preacher every few years so, when he got the call from the folks in McKinney, he was ready for a new challenge.

We had a big Dodge touring car in the late '20s, large enough to fit the nine of us, but the drive from Hobart to McKinney, Texas, still took two days after factoring in visits with some of the Estes clan along the way. I remember driving up to the manse, which sat side by side with the church on Mounts Avenue. The church itself dated back to Civil War days and was in pretty rough shape, but the manse seemed big enough for all of us and the bag swing hanging from a branch of a huge shade tree in the front yard let me know there was a special place for me in the new house.

We piled out of the car to be greeted by the church elders, and Mama was relieved to discover they had stocked our new home with staples piled high in the pantry. Southern hospitality is no myth; the ladies of the congregation brought endless covered dishes to last until we could get unpacked and settled, so the transition to a new church family was almost seamless.

McKinney is only thirty-two miles north of Dallas, so today it's undoubtedly a bedroom community of the big city, but back then it still had the flavour of an old Texas county seat. It had been named for Collin McKinney, one of the signers of the Texas Declaration of Independence in 1836. In 1845, the Republic of Texas was annexed to the United States, staunchly committed to slavery, with its constitution making illegal the unauthorized emancipation of slaves by their owners. William Davis heard the news and emigrated out of the Old South looking for fertile land. He brought his slaves along anticipating the day in the not-too-distant future when the extension of slavery would be the issue that would bring Thomas Jefferson's version of equal rights to a reckoning. Reasoning, I suppose, that north Texas was far enough away from the hotbed of political fisticuffs over the states' rights issue, he bought 3,000 acres of good cotton-growing land and, in 1849, donated 120 of them for a town site. Ten years later, on the eve of the Civil War, the population of McKinney had ballooned to almost 5,000.

When we arrived in 1928, it was still full of cotton mills and gins, and it had a cotton compress and a cottonseed oil mill along with banks, schools, newspapers, and, dating from the 1880s, an opera house. Before long, Preacher was deep into plans for a new church building, and he moved the congregation to the theatre downtown so he could get to work clearing the site. Evidently Papa was just as successful cheering along the building campaign in McKinney as he had been in previous communities, and the McKinney congregation quickly pledged the full $25,000 it would take to build a two-storey brick church, complete with classrooms, a women's parlour, a large dining room, and a private study.

That didn't mean, though, that it would be impervious to the cyclones that roared through north Texas every spring. There was a good-size storm cellar between the manse and the church, and we came to recognize that when the chickens in the yard started getting restless in the approaching wind, we'd better head for that cellar. Remembering those times now I suppose I was frightened, but my father would always say that we were being watched over and cared for, so it really just seemed like an exciting adventure.

When they excavated for the foundation of the new church, the builders pushed the rich black soil over toward our house and, to our delight, it was absolutely full of tarantulas. We had a grand old time catching them in fruit jars but when Nannie discovered what we'd done, she about had a fit. So naturally my sisters and I blamed it on brother Charlie.

Poor Charlie, surrounded by five yattering sisters; can you imagine anything worse? Even our mother knew how difficult we all were – with the exception of our oldest sister, Lillian, that is. She was the perfect one. Whenever Mama was at the end of her patience with us, she used to shout, "Eleanor! You girls! Settle down!" I suspect she thought of Lillian as her ally in the fray, so Eleanor, the next in line, must be the one leading us astray.

We had left our oldest brother, John Dillon, back in Hobart to complete his final year of high school. My two oldest sisters, also of high school age, were starting to chafe a little against Papa's old fashioned sense of fashion. This was the era of the flapper girls with their bobbed hair, short skirts, and decidedly progressive behaviour. Shockingly, big-city girls back East were reported smoking cigarettes, drinking bootleg whiskey, and dancing the Charleston – showing their legs in a most unladylike way.

And then along came Cousin Willie. Preacher's first cousin lived in Itasca, Texas, not an exceptionally cosmopolitan town, but the day she arrived for a visit all sorts of havoc ensued. She was pretty and vivacious and we were all fascinated by her, especially when she decided my big sisters needed a twentieth-century makeover that would include cutting their long braided hair.

It may have been a small matter to Cousin Willie, but to us it was revolutionary. For generations of Southern women, hair was *never* cut. Little girls wore pig tails tied with ribbons until their hair grew long enough to braid and wind into neat little buns atop their heads. Sun bonnets were meant to keep the sun off their faces, of course, but they were also helpful in keeping their hair clean in the days when baths never came more than once a week. Those braids tucked into their sun hats kept their hair relatively dust free and up off their necks in the hot summer.

Bob their hair? Mama was probably flabbergasted when Willie suggested it, but she really couldn't think of a good reason to forbid it. Besides, what could Papa say? Willie was *his* cousin, after all. Truth be told, Mama was always more reasonable than Papa when it came to this sort of thing so, maybe a *little* reluctantly, she gave her permission – provided Papa agreed. However, when Willie armed herself with the shears, my sister Eleanor was the only one brave enough to go ahead with it. Lillian decided she wasn't quite ready to take the big step into the flapper age. But, bobbed or not, the older girls were growing up, and it wouldn't be long before they would need to go off to college, and that needed very careful consideration.

Much to my father's credit, there was never any thought given to educating only the boys. In her youth, my mother had been a teacher and, since the day she and Papa married, she was a full partner in their ministry. Of course, the girls would go to college. The only problem was figuring out how to afford to educate all seven of us.

Preacher successfully completed the big new church in McKinney, so was again looking for new challenges, but this time he needed to be even more strategic in his choice of locations. He would need to look for a congregation in a college town. And he would have to find a college sympathetic to the economic realities of a preacher's life.

Coincidentally, an old friend of Preacher's had situated in St. Louis and was serving as Secretary to the Presbyterian Synod. He began writing to my father about a congregation without a pastor in Rolla, Missouri – deep in the lushly wooded hills of the Ozark Mountains. The congregation wanted a new building and the farmers hidden back in the hollers needed a missionary. "Oh, and one more thing," the search committee wrote, "Rolla is the home of the Missouri School of Mines and Metallurgy. The town really needs someone who can work with the college boys as well as the farmers in the hills and hollers." When Preacher got out the map to see just where Rolla might be, the deal was settled; it was halfway between Nannie's family in Illinois and his back in Texas.

I was seven years old by this time and had not yet gone to school since, in Texas, children started later. As you can imagine though, as the youngest of seven, I had lots of siblings to read with me so I was more than ready to start school the September we arrived in Rolla.

It was a typical little college town. The college dated from 1870, and it was even then regarded as an excellent engineering school. The manse was surrounded by fraternity houses as well as by the junior and senior high schools. But even better, it had a big porch swing where the college boys who came courting my older sisters could pass the time until Nannie called them in to join us for supper.

She kept a permanent soup pot on the back of the stove and could throw in a handful of beans or fix hot biscuits any time of the day or night, should anyone – students or hobos off the trains – unexpectedly arrive. They must have thought the home cookin' was worth the price because they inevitably stayed to dry dishes or bring in the wash from the clothesline or carry in the coal we'd collected from the tracks on the edge of town. Times were tough in Rolla, and if the trains lost a little coal passing through town, we could certainly find a use for it in our furnace.

The congregation in Rolla was so good to us I don't ever remember actually going to a grocery store. Even though they must have been suffering too, the ladies of the church always came up with an extra chicken or some produce from their gardens. Being the youngest of five girls, I'm sure I never had anything new to wear until I was practically grown. But in Rolla, the hand-me-downs were at least new to me.

None of us ever had any walkin'-around money; I'm sure the concept of an allowance would have been totally incomprehensible to any of us, my parents included. Whatever salary my father made could scarcely cover the necessities and, though my mother played an equal part in their ministry, she received no salary at all. However, when weddings were held at the manse, rather than at the church, it usually meant the father of the bride was carrying a shotgun to make sure the groom did the right thing by his daughter. In those cases, it was the custom for the father of the bride to pay the preacher's wife a small gratuity in thanks for providing the little wedding party with coffee and cake following the young couple's wedding. Nannie would discretely tuck the money away in her bodice to use for her necessities, pinning it to the chemise under her dress for safekeeping until she found a worthwhile place to spend it. Hence, the term 'pin money.'

I started the first grade a head taller than my fellow students, but when the teacher realized I could already read and print, I was bumped up to join the rest of the students who were my own age. It was there that I had my acting debut. It was my big chance. I was to play the starring role in the Thanksgiving pageant, the Princess of the Harvest. I rehearsed and rehearsed, but on the night of the performance as I marched proudly across the stage, my head held at an imperious angle no doubt, I fell over my own feet and dropped the ear of corn I was supposed to present to the Indian brave. I was mortified. I still cringe remembering it.

Still though, the most fun to be had was back at home where the engineering students gathered around the table so my sisters could help them with their English assignments. Or, if the older girls weren't around, they'd pull taffy or make cocoa with me. In the summer, our neighbour would let me have a bowl of strawberries if I'd weed the patch for him, and then we'd all line up on the porch to take turns cranking the handle on the ice cream freezer. To this day, I can close my eyes and summon the taste of those sweet summer strawberries and anticipate the frosty-cold strawberry ice cream that followed.

And when Papa bought our first radio, even more visitors came by. They'd gather around to listen to the political conventions, or the football games and music broadcasts from Chicago. The radio was a big Atwater Kent table model, complete with headphones, and it would become a focal point in our family in the coming years, but, when he bought it, no one could have anticipated how the news of the world coming to us via that radio would soon consume *all* our attention.

Preacher was busy trying to inspire the dwindling Rolla congregation to remodel and enlarge their little church to accommodate the burgeoning population of young people, but money was scarce, so a minimal amount of work was completed. At the same time though, Preacher, accompanied by a Presbyterian missionary who carried along a portable pump organ, was making twice monthly trips into the Ozark hollers to preach at revivals.

Nannie once wrote, "Sometimes they would drive their Model T up damp creek beds and walk the rest of the way to hold a mission class on the front porch of some woodsman's home where the folks from miles around would be waiting." Those little ramshackle frame houses with sleeping lofts for the children and steeply pitched roofs overhanging extended front porches still dot the Ozark hills. In the autumn, you can spot them through the trees as you travel the back roads through the soft orange, yellow, and pinkish-red pastels of the falling leaves.

Back then, most of the people living in the hollers were very poor, but few ever showed much interest in moving down to the bottom where twentieth-century trade and commerce was taking place. Their ancestors were the Scotch-Irish who, for the most part, arrived in the Old South in the early 1700s skipping over the Virginia planter class altogether. They went straight into the mountains of Appalachia, and some worked their way south and west as far as the Ozarks of Missouri and Arkansas. Those who stayed there liked the relative isolation of the hills and hollers and had no inclination to move along. They could hunt deer, and most kept a few hogs for slaughter in the fall so they could make it through the winter. And no doubt there were some who kept a still to make moonshine for a little extra income.

There are all kinds of academic studies on their distinctive mountain speech. Some say it's eighteenth-century Old English but, speaking as one whose own Southern accent has caused comment,

I can pretty confidently say that everyone in the South speaks with *some* kind of regional dialect. The only difference is that those who have chosen to stay relatively isolated tend to keep their distinctive speech patterns a little more true to their origins.

Whereas a Texan might say, "Y'all come; I'm fixin' to fry up a chicken. Maggie, you might could bring a salad," a woman from the Ozark hills inviting her friends from a neighbouring holler to supper on a chilly evening would say, "You'ns come along and bring wraps fer yer young'uns. I liketa froze last night; it's airish over yonder and it's commencin' to snow."

Rolla is still a little college town and the school, although re-named, is still regarded as one of the best schools of science and engineering in the Midwest. We were all sorry to leave Rolla, but I think it eventually dawned on Papa that his five girls weren't likely to be interested in what this particular college was offering. He would have to find another college town – one that hopefully offered courses in the liberal arts. So we left Lillian and Eleanor behind, one in St. Louis in nurses training and the other at Missouri Valley College, and made our way back to Texas where a new congregation was waiting.

CHAPTER FOUR

If It Rains

It was 1930. Denton, Texas. The stock market had crashed the previous October. Herbert Hoover was president of the United States, and more than half of all Americans were living below the minimum subsistence level. Unemployment had hit 8.7 per cent. Within three years, it would climb to almost 25 per cent. And in Texas, the Depression arrived with unrelenting dust storms.

You've heard of the butterfly effect, I'm sure. I was only ten years old in 1930, and chaos theory was still to come, but I certainly witnessed its effects throughout that decade. What happened, from hindsight, was a predictable disaster. During World War I, more than a million acres of grassland in the Midwest were ploughed under and planted with crops to feed the armed forces. Then, throughout the decade of the '20s, when agriculture prices bottomed out and farmers were desperate to increase their incomes, they over-ploughed and over-planted those fields – fields that were really suited only for grazing.

It wasn't that they didn't know about soil conservation. The federal government, in fact, encouraged them to conserve soil fertility and stop erosion, but times were so bad during the Depression that landowners couldn't afford to use methods that might not pay for several years, and tenant farmers weren't about to invest any money in land they didn't own.

Then the butterfly metaphorically beat its wings at the precise moment to cause climatic chaos. And along came the drought, the heat, and the catastrophic wind.

When I was twelve, fourteen monster dust storms were recorded on the Plains. The next year, there were thirty-four, the following year thirty-eight. The year I was fourteen, it was estimated that 100 million acres of farmland lost all or most of the topsoil to the winds. At its worst, you could see the storm roiling in like a giant black tsunami hundreds of feet high — mercilessly intent on drowning everything in its path. Despite the heat of summer, doors and windows had to be sealed tight against the wind and dust. Still, butter sitting uncovered on the table would accumulate a fine coat of dirt.

We certainly weren't the hardest hit. Denton is in northeast Texas, north of Dallas. The worst storms were in the west Texas panhandle where farmers reported that the wind sucked the seeds out of the ground and blew tumbleweeds into fences so the dust drifted up and covered the fencerows altogether. A reporter from the Associated Press covered one of those storms. "We live with the dust, eat it, sleep with it, watch it strip us of possessions and the hope of possessions. It is becoming Real. Three little words achingly familiar on the Western farmer's tongue rule life in the dust bowl of the continent — if it rains."

The dust storms. They're what I remember most vividly about the years of the Depression, not the financial hardships. In fact, when we arrived in Denton on Labour Day in 1930, we were all thrilled to see a beautiful two-storey frame house surrounded by a huge shaded porch on two sides and an upstairs sleeping balcony for the hot humid summer nights. The manse sat high on a hill near the junior and senior high schools, and it was only about six blocks from downtown Denton. Plus, it was fully five blocks away from Cumberland Presbyterian Church where Papa would be preaching. Strangely though, we all kind of missed living next door to the church. However, with nine rooms and two baths, it was far and away our most luxuriously large home. Preacher had a study, we all had huge bedrooms and the screened-in back porch easily had room for the old oak table as well as Mama's sewing machine. That house still stands – it's been designated as an historic site.

Denton was, and still is, a college town. Home to both the University of North Texas and Texas Women's University, it was the ideal location for our family of students ready to launch into professional careers. My sister Eleanor – with her recently bobbed hair – enrolled in the University of North Texas, then a normal school for the education of teachers, and the rest of the younger brood enrolled in Denton's public schools.

The porch swing had pretty much constant traffic in the five years we lived in Denton because the youth group of the church enlarged considerably with the arrival of our family and the subsequent arrival of the university students who gravitated to Nannie's hospitality. It was obvious that the old church with its red brick sanctuary was in need of major renovations, but, unfortunately, prior to October, 1929, the recklessly optimistic congregation had purchased a large corner lot with the idea of rebuilding. By the time Preacher received their call, it was clear to everyone that the debt they had incurred to purchase that lot would have to be cleared before any rebuilding or even renovations could be considered.

Once again, it was the women of the church who rose to the challenge. And, to their credit, they did accomplish a small miracle. Their fundraising campaign was successful in meeting many of the payments that first year. But the three-inch headlines that had announced the economic meltdown in 1929 only got worse as time passed. In 1931, unemployment rose to almost 16 per cent. Preacher announced to the congregation that he would take a voluntary reduction in salary provided that the same amount of money would be pledged on the new location.

But regular tithing continued to fall off and Sunday offerings were small. With three children in college and two in high school, Preacher's sacrifice didn't go unnoticed, but the simple fact was that the congregation couldn't possibly contribute money they didn't have. How Mama did it I'll never know, but every Sunday at noon the old oak table was still stretched to its limit to include all the visitors who happened by.

One time, Kiowa Chief Lone Wolf arrived unexpectedly. He had become a great friend of Preacher during his ministry back in Oklahoma and had come to Texas to donate a buffalo to the McKinney Zoo. He had named it Charles William Estes in honour of my father.

Most of the visitors, though, were students. During the most desperate years of the Depression, as many as nineteen students lived with my family for at least a part of their school terms, and three of them boarded for the duration of their enrolments. Standing back in the fullness of time, what I remember most about those students gathered around the table was the fun we all had, not whether we actually had enough to eat. We laughed; we all sang. My sisters Ann and Eleanor both had beautiful alto voices and Ruth and I, the youngest of the brood, were sopranos. Both Charlie and Papa were tenors, and Mama could accompany us on either the piano or the organ and my oldest brother, John Dillon, played the trumpet, so music was virtually the required final course of every mealtime gathering. It hardly mattered what kind of music was requested, we could do it all: popular music, rounds, parodies. And naturally we all sang in the church choir, too.

I went through junior and senior high school in Denton. All of us were busy with our extracurricular sports and clubs, and, by this time, it also fell to me to help my brother Charlie look after Lady, Papa's Jersey cow. I suspect that Lady played a pretty important role in our family during those years in Denton. Free milk would have been an enormous bonus for a family as large as ours during those years. I do know that Preacher joined the Denton Farm Club and the Jersey Cattle Club, even serving as its president for one term. He volunteered much of his time with the 4-H Club for the boys and girls in the county, undoubtedly knowing how important it was for the children to learn to be successful farmers in those difficult times.

And, increasingly, Mama's lessons in self-sufficiency were also paying off as my older sisters were often called upon to run the household when both she and Preacher had to be away on church business. Of course, this isn't to say that it exactly ran like clockwork on those occasions. Like any household full of teenagers, if given a chance to slack off a little we were all more than willing to cut corners. And, since our brother Charlie was the only male in residence by this time, he had to take the brunt of his sisters' teasing, and most of the time he was pretty good-natured about it – at least until the Lydia Pinkham poisoning episode.

For anyone under the age of ninety, I should probably preface this story by explaining who and what Lydia Pinkham and her medicinal compound were. Oddly enough, Lydia (Estes) Pinkham was a distant relative, although I doubt my parents ever knew of that connection. Her ancestry in the United States dated from the seventeenth century, and her family had been neighbours and close friends of William Lloyd Garrison, the famous Massachusetts abolitionist. So, by the time Lydia was a teenager, she was actively involved in the anti-slavery movement and she also became a strong advocate for the early feminist movement.

The other thing you should know about Lydia is that, like most women of her era, she had very little faith in the medical establishment, and she was inclined to brew up folk remedies for various minor ailments, particularly if those ailments related to female complaints. So, mixing up a little pleurisy root, life root, fenugreek, unicorn root, and black cohosh, plus a generous dollop of alcohol, Lydia cooked up a recipe that brought nineteenth-century women flocking to her door. And by the twentieth century, Lydia Pinkham's Compound was being very successfully marketed from a family business out of a Salem, Massachusetts, factory.

I'm sure the only reason that Mama kept the pantry stocked with Lydia Pinkham's was because our family of teenage girls went through multiple bottles of her tonic every month and it was cheaper to buy it in bulk. However, my sisters and I preferred it served chilled.

Nannie and Preacher happened to be away at a church meeting one particular October, so, for reasons of efficiency, one of us girls decided to pour two or three little bottles of Lydia Pinkham's into a milk bottle and keep it in the icebox.

Charlie, meanwhile, was at football practice.

Later that afternoon, he came home hot and thirsty and headed immediately for the icebox and, like all teenage boys, never bothered to find a glass. He went straight for the milk bottle, upended it, and drank the entire quart before he realized we were all watching him in horror.

From that time on, whenever we wanted to get his goat we called him Charlene. And, many years later when we told that story on him, he called us Charlie's Angels. (I think he was being sarcastic.) Yes, we were all growing up. During our time in Denton, four of my brothers and sisters graduated from college and two had married.

By this time, I was old enough to get in on the dating intrigue but, as you can imagine, Papa's rules about courting were pretty discouraging and more than a few young beaus were scared off the front porch before they could even make it through the front door. My older sister Ruth was smitten with young Tom Mitchell, but *he* was so frightened of my father that the closest he ever made it to the house was a half-block down the street where he hid behind a fence hoping that Ruth might venture outside. Finally, I was enlisted to be the lookout. When I heard Tom whistle for Ruth, my job was to divert Papa's attention while she slipped out the door to meet him. It worked pretty well, I guess; they were married a short time later and lived happily ever after.

It was 1935 when Preacher finally had to admit to himself that the economy couldn't support a rebuilding campaign, even though the congregation was growing at a healthy rate. However, there were the diehard optimists among the flock who insisted that God would provide – eventually – if only he could hang on and continue to serve. But Preacher was no longer a young man. At sixty-one, he had had to face the reality that the Denton church couldn't financially support an assistant minister to help him attend to the increasing needs of the congregants and that he would have to find a smaller church. I would be starting my senior year of high school in the fall.

But, as I like to say, I am nothing if not resilient. Even I know how devastating it can be for adolescents to be uprooted from all their friends, but this had been a fact of life for all of us as we grew up. It wasn't that we learned to keep our friendships superficial. It was simply that we learned to make friends quickly and to appreciate each new adventure as it came. And too, every congregation had been an extended family who genuinely cared for us so we learned to expect the best of everyone we met.

Preacher responded to a call from a tiny, struggling church in Eastland, Texas, in the spring of 1935. Most of the congregation had moved away during the worst years of the Depression, but Franklin D. Roosevelt had been elected and almost immediately established make-work projects like the Civilian Conservation Corps, the Public Works Administration, and the Tennessee Valley Authority, at least slowing the free-fall of the plummeting economy. For the first time since 1929, there was a glimmer of hope and Preacher's irrepressible optimism returned. His job this time would be to rebuild the congregation, not the church.

Eastland is a tiny town about a hundred miles southwest of Fort Worth, and its claim to fame when we were there – even now, I suspect – is a horny toad by the name of Old Rip. What's a horny toad, you ask? Well, if you're going to believe this story, I'd better tell you a little bit about Texas horny toads.

First, horny toads aren't toads at all. They're not even frogs. They're lizards. And yes, they do have horns as well as scales. They're basically lazy. They're sit-and-wait predators. And if they're threatened they're likely to just sit there, hoping you'll not notice, I guess.

But if you're some especially hungry critter and insist on poking at it, it'll puff up its body to make it look hornier and thus more difficult for you to swallow. Should you appear to be considering pursuing this course of action anyway, the horny toad will then do something really disgusting. It'll squirt blood at you from its eyes.

The story goes that, when the Eastland courthouse was built in 1897, a horny toad was sealed in the cornerstone of the building. In 1928, when the current courthouse was being built, the original cornerstone was opened and Old Rip was found alive and undoubtedly spitting mad.

You can imagine the notoriety. I'm told he toured the country and, at the pinnacle of his fame, he received a formal audience with President Calvin Coolidge. However, the celebrity and the paparazzi were apparently too much for Old Rip and he died in 1929. His remains were placed in a glass casket and, should you wish a visitation, they say you can find him on view in the present courthouse.

Remind me to tell you about Jackalopes later on....

Eastland was unfortunately a boom-and-bust town from the word go. It had been sparsely settled by immigrants from the Old South just prior to the Civil War, but there were still frequent raids by the Comanche and Kiowa people and, following the war, the population declined. Eventually though, more settlers came to plant corn and cotton and to build cattle ranches, and, by the early 1880s, the railroad arrived. Then, with a booming cotton economy in the early twentieth century, it looked like Eastland was the place to bank on. However, a boll weevil infestation crippled the cotton production in about 1916 and farmers left the area in droves.

Then, almost on the heels of the last departing cotton farmer, a major oil discovery was made in Eastland county, which set off a spectacular boom that lasted into the 1920s. Thousands of speculators and wildcatters flooded into the area; the population more than doubled. But by 1922 the oil boom was over, too.

Nothing however, was more devastating to Eastland than the Depression. Cotton production came to a virtual standstill, oil production barely limped along, but when Preacher arrived in Eastland, he was very interested in learning more about the oil industry. Little did any of us know that this education would be so influential in how my life would eventually turn out. But I'm getting ahead of myself.

What Preacher discovered in 1935 was a tiny church growing smaller with every passing month. There was no question of growing the congregation. People were leaving and no new Presbyterians were arriving. No one could make a living in Eastland. We were all very poor. I worked at the drug store after school and cleaned houses and babysat to make a little extra money. But I also played basketball and sang in the church choir and was in the drama club. And I met lots of boys who played football, so I was a pretty typical high school girl and enjoyed every minute of my senior year at Eastland High.

After I graduated in 1936, I went back to Denton to start college. However, I was only able to complete one semester because Papa simply couldn't afford to pay any additional tuition and I had to drop out. I came back to Eastland and starting working odd jobs as I could find them because I really wanted to be a nurse and I hoped I could save a little money and maybe get to return to college one day.

Papa faced the fact that the Eastland congregation could no longer support a minister, and he began to consider other options. He had never strayed far from his roots as an itinerant preacher, and the Depression years had seen the resurgence of evangelical revival tent meetings across the South, so when he heard that the famous Gipsy Smith was coming to preach at Abilene, he made a special trip to see him.

Smith was born in a tent in England to a gypsy family that made its living on the road selling notions from their wagon. His father was in and out of jail for various petty offences and while there met a prison chaplain who introduced him to the gospel, and eventually the whole family converted at a Salvation Army mission meeting. As the boy grew in the faith, he taught himself to read and write and began preaching and singing the gospel on street corners and mission halls. Soon, huge crowds were assembling to hear him and, within a very short time, he began conducting evangelical crusades around the world, which eventually brought him to Abilene, Texas, in 1936.

Papa never forgot hearing Gipsy Smith. Had he been a younger man, I have no doubt he would have gone back to tent meeting evangelism after that powerful experience. In the end though, Preacher decided to accept the call to a church in Winters, Texas.

If we thought the dust storms had been bad in Denton, we were in for a real shock.

CHAPTER FIVE

Hello, Charlie!

Winters is south and west of Abilene, deep in the dust bowl. By the time we arrived, the wind had blown pretty much non-stop for years. Worse was the drought. By 1937, the water table had about dried up and what remained was so alkaline it was barely potable. It tasted dreadful and it was so hard that it was virtually impossible to make suds to wash our clothes.

The large red brick church was in good repair though, and certainly adequate for the members of the congregation, as was the manse for our now-small family of four. I went to work that year cleaning houses again and picking up odd jobs when I could, while my older sister was able to go back to Denton to resume college in preparation for a career as a teacher. But my father was obviously in failing health. He was diagnosed with pernicious anemia, although frequent transfusions seemed to revive him and he struggled on as he always had.

The manse had a wide expanse of lawn between the house and the church so, just as they had at all their postings, Nannie and Preacher resumed the summer garden parties for the town's children. And there were lots of them because Winters attracted great numbers of migrant workers at cotton-picking time. White, brown, and black children roamed the streets while their parents worked, and some inevitably got into trouble. Occasionally Mama and Papa were called for assistance with " delinquent" children, but both of them knew that most of those troubles could be solved with a little extra attention. On Saturday afternoons, Mama would set out the ice-cream freezer and bake a big cake, and the children would assemble on the lawn to sing and play games and have fun.

The garden parties attracted so many children that eventually Preacher and Nannie needed a little extra help on Saturday afternoons so they appealed to the congregation for volunteers. A few stepped up but, much to Preacher's consternation, most made it clear that they opposed "missionary work." They had hired him to devote his time and effort to the older members of the congregation, not for those "dirty youngsters." It was this point of friction between Preacher and the elders of the church that eventually caused him to resign.

For the first time, he had no specific plans. But, as we all knew, God opens new windows of opportunity when these things happen. Indeed, Preacher was so unconcerned about our financial future that he had negotiated with the powers that be at Trinity University in Waxahachie to enrol me as a full-time student and to give me some financial aid. Plus he was able to find a job for me waiting tables in the dining hall that would help defray the other costs of my education, so in September, 1938, I started back to school. And almost immediately, a new future opened for Nannie and Preacher when he was offered the pulpit at Whitesboro, Texas. They would serve there very happily for the next ten years.

Trinity University is now in San Antonio and it's still affiliated with the Presbyterian Church. In 1938, however, Trinity was in Waxahachie, where it had been since 1902 when it had relocated from its first site in Tehuacana, Texas. It had been founded there shortly after the end of the Civil War by a few hardy pioneers from Cumberland Church stock who believed in the transformative power of higher education, particularly if that education was absorbed far from the hurley-burley of commerce and other distractions. As a result, students and faculty could only get to the university by horse-drawn carriage from the train station that was six miles away.

It was a co-educational school from the beginning, undoubtedly thanks to its Cumberland Presbyterian roots, and it had a decidedly progressive curriculum with literary societies for discussion and debate. However, by the turn of the twentieth century, it was clear to the trustees that the school would have to relocate to survive, and it was moved to Waxahachie – a cotton-growing community and a railroad hub. At the time, it was one of only four accredited colleges in Texas.

Unfortunately though, the fall-out of the 1929 financial disaster meant that colleges were devastated by declining enrolments and, by the time I arrived at Trinity in 1938, it had been placed on probation and was teetering on the brink of collapse. Whether I even knew that at the time, I don't remember now. I just knew I was very lucky indeed to be starting over. After two years of general studies, I could work toward my nursing degree – as I'd always hoped.

Mama and Papa drove me to Waxahachie, and we all sat down with the dean to decide which, if any, of the courses I'd taken back in Denton would transfer, and where I might be most useful. I enrolled as a freshman, was assigned to a room in Drane Hall, and met my roommate, and was then introduced to Mr. and Mrs. Ragsdale, who ran the dining hall. They were happy to give me a job waiting tables for the freshmen boys and told me I would work five days a week and wrap sandwiches for them on the weekend. That sounded like a walk in the park! I was used to feeding the multitudes, thanks to Mama's hospitality, so a couple of tables of freshman boys was hardly worth notice. So, after settling me in my dorm, Nannie and Preacher left me to get acquainted with Waxahachie.

It was a pretty little town – hilly and full of Victorian gingerbread houses back in those days – and the town square had several churches and a beautiful big stone courthouse surrounded by huge oak trees. Today, it's a charming southern suburb of Dallas that has retained the old-fashioned feel of a wholesome little community, where pink-blossoming crape myrtles shade wide neighbourly streets.

Most of the students when I was there were kids from cotton farmer families because Waxahachie is right in the middle of the nation's largest cotton-producing county. And even though it was a place where everyone knew and looked after everyone else, the college made sure the freshmen weren't corrupted by the exposure to big-city living too quickly. For the first semester, we weren't even allowed to *speak* to upperclassmen. And of course all the girls were strictly monitored by Mrs. Dodd, the Drane Hall matron, who locked the doors at ten every night. However, despite all the safeguards, I'm proud to say I was almost immediately chastised for contravening the rule against fraternizing with upperclassmen.

The tradition at Trinity was that during the first semester the second-year students broke in the freshmen with harmless little pranks and reminded us that we were too insignificant to address them in any way. But one of the sophomore girls recognized that I probably wouldn't be easily cowed into submission and decided that she should show me the ropes. She and her upperclassman friends piled me into her car and we drove downtown to a dance hall that I'm *sure* Preacher would never have approved of.

And that's where I met Charlie. He was not only an upperclassman, two years older than I, he was also a football player. And even better, he knew how to dance. And, by the end of that evening, so did I. Charlie walked me back to Drane Hall and Mrs. Dodd met me at the door. Not only was I late, I was obviously guilty of a more serious infraction and she let me know it with both barrels.

I obviously wasn't much dissuaded by her lecture because Charlie and I, by the end of that first semester, were an item, despite the fact that I was very busy with both classes and work in the dining hall. I took the usual array of first-year courses: English, biology, French, public speaking, and bible. I confess that I flunked biology that first semester, but I still maintain that it was because the prof mumbled and I couldn't understand a word he said. However, I loved English and was good at it.

Classes started at nine o'clock, but I was up by six to get into my waitress uniform and to the dining hall by seven so I could be finished cleaning up in time for my first class. I remember that the meals were pretty Spartan, especially for all those ravenously hungry farm boys. But we always had lots of fried okra and beans of every size, shape and colour.

I'd dash back to the dining hall at noon to wait lunch tables, then run back to be in time for my afternoon classes. Most days, there'd be a little break between the last class and the dinner hour, so, if Charlie didn't have football practice, we'd sit on the lawn under a shade tree to study together. And on the days he did, I was there to watch because I'd joined the Lancerettes, the pep squad for the college teams.

We hung around with three or four other couples that year. They called us Sweet-Lola-and-Charlie, and if we happened to be late coming home, my roommate would make sure our dorm room window was unlatched so I could climb in. Once in a while, Charlie would borrow a car so he could take me home to visit his family in Ferris, Texas, and at Christmas we drove to Whitesboro to visit mine, and I suppose everyone thought we were destined for marriage once we graduated.

In fact, when we both came back for the second semester, we took up just where we'd left off and spent even more time together since Charlie wasn't playing football and, as centre, he was too big to play basketball. However, my sister Eleanor was due to have her second baby in March and Preacher insisted that I leave school and go to help her through her recovery in Denton. Charlie dutifully borrowed a car and drove me up there then back again to Trinity a few weeks later.

I worked hard to catch up with the classes I'd missed, so by the end of term in June, I was ready to go work at a Christian camp in north Texas that Preacher had found for me. Charlie had to go to football camp at Trinity all summer, so our plan was for me to finish at the camp and join Charlie back at Trinity where I could work in the dining room to support myself. That way, we could see one another in the evenings, and we'd both be ready to start the fall semester together. Charlie would be a senior.

Then Preacher interfered again! This time he announced that I'd have to spend the rest of the summer with my sister Ann in Olney, Texas. She was a new bride and needed some company. I was devastated. Why did I need to babysit Ann? She was a grown woman; she could find her own friends. I wanted to go back to Trinity to be with Charlie. But there was no way I could budge Preacher once he got an idea into his head.

So very sadly, I wrote to Charlie and let him know – then packed my bag for Olney. It didn't take much packing in those days; I only owned four hand-me-down dresses plus a skirt and sweater. Anyway, Preacher picked me up for a very stony-silent drive out west to deposit me at Ann and Ed's home.

Olney was a little nondescript town in north central Texas until the 1920s when a plentiful supply of crude oil was discovered, and then a huge gusher blew in and oil derricks sprouted like weeds. The town, shall we say, got to be pretty rough and tumble after that. Saloons and houses of ill repute took root almost as fast as the oil derricks until a law-and-order sheriff arrived to whip things into control, so by the time I arrived it was pretty dull.

Ann and Ed took pity on me as I moped around missing Charlie with nothing to do, so finally, on June 24, they planned a bridge party to introduce me to some of their friends. I, of course, had never dealt a hand of cards in my life because that was another of Preacher's taboos, but Ed said that he'd met a fellow on one of the seismic crews outside of town who knew how to play and would teach me....

CHAPTER SIX

Hello, Ted! Goodbye, Charlie

Truth be told, I felt like Papa had sent me to Ann as an ambassador to try to make peace. After she graduated from college in 1936, Ann got a job at a newspaper in Olney and almost immediately met Ed who was employed at the Chevrolet garage across the street from her office. They fell madly in love and, when she came home to Eastland for Thanksgiving that year, she brought him along and introduced him to Preacher saying, "This is Ed Hart, my husband."

Papa and Mama were shattered. No one in our family had been married by anyone other than our father – and for very good reason. He would have taken it as a personal affront. He made that very clear to everyone, including Ann and Ed. But, since then, three years had passed and he was beginning to mellow. It was time to let bygones be bygones.

I'm sure I wasn't exactly pouting about having to entertain some friend of Ed. It's not like me to sulk. But I'm equally sure I wasn't looking forward to a boring evening with my sister's married-couples' bridge club. Oh well, once they all leave, I probably thought, it'll be something I can write about in tonight's letter to Charlie.

I helped Ann fix something for her share of the supper and changed my dress just as people started arriving, so I didn't really have time to worry about learning some stupid card game. All the couples arrived, introductions were made, and Ann and I set up the tables and arranged a buffet of all the pot luck contributions, and then there was another knock at the door.

Ed went to answer it and, just as I turned around, in walked the spitting image of Errol Flynn! He had come straight from the golf course – tall, tan, dark curly hair, beautiful beige suit, yellow tie. "Lola," said Ed, "I'd like you to meet my friend Ted Rozsa. He's working on Shell's seismic crew just outside of town and he tells me he's a bridge player."

I was instantly smitten. If I looked the way I felt I'm sure I was lit up like a Christmas tree! He was drop-dead gorgeous and gentlemanly enough not to laugh at me at least until I regained my composure.

The rest of the evening still remains a blur. We were paired off as partners for the bridge game, and he must have coached me through it somehow because at the end of the evening we had won first prize. All I can tell you is that after everyone left, I didn't write that letter to Charlie.

And I didn't write one the next night ... or the night after that. I was far too busy agonizing over whether I would hear from Ted again. But finally he called and asked me to a picture show, which for the life of me I can't remember. And the next night he said that a couple he knew was planning a fried chicken supper that evening and would I like to go with him. Would I? You bet I would!

Then Charlie called me. When was I coming back to Waxahachie? I'm embarrassed to admit that I didn't have the courage to tell him that it was looking less and less likely that it would be any time soon.

Ted was finding reasons to come into town almost every evening, and then he started telling me about the nomadic life the crew had to live, picking up and moving camp every few weeks, until finally one night, as we sat in his car, he proposed to me.

Before I had a chance to accept, he immediately launched into all the reasons I *shouldn't* marry him. Life on a seismic crew is unsettled ... it's a constant migration from one dusty little community to the next ... the move to a new field comes every six weeks or three months … you'll have to live in close quarters with the crew who'll become your family with all the good and bad that goes with it whether you want that or not … and there'll be times you'll have to spend alone because I'll be on fields where there's no housing of any kind … and …

I had to interrupt him to say yes. I was nineteen. Ted was twenty-four.

He wanted to go to Oklahoma and get married without any fuss, but I told him my father was only now getting over the fact that Ann and Ed had run off and married without any fuss. "It's not that a big wedding is something that I've ever wanted, but Papa would *never* recover if I ran off, too." We'd have to go home to Whitesboro so Ted could meet my parents.

I finally wrote to Charlie.

And then I discovered that Ted wasn't just another pretty face. He was the superstar second son of John and Lela Rozsa and had been raised with a work ethic that wouldn't quit. His father, a Hungarian immigrant, had arrived at Ellis Island a penniless young man with dreams of starting over in a place where he could make a life for himself without the entanglements of the past. He worked for a time in New York apprenticing as a barber to learn the trade and shortly thereafter took his new skill with him to Grand Rapids, Michigan. John married Lela and they had three children while they lived in a little house on the outskirts of town. The house had no electricity, and their children learned to read by lantern light. In time, though, the city's movers and shakers offered him an opportunity to own his own barbershop in the Businessmen's Club, and John learned from them what it would take for his American children to get a foothold on the ladder to financial success.

From the beginning, it was made perfectly clear to Ted that he would go to university, and that he would have to win a scholarship to do so. He finished at the top of his high school class in 1933. And, since he graduated with straight A's, Michigan Tech awarded him a scholarship that would cover his tuition. However, Tech was in Houghton so he would have to feed and house himself for four years because his family was unable to cover his living costs. It didn't take him long to look at the projected budget and decide the only thing that would work would be to complete the four years of the BSc in Geological Engineering in two and a half years. So he did – after taking a 50 per cent overload just because he was interested in anything they had to teach him. He graduated with highest honours in 1936.

Stacked up against Ted Rozsa, I'm afraid Errol Flynn was coming in a distant second.

When I think about it now, I realize that Preacher's instincts were probably acting in cahoots with a higher power that knew very well I wasn't meant to be the wife of a Texas cotton farmer. Every time he whisked me away from Trinity and put some distance between Charlie and me, I think Preacher knew that eventually I'd discover that myself. So when I wrote to my parents and told them about Ted and our plans to come to Whitesboro in hope that Papa would marry us, I'm pretty sure Preacher offered up a quick prayer of thanks. And when he shook Ted's hand, he told him he knew I had made the right choice.

In 1936 jobs were scarce in the industrial north. More accurately, there was 40 per cent unemployment in Michigan, so jobs weren't just scarce, they simply didn't exist. But in Oklahoma, the 1927 boom in petroleum production had reached 762,000 barrels a day, making it the nation's largest producer. The huge discoveries had everyone excited and Shell Oil was intent on extending their exploration to other possibly productive sites in the state. So Ted, with the ink barely dry on his diploma, let Shell know he'd like to be one of those explorers.

Oil seeps had been recognized in Oklahoma long before white settlers came along, but as soon as they arrived they learned to scoop it up to fuel their lamps and collect dip oil to treat their cattle for ticks. However, it didn't take long for some enterprising entrepreneur to exploit its real potential, and the first commercial well was drilled in 1896 near Bartlesville. That discovery well, as well as many subsequent finds, spurred the movement toward statehood in 1907 and brought Oklahoma into the club of major worldwide oil producers.

Shell hired Ted to be a computer on a seismic crew. His job was to help prepare the records and make the computations for surface corrections, for elevation corrections, and for weathering corrections. What they were doing was teaching him the trade because he'd had no experience or education in the field at all and, being the kind of student who is constantly seeking out new information, Ted thrived on it.

What Ted had been trying to tell me, though, was that life in those little boomlets scattered across Oklahoma was less than genteel. Usually, what happened was that some wildcatter would ignite a frenzy of speculation that would unleash the swarming bands of land-hungry land men trying to devour the most promising plays. Then the roustabouts would arrive to start drilling, but, with nowhere to live, they'd be sleeping in any vacant room, whether that room was in a hotel, a tent, somebody's barn, or in the local pool hall under the table.

Most of those migrant workers were unmarried, of course, so to attend to their recreational needs, business men and women followed close on their heels to set up establishments to cater to those necessities, and saloons and bawdy houses sprang up like tumbleweeds in spring. If the boom was short-lived, civilizing forces like schools, churches, and local law enforcement never had a chance to take root. However, if fortune smiled and the discovery proved bountiful, families arrived and brought along stability and those little hamlets became towns. Unfortunately, that didn't always happen and many boomlets died almost as quickly as they were born.

Ted was twenty-one and determined to put his education to work. He joined the other young guys on one of Shell's seismic crews in the summer of 1936. Their job was to relate the geophysics to the geology. Everything was to be done out in the field.

Unemployment in the United States, though beginning to improve, was still almost 17 per cent, and across the Atlantic the news was far worse. In violation of the Treaty of Versailles, Germany had just reoccupied the Rhineland. Ted was very glad to have a job. He had a chance to learn fast and an opportunity to be in on some of the technological innovations that would revolutionize the industry.

Three years later when he proposed, he was a seasoned veteran of exploration seismology and knew exactly what he was offering me. In fact, no sooner had I written to Mama and Papa letting them know we'd like to be married in Whitesboro at Christmas, Ted got word that his crew would be relocating to Stroud, Oklahoma, right away. My heart sank; I knew it was too far away for us to see one another – at least on a daily basis. And practically in the next mail, his father wrote to say he couldn't leave his barbershop during the Christmas season, and would it be possible for us to get married during the Labour Day weekend instead? The only practical thing to do was to get married and go to Stroud together. We had known each other barely three weeks.

We said our goodbyes to Ann and Ed, who were looking mighty smug about their matchmaking talents, and Ted drove me to Whitesboro to meet my parents. They obviously approved of *this* choice and Preacher and Ted established both a respect and fondness for one another that would last a lifetime. But almost immediately Ted hit the road for Stroud, leaving me in Whitesboro to pine away the few weeks left until Labour Day and our wedding.

I went to work in a dry goods store in Whitesboro to keep busy since weddings in those days most definitely didn't require any planning. There was no money to spend on all the accoutrements that seem required for a wedding today, so I was at best looking forward to gathering my family for a simple service and a farewell lunch. But that was before our church family and friends in Denton got word.

We all felt that Denton, where we had spent the happiest growing-up years, would be home. It was where our parents dreamed of perhaps retiring one day, and where all of their children would gravitate for special occasions and, in the best of all worlds, to finally settle – all of us together. So maybe it wasn't really all that surprising when the Denton congregation insisted on throwing me a bridal shower.

And then, on the Friday before Labour Day, everyone started arriving at my parents' home in Whitesboro. Ann was to be my matron of honour, of course, so she and Ed came first, then Mac McKenzie, Ted's closest friend on the seismic crew came to stand as his best man. John and Lela Rozsa, Ted's parents, along with his sister Theresa, drove in on Friday evening, September 1, having just heard that Hitler's fifty-two divisions with some 1.5 million men including six armoured divisions had invaded Poland. For the first time in a very long time, John felt an agonizing kinship to the people he had left behind so long ago, and we all huddled around Papa's radio to hear the relentless updates on the word's inevitable plunge into war.

On Sunday, I'm sure my father preached a very different sermon than he had planned earlier in the week, but at its end he announced from the pulpit that his youngest daughter was being married the next day and he invited the entire congregation to attend. And taking him at his word, they all showed up at the church the next day to help us celebrate my wedding.

Papa had bought me a new outfit and, since it was to be a fall wedding, he reasoned that an autumn dress of rust-coloured wool would be both pretty and appropriate. (Even he knew that one puts away one's white shoes after Labour Day, for heavens sake!) However, since the day of the wedding dawned at 105 degrees and as humid as only east Texas can be at that time of year, that rust-coloured wool dress was pretty limp by the time I had donned my little black hat and orchid corsage for the march down the aisle accompanied by my brother Charlie. Poor Ted was equally overdressed. He had also bought a new serge suit for the occasion – double breasted, back belted.

Worse yet, neither of us had the good sense to change our clothes following the ceremony so we both sweated through the chicken salad and wedding cake luncheon that the ladies of the church served to all of us at the manse. Mercifully, most of the guests left after lunch, and I packed up my little suitcase containing all my worldly goods to start my married life – *still* wearing that cursed wool dress.

You might think our honeymoon was perhaps less than storybook perfect. But let me assure you, by Texas' standards, it couldn't have been better. Ted had to get back to Stroud the next day, so we drove over to Wichita Falls on the way to meet his crew so we could all watch the big high school north/south football game together. Let me just say, in case you don't know about high school football in Texas, this was a *really* big deal!

*Every*body goes to the high school games in Texas: parents, grand-parents, siblings, aunts, uncles, cousins, distant relatives, and totally unrelated fanatics. Normally the games are scheduled on Friday nights, and for years it has been against association rules to permit television coverage of the games because it might affect ticket sales to the games. Back in 1939, of course that wasn't an issue, so the stands were packed on Labour Day Monday when we arrived dressed in our wedding finery. What with the very limp corsage still pinned to my wool dress and my now less-than-perky little hat, it was obvious to everyone that we were newlyweds, so we were subjected to all kinds of attention. And when we got up to leave, everybody seemed to know we were on our way to find a motel.

All I'll say is that *our* storybook wedding ended with a perfect happily-ever-after.

The seven Estes children, Oklahoma, 1920.

Preacher and Nannie Estes with their brood of chicks.

Sweet Lola upon high school graduation.

Lola at Trinity University in Waxahachie, Texas.

Lola at nineteen, wearing her wedding-day finery.

TED, THE GROOM.

CHAPTER SEVEN

And So We Begin

Stroud, Oklahoma. It was everything Ted had warned me about; a tiny hopeful boomlet just south of Tulsa where, in the fall of 1939, the wind was still blowing and the sand was still drifting. Today there are fewer than three thousand people in Stroud, but we arrived not long after Route 66 brought all kinds of rest stop amenities like motels and gas stations and restaurants.

Back in 1915, the legendary outlaw Henry Starr, along with his sidekick Lewis Estes (no relation, I hope), and six other bad guys attempted to rob two of the town's banks simultaneously. But the town heard about the dastardly deed while it was in progress and quickly took up arms, forming a citizen posse. They ran down Henry and his pal Lewis, wounding them both in a gun battle, but the rest of the gang escaped with all the money. Henry and Lewis were the only two of the eight culprits who had to go to the state penitentiary. Not much had happened in Stroud since, at least not until Shell got interested in what might be percolating beneath the subsurface geology.

Miraculously, Ted's party chief on the seismic crew had found a duplex for rent in Stroud so he and his wife snatched up one side and alerted Ted that the other side was available. It was a little grey-shingled house with a bright, sunny kitchen, and I discovered that if I opened the front and back doors at the same time, the dust would blow right through. We moved in with my one suitcase and one small box of wedding gifts. Fortunately, Ted had a chair, a lamp, and a folding table because, although it was advertised as furnished, the three-room duplex really only came with a bed, a couch, and a night table. We loved it! It was perfect. We were well and truly married.

However, I think if you'd asked either of us if the Depression had finally come to an end, we'd have laughed out loud, especially from our point of view in that dusty little town in central Oklahoma. But the fact was, the country *was* getting back to work in 1939, largely because of the ominous war cloud looming on the horizon.

The day we got married, the British declared war on Germany. And the next day, the United States publicly declared neutrality.

But President Roosevelt borrowed a billion dollars in 1939 to rebuild American armed forces and, by December of 1941, manufacturing had shot up by a phenomenal 50 per cent. So I'm pretty sure the multinational oil companies were very aware of what was happening. Shell's regional head office in Tulsa was pulling out all the stops; exploration was their top priority.

The Shell seismic crew had been sent to Stroud to check on some likely-looking plays, so the crew's job was to take the next step – to help head office decide whether to drill. Drilling, as you know, is very, very expensive. I've been told that about 85 per cent of "likely-looking" comes up dry, so the oil business is not for the faint of heart. It takes a gambler's instinct combined with a very sober second thought to take those well-informed risks that may, just may, pay off.

Ted's crew consisted of two crews working together: the field crew and the office crew. The field crew had a land man whose job it was to negotiate access to the site with the property owner. He was actually sent out ahead of the crew by the Tulsa office, but he hung around for the duration of their assignment to take care of any difficulties that might arise. The other guys on the field crew, who came to be known as jug hustlers, used truck-mounted drilling equipment to drill a series of holes for the dynamite anywhere from 60 to 300 feet deep at designated locations mapped out by the office crew – the party chief, his assistant, the geologist, and the geophysicist – who did the actual science of the work. Then the reel truck crew would lay out cable a quarter of a mile on either side of the shot hole and drop the geophones so the jug hustlers could attach them to the cable. The shooter would load the holes with the appropriate amount of dynamite and, at the direction of the scientists, set off the charges sequentially. The reverberations of the explosives echoing through the different formations of the successive rock layers below would be recorded through the geophones onto a long piece of photographic paper.

The next step was to wash the records – prepare the photographic paper for an analysis of the tracings by the geologists and geophysicists – and that was the stinky part. Occasionally, when no one else was around, I would go down to the office to do that part for Ted, and I swear those tapes must have been washed in formaldehyde. Then the crew would rush those records back to the Tulsa office where they were added to the rest of their information about the site's drilling potential.

The crew worked together, travelled together, and most often lived together. Exactly as Ted had warned, we were a big family. We had all the positive benefits as well as all the inevitable problems that go with that close relationship, so I felt right at home. Mostly, we were young, full of energy, excited about our futures, and enthusiastic about the adventure. Some had families of small children, but at that time Ted and I were among the few childless couples. However, most of the crew were single guys. The little towns didn't have much in the way of recreation so we made our own fun, and the wives tended to be the crew's good-will ambassadors so we all got to know the local people, too.

The first thing I did, of course, was to find a church family and offer to sing in their choir. Then I found the grocery store. This was a real novelty; I'd never had to shop before. The ingredients for most of our meals back home just magically appeared in our pantry so it was kind of fun learning that I could cook anything that Ted and I might like. I remember that eggs were 10 cents a dozen, but pork chops were horrifically expensive at 10 cents each. Our rent was $20 a month, so Ted's salary of $95 had to be budgeted pretty carefully to ensure we had gas money to travel back and forth to Whitesboro for visits.

But just as I was getting thoroughly nested in my new home, Ted came in one evening to announce that we'd be moving. It was November 2. Our stay in Stroud had lasted two months. I remember thinking, it's a good thing I was raised by an itinerant preacher who believed he should be able to accomplish what he'd set out to do in five or six years. I guess geophysicists just work a lot faster. Obviously, Tulsa hadn't been much impressed by those tapes. We were on our way to Winfield, Kansas.

Compared to Stroud, Winfield was a metropolis. Today it has about twelve thousand people and it's probably not much larger than it was back in 1939. But when we drove up there I was relieved to see that we weren't too much farther away from my family than we had been in Stroud because Winfield sits practically on the northern border of Oklahoma, almost directly north of Whitesboro, where my family would be gathering for the upcoming holidays.

It's a beautiful little town situated along the Walnut River and Timber Creek. In fact, it's been named as one of the best one hundred small towns in America, and Ted was very pleased to discover that it had a wonderful golf course that today advertises itself as having "carpet-like fairways with feisty bent-grass greens." He'd played a lot back in Michigan and was an exceptionally good golfer, but life on a seismic crew hadn't given him much of an opportunity to work on his game.

However, first things first. We had to find a place to live and that was getting harder and harder because these small town landlords had figured out that seismic crews were notoriously unreliable. Leases meant nothing. We might stay for a year, but then again, we might be there only a few weeks. Who knew? I would patrol the streets looking for rental signs, but no matter how charming I was, once the landlord discovered what my husband did for a living, the door would be slammed in my face.

Finally, though, I found an upstairs apartment with three rooms and a bath – plus a door that opened on a Murphy bed. I liked to call it our guest room. It was across the street from a little convenience store and not too far from a Presbyterian church. And best of all, it was only $20 a month. The rest of the crew was very envious of our good luck because all the oil companies seemed to have discovered Winfield at once, so there was very little housing of any kind to be had by anyone.

By that time, I had my new-town routine pretty well under control. I'd set off for the church first, find out when the choir was scheduled to practice, and promise I'd be there on the assigned evening. Then I'd start introducing myself to the merchants around town. One of the wives on the crew, however, just never seemed to get it. She had no interest in meeting the locals and was completely convinced she would have nothing in common with any of them, so of course she was very lonely with her husband out in the field much of the time. I was discovering though how much Mama had taught us about making good friends quickly and getting involved in a helpful way in whatever community we happened to land. Quite frankly, that may have been the best life lesson I ever learned.

Within a very few weeks, we were off to Whitesboro to celebrate Nannie's birthday and of course went back for Thanksgiving and Christmas. Yes, I know. I suppose I really wasn't trying too hard to wean myself away from my family. But when we'd go back home for special occasions, *every*one in the family was there. The old oak table was stretched to its limit to accommodate not only all my brothers and sisters but also their spouses and babies, and whichever members of the congregation were too far from their own homes at the holiday season. My heart was still there. And to add to the poignancy of our warm family reunions, the talk inevitably turned to the sadness of war where other families were suffering unimaginable grief.

That Christmas of '39, we talked about the fact that British conscription had increased to cover men between the ages of nineteen and forty-one, and I know that Ted and his brothers-in-law worried about whether they would get to do their part, too. Ted, of course, was working in an essential industry and was needed at the home front, but I was hearing about more and more of my Trinity classmates who were considering joining the Canadian troops that had already arrived in Europe.

We drove back to Winfield after the holiday to settle in to winter in Kansas, and before long Ted asked whether I'd like to go with him to Tulsa. He'd set up a meeting at the regional office to discuss the possibility of heading up his own crew as party chief, so I roamed the big city and had a wonderful time window-shopping and people-watching. By the time we were ready to go home, however, a norther blew in and we knew we'd better get on the road fast. The storm worsened with every passing mile, and before long the snow was coming at us horizontally. We were in a white-out. I'd been a pretty self-confident Texas driver for a long time, but this was my first blizzard, and it had me scared to death so, even though Ted was driving, my knuckles were white and I was offering up fast and fulsome thanks that I'd married a Michigan man who knew how to handle it.

Spring came eventually though and with it the premiere of *Gone with the Wind*. Now I'm sure this wasn't its *first* premiere; I think that one was in Atlanta. But they must have released it all over the country at about the same time – along with its over-the-top publicity about Clark Gable and Vivien Leigh. Everyone was excited about seeing this new movie, so much so that the party chief gave the whole crew the day off so we could all attend.

We knew it was almost four hours long so the women all packed picnic lunches for the intermission and we made a day of it. I know all the hoopla sounds silly now, but *Gone with the Wind* really did make movie history. It was the longest sound movie ever made at that time, the first feature film shot in Technicolor, it received ten

Academy awards and, to this day, no movie has ever made more money. It cost $3.85 million to make and its box office take was $400 million. And, speaking as a Southerner, it was darn good Civil War history too, except of course that it sentimentalized slavery. But when Scarlett stood there in her ragged dress on the burned-over fields of Tara and, with her clinched fist held high, vowed, "As God is my witness, I'll never go hungry again!," I could hear generations of Reconstruction-era Southerners pulling themselves up by their bootstraps and living another day by the sheer force of will.

Ted loved it too, and we watched it again several times after it came out on TV. But ironically, I think he might have identified with Scarlett's stubborn refusal to submit to insurmountable odds even more than I did. I had grown up with six closely spaced siblings in a noisy, laughing, singing, story-telling, fun-loving family. But Ted had been raised by parents whose two primary values were the importance of education and hard work. They were both lovely people, but they made it clear that the subject of their extended families wasn't open for discussion. Dad Rozsa said that the last day he ever spoke Hungarian was the day he landed on Ellis Island. "The first day of my life started at that moment," he said.

You cannot imagine how very different our backgrounds were. My family revelled in one another. We all talked at once and told stories on each other and learned about those who had come before us from parents who were not only natural-born storytellers but were also professionally trained to teach the history and values and ethics of their forefathers through storytelling. All of us adored our parents and each other, and we were wrapped in a close nurturing bond that was made even stronger by the church communities we lived among and who cared for us all our lives. What we learned were the people skills.

Ted's parents were, of course, very proud of their three exceptionally bright children. Both Ted and his brother John earned scholarships to Michigan Tech in the hardest years of the Depression. They had to get in and get out fast because there was no money to keep them there any longer than absolutely necessary. There was no time for recreation or entertainment anyway, but clearly they were only there to get an education – the best education that could lead to the best job opportunities. What Ted developed was an eclectic intellectual curiosity along with a very strong work ethic. Both served him extraordinarily well his entire life.

On April 15, Ted came home to announce we were moving again. We had been in Winfield for six months, an eternity in seismic speak.

CHAPTER EIGHT

On the Road Again

… just can't wait to get on the road again!

Seismology was a pretty new technology back in the early '40s. What it made possible was a look into structures buried too deep to be found otherwise, so geophysicists were able to find hundreds of new anticlines and other oil traps that had never been discovered before. All the big oil companies were taking a second look at formerly productive fields that had seemingly run dry, so we were on the move … again.

Bristow, Oklahoma. It was getting pretty clear that we weren't going to sink roots any time soon, so I figured I'd better get a little more efficient about the transition process. I've always admired the Indian women who could pack up their teepees and all their worldly goods and have them lashed to the back of a horse before breakfast. If I was going to be a nomad, I figured I'd better learn the tricks of the trade. Let's face it, we were accumulating more stuff; somehow I'd have to find a way to haul it along.

The dynamite for the seismic teams was packed in sturdy wooden crates for transport to all the sites, and I'd had my eye on those boxes ever since I'd been introduced to the field crew. I figured they'd make terrific end tables, and so what if the word DYNAMITE was stencilled in big red letters across the tops and sides. With a pretty piece of fabric draped over them, no one need know what they really were. So, sing-songing the Depression-era mantra to *use it up, wear it out, make it do, or do without*, I'd managed to expropriate quite a number of them. I knew if I threw a nice white table cloth over a few stacked boxes, my dinner guests never had to know what they were actually eating on.

But now that we were moving again, I realized they could serve a dual purpose. They'd make excellent packing boxes, too. I could wrap up the dishes in the linens and stuff everything into the dynamite crates so securely that nothing would even rattle. And, should some hapless volunteer be commandeered to help us load up the car, that giant red stencil would undoubtedly catch his attention. He sure wasn't likely to drop it. It was foolproof. We'd never break a single thing.

Bristow, Oklahoma: home of Gene Autry, the singing cowboy. We didn't have far to drive; Bristow is just south of Oklahoma City and there's not much to it. It was just another little community that was attracting lots of renewed interest by the oil companies because of its past performance in the boom of the late '20s.

This time, though, the whole crew was able to move into the same apartment complex. Ted and I claimed a downstairs unit with two bedrooms and, best of all, that extra bedroom was an actual room, not a Murphy bed, so I had hopes of inviting my family for a visit one day, should I ever acquire a telephone. Getting a phone was a major challenge in those days, particularly if you were of no fixed address, like we were. But I even found an extra chair so my potential guest wouldn't have to sit on a dynamite box.

The apartment had a big yard with a garage. Ted had the bright idea that we could build a trailer to haul all our stuff when it came time for us to move again. He had a company car by this time and I was driving his old one, so he thought he could find a two-wheel axel on a trailer bed that we could convert to something that would serve our needs. Between the two of us, we built up the sides and made it to fit what furniture we'd accumulated as well as all the dynamite boxes.

Ted found a nearby golf course, which made him very happy, and while we were there he also took flying lessons and got into photography in a big way, so when he got word that he had been promoted to assistant party chief and had a new crew to meet in Decatur, Texas, it seemed like our three months in Bristow had flown by. Both of us could hardly wait to try out that new trailer.

I was really excited about the move because it would mean we'd be close to my parents in Whitesboro, but since Ted had a few days off, we decided we could drive up to Michigan to visit his folks first – if we hurried.

I shifted into overdrive. After all, I was the packing queen by this time. Out came the dynamite boxes, dishes, linens, kitchen utensils, laundry equipment, pots and pans, foodstuffs, books, photography equipment, the clothes, shoes, golf clubs…. I was a machine. Wrap the dishes in newspaper, layer the books with lighter clothes, stuff the condiments from the ice box where they'd fit, etcetera, etcetera, etcetera, and load it all into the trailer with the furniture.

By the time we finally bounced down the road to Decatur, I was glad to be getting somewhere I could unpack and get settled again, even though home would be another dusty, windy duplex right on the highway. The trucks would be roaring by day and night, but we were close to my family and I knew we'd have lots of company, so I was eager to unload the trailer. Ted started hauling in the furniture and then the dynamite boxes, but he was somewhat puzzled by the gloppy yellow drip that was oozing out of the box packed with the linens. The smell was pretty awful, too. One horrified look and I knew what I'd done. I'd been in such a hurry to pack everything I hadn't bothered to screw the lids tight on the condiments so, when I crammed them in upside down with the linens – so they wouldn't break of course – , one of the mustard jars oozed. And throughout the long drive, it kept oozing. By this time the jar was bare and dry. The linens weren't.

My family did visit, of course. In fact we had lots of company during our six months in Decatur. Most of them were kind enough not to comment that our house smelled like a county fair hotdog stand.

The trailer was perfect, though. We lashed it to the back of the car and loaded it up. We were, (sing it with me Willie!) on the road again. We just couldn't wait to get on the road again ... because this time we were headed back to where we'd begun.

We had been married eighteen months. All that time we'd lived with our family of crew members, hopping back and forth between isolated little towns scattered across Texas, Oklahoma, and Kansas, wrapped in a protective little cocoon. Did we really know what was happening in the world around us? Oh, most certainly we heard the news on the radio and read the headlines, but it was very far away and there was a strong movement toward American isolationism following Germany's invasion of Poland. There just didn't seem to be much political will to get involved in somebody else's war.

But over the last year, the headlines grew more frightening day by day. In March Finland surrendered to Russia; in April Denmark surrendered to Germany and Germany invaded Norway. Winston Churchill became the new prime minister of Britain, replacing Neville Chamberlain in May – while Adolf Hitler invaded the Netherlands. Then Belgium. Then Paris.

1940 was an election year in the United States. Franklin Roosevelt was up for re-election against Wendell Wilkie, an avowed isolationist, and a poll taken that fall indicated that even though Americans were mighty impressed with British courage in the face of overwhelming odds, 83 per cent still didn't think the United States should get involved. A week before the election, Roosevelt declared, "I have said this before, but I shall say it again and again and again: your boys are not going to be sent into any foreign wars."

Hindsight makes it pretty obvious that Roosevelt was only promising what was expedient for the purpose of getting re-elected. Merely weeks later, in his final fireside chat of 1940, he said, "The history of recent years proves that the shootings and the chains and the concentration camps are not simply the transient tools but the very altars of modern dictatorships. They may talk of a new order in the world, but what they have in mind is only a revival of the oldest and worst tyranny.... In a military sense Great Britain and the British Empire today are the spearhead of resistance to world conquest. And they are putting up a fight which will live forever in the story of human gallantry.... The time has come for America to be the great arsenal of democracy."

On January 10, 1941, he introduced Lend-Lease into the United States Congress. In February, we were on our way back to Olney, Texas. Ted's job was to make sure the United States could fuel that arsenal.

My job, yet again, was to find us a place to live and that was getting more and more difficult because so many oil companies were converging on these little towns all at once and housing was less than scarce. However, there was a partially furnished house that we could have for about four months, so, since I knew we could be long gone in that amount of time, I took it.

But wouldn't you know, the owner came back to reclaim it just as he said he would and we ended up being thankful for a two-room apartment behind a garage. The only positive thing about it was that it was on the ground floor. Anyway, we weren't to stay long in that little apartment because I was, shall we say, highly motivated to find someplace cooler. By that time I was very pregnant. It was July in west Texas. You cannot imagine the heat. I finally found a wonderful little duplex, blissfully cool, but practically before I could even unpack all the dynamite boxes, Ted came home to tell me we had been transferred.

Living in Olney again, despite the heat, was wonderful. I had had an earlier miscarriage so everyone was pampering me through this pregnancy, and I saw lots of my mother as well as my sister Ann, who was also expecting and due about three months ahead of me, so I have very happy memories of that little town. It was chock-a-block with people just like us who were all working the oilfields in various capacities. Olney became famous for its One-Arm Dove Hunt long after we left there, but this story's worth telling because it's a quint-essentially Texas-Roughneck Tale.

The Dove Hunt was the creation of two local residents, Jack Northrup and Jack Bishop, the One-Armed Jacks, each of whom had a limb amputated at the shoulder because of oilfield accidents.

While sitting at the local drugstore, in order to harass two eavesdropping strangers, the Jacks loudly began discussing how they planned to go dove hunting with their muzzle-loaded shotguns and bolt-action rifles. This loud-talk bravado was meant as a joke, of course. Either gun would be next to impossible to operate with only one arm, but eventually the Jacks did hold an actual One-Arm Dove Hunt. It was attended by six Olney residents who had lost arms, mainly due to oilfield accidents, as well as others who had heard of the event through the grapevine.

The event grew quickly, so the Jacks expanded the event to two days and included such features as one-armed trap-shooting, one-arm horseshoes, cow-chip throwing, and a 10-cents-a-finger breakfast on the day of the hunt. It's become quite the little revenue-generator for the town of Olney.

By October, Ted and I were on the road again. This time to Jacksboro, Texas, which was only a forty-minute drive from Olney so I could go back there for my pre-natal visits and to see Ann. Living accommodations in Jacksboro weren't exactly five star, but we finally found a lean-to that had been built by some enterprising landlord who knew a seller's market when he saw it. Practically anything with a roof would rent at whatever price the landlord imagined the market would bear. Frankly, Scarlett, we were glad to get it.

Truly, it was a lean-to the old man had built on the back of his house; he was using the rental revenue to support himself in his old age. He and his daughter lived in the actual house and the walls between us were so paper thin we could hear them talking to one another. Thankfully though, we were hardly ever there, what with Ted working out in the field and me going back and forth to Olney to see Mama and Ann.

Mama was still in Olney on November 30, 1941, helping Ann with her new baby boy when our daughter was born. I named her Ruth Ann after my two closest sisters because my sister Ruth never stopped complaining that she wasn't given a middle name like the rest of her siblings. The baby was happy and healthy and I was just fine, but in those days they kept new mothers in the hospital for ten days following delivery. While we were still there, the news came that the Japanese had bombed Pearl Harbor. On December 11, the United States declared war on Germany and Japan.

Oil exploration shifted into high gear.

Baby Ruthie and I left the hospital for Whitesboro so she could be cuddled and petted and I could complete my recovery through the remaining weeks of December. Preacher's parishioners brought us extra chickens and produce and covered-dish suppers because my large extended family now included high chairs full of toddlers and infants. We all huddled around Papa's radio every evening to hear how the country was mobilizing for war. Many of my Trinity classmates were signing up, mostly for the Marines. We all knew that it was unlikely we'd ever see some of them again.

Ted finally arrived for a few days of Christmas holiday, and, as always, it was hard for me to leave, but it was time for *our* little family to go back to the ramshackle lean-to in Jacksboro. I'm very sure the proprietor was no happier to see me coming with my newborn, who as yet hadn't figured out the difference between daytime and nighttime, than I was to see him and his *equally* noisy daughter. Thankfully though, before we had been back in Jacksboro a week, Shell decided to move its seismic operations farther west to Midland.

Midland – so named because it's halfway between Dallas and El Paso. Ted had been promoted to assistant party chief and would be working in the district office, but housing was still going to be a challenge, so we were instructed to check into the Alamo Plaza Motel until we could find a place to live.

Remember the Alamo. You'll be hearing about it often.

Midland wasn't a major metropolis by any stretch of the imagination, but it was definitely the biggest city we'd been assigned to so far. Smack in the middle of the west Texas desert, it's been called the High Sky City because it rests on an absolutely flat horizon of sand, unimpeded by anything other than an occasional tumbleweed that might take your eye off the dazzling, brilliantly blue sky. It's an indescribable blue that you'll never see anywhere else. And it's that same colour every day since clouds are practically unheard of in west Texas. Against that sky, nothing can compete. Even now, the giant office buildings of downtown Midland seem somehow false-fronted, as if they they're only a temporary movie set destined to be torn down so the sky can take over again, like it's supposed to.

Mac McKenzie, Ted's party chief, and his wife Elizabeth invited us to dinner one evening to get acquainted with some of the other Shell people. But while I was reaching for something behind me, I slipped and fell on my tail bone. If you're cringing at this point, I know *you* know how that feels! The baby was so little that she still required round-the-clock attention and I, of course, was in terrible pain and hobbled by crutches. Elizabeth, bless her heart, found a young girl to help me with Ruthie and before long we inherited one side of a rental duplex from a geologist who had been in the Naval reserve and was called up to active duty.

Once I could start creeping along without my crutches, I discovered the Presbyterian church and volunteered to sing in the choir on the Sundays when Ted might be home to look after the baby, and I started exploring the town and introducing myself to my neighbours. And, once springtime brought green grass, Ted and Mac discovered they could slip away from the office for an occasional round of golf.

Neither of them knew it then, but that grass wouldn't stay green very long. Once the heat of the summer arrived it would burn like straw. The heat of the pavement could quite literally fry eggs. Seasoned veterans of the west Texas summer taught me to wear oven mitts so I could hold onto the steering wheel of the car. They were the ones I went to for advice on whether to open the windows in the house so we could breathe, or to close them to keep the sand from blowing in and drifting up the walls. In the east Texas humidity, we used to complain that we could never really get dry after bathing in the morning. In west Texas we were plenty dry; venturing outside was like stepping into a blast furnace.

Not that that ever stopped either of us from thoroughly enjoying our Midland assignment. Ted had always been an avid chess player, and he went back and forth several times to Dallas and Fort Worth for weekend tournaments. Then he started a penny postcard game with a chess master who was a professor at Baylor University. As each decided on his next move, he'd mail the other a postcard describing it. My great-grandchildren are completely confused when I tell them this story. "What's a penny postcard? Why didn't they just Skype each other?"

Oh well, time marches on ... and so did we.

CHAPTER NINE

On the Home Front

Shell was evidently tired of looking at worked-over geology in Texas so they promoted Ted to party chief, gave him a new crew, and decided we should go north to Vandalia, Illinois.

I'm sure I must have groaned audibly when Ted told me. Illinois would be very far from Whitesboro. I bundled up Ruthie and made a hurried trip to Whitesboro to say goodbye to my family, and by the time we'd made it that far, she was having a wonderful time with all her toys in her backseat play pen. Both of us were singing every song I'd ever learned as we drove along, and the whole trip had become a delightful adventure. After we left Whitesboro, I drove on up to Illinois looking forward to visiting with my grandmother and elderly aunts and to introducing them to the baby, but all they did was cluck at me for taking her on such a dangerous trip all alone and fuss at Ted for allowing me to do it. From my perspective, though, it seemed pretty odd that these intrepid pioneer women would have even given it a second thought.

Vandalia is about sixty miles directly east of St. Louis. I kind of wondered whether those Yankees thought we were carpetbaggers when we all descended upon them to plunder their resources. But, if you know your petroleum history, you'll remember that the Illinois Basin had been plundered long before. It all began back in about 1905, peaking three years later at 34 million barrels a year, becoming the third most productive area in the United States before it declined again. But, what with the advancements in seismology, Shell wanted to be there in September of 1943 to see whether any more oil could be wrung out.

We moved into a motel at first, and then quite quickly found an absolutely perfect house. It was big, with cavernous rooms and a huge yard. We unloaded the trailer and the dynamite boxes and then Ruthie and I started to explore. For about twenty years back in the nineteenth century, the little town of Vandalia was the state capital, and Abraham Lincoln started his political career there, but when we arrived it was teeming with transients all looking for the same thing.

However, Shell changed its mind, I guess, because within six weeks we were on the road again, this time to Bay City, Michigan. Well, I thought, at least we'll be closer to Ted's folks. When we arrived, I realized my Michigan geography was a little sketchy. Michigan is a big state and Grand Rapids might have been relatively closer than Midland, Texas, but it was hardly next door to Bay City.

We moved into a little cabin right on Lake Michigan which, in the summer, would have been wonderful. However, by this time it was late fall and cold and rainy, so we moved back to town to a three-room apartment in the upstairs of a house. We stayed there almost a month until I found a perfect house with two bedrooms and a huge yard.

I was so proud of myself. This was absolutely ideal for all of us. There was lots of room and Ruthie was learning to walk, so she would have ample roaming space. I unpacked, made up the beds, and within a couple of hours realized I might have been less than thorough in my initial assessment. As I tucked Ruthie into her crib for the night, I ran the water into the tub looking forward to a long relaxing bubble bath after the move. I stepped in with one foot – yelped – and stepped right out again. No hot water. Wrapping myself in a towel, I ran to the kitchen to test the hot water faucet and decided the landlord had turned down the thermostat on the tank. Then, just moments after the ink dried on the lease, I discovered there *was* no hot water tank. This was long before anyone had thought of disposable diapers, so the diaper pail was by this time brimming over and a crisis was at hand.

For a solid year we lived in that house, with a bucket of water permanently simmering on the back burner of the stove. Don't talk to *me* about your housewifely trials and tribulations! At least not until you've lived a year hauling hot water.

The year wasn't wasted though. I spent every free moment trying to find something else and finally jumped at the chance to rent a duplex on, would you believe it, Park Avenue. It was kind of dingy but it had an actual washing machine in the corner of the kitchen and came complete with a hot water tank. Ruthie was, by that time, out of diapers and life was good, despite the war rationing.

To get a book of ration stamps, we had to appear before a local rationing board and each person in the family — including babies — received their own book of stamps. If you wanted to buy gas, the driver had to present a gas card along with the ration book plus cash. If you were caught sightseeing or aimlessly driving with no apparent reason, you could get fined. Every drop of fuel was essential for the war effort.

Tires were the first to be rationed, then gasoline to further discourage people from using their cars. By 1943, you needed ration coupons to buy typewriters, sugar, bicycles, clothing, fuel oil, coffee, shoes, meat, cheese, butter, margarine and lard, canned foods, dried fruits and jam. Lots of communities had big Victory gardens so families could keep produce on their tables and share it with others, of course. And, since silk and nylon were rationed too, more than a few women took to drawing black lines down the backs of their legs to make them look like they were still wearing stockings. Some things you just couldn't get at all, like new cars and appliances. Everything coming off the production lines was directed toward the war effort.

Our next stop was Alma, Michigan, in March of 1944. The only thing we could find there was a two-bedroom apartment owned by the local mortician.

June 6 was D-Day. It was beginning to look like the tides of war were finally turning. We stayed in Alma through the summer, though, and then moved to Flint, the big-city manufacturing hub where the war effort was booming along at maximum capacity.

Flint, thanks to the burgeoning automobile industry of the early part of the century, was ideally set up to convert to wartime production and, the young woman who rented us her home told us that since her husband had been called into service, she was going to work in one of the factories.

In Michigan though, the story of Rosie the Riveter wasn't quite the sociological transformation that it was in the rest of the country, simply because it had always been a blue-collar working-class town and women had been part of that workforce for the previous twenty years or so. The only difference was that, prior to the war effort, women hadn't been employed in so-called 'male' jobs, so a propaganda campaign targeted young women telling them that women could be "militant partners in the struggle to defeat the enemy … heroines who helped their men in wartime." Clearly, the War Manpower Commission was setting them up for short-term employment. Following the war, the men would take their rightful places back in the economy.

Be that as it may, women eagerly signed on. Young women, married women whose husbands were overseas, older women – all stepped up to offer their services and were in fact extremely good at the "male" jobs they were expected to do. Most loved every minute of the experience and knew what they were doing was of critical importance to the Allied forces so, in hindsight, it might be hard to understand why most American Rosies retreated dutifully back to their kitchens after the war was over. In truth, though, this blip on the historical timeline of women's history, was really just a blip. What that experience accomplished in the long run, though, did make a very important difference. It showed that women *could* do it all. They *could* go to work and be successful in important positions of responsibility, manage their homes, and raise their children – all while helping to win a war. It would just take another twenty-five years and another generation for their daughters to mobilize and make it happen again.

We stayed in Flint for just over a year. Our house was practically brand new and it was completely furnished. It had two bedrooms, hot water, and neighbours with two teenage daughters eager to babysit, so we often drove over to Detroit to see the baseball games and hear some of the big bands and jazz greats of the era. My childhood friend from Denton, Louise Tobin, had run off to New York when she was only sixteen to be a jazz singer and I always hoped I might find her on one stage or another.

We stayed there through the end of the war – at least the war with Germany – until we moved back to Bay City for four months. Then, since Ted was called back to the Tulsa office for a temporary posting, Ruthie and I stayed with my parents in Whitesboro through Christmas until, on January 1, 1946, we were transferred back to Midland.

At last, the war was over. And our days on the seismic crew seemed to be over, too. Ted was to move into the district office, and we knew the drill. We drove right back to the Alamo Plaza Motel and, since the war's end had brought thousands of servicemen back home, I knew that finding housing was going to be a Herculean task, despite the fact that Shell had promised Ted a company house.

I needn't have worried. I'd barely transferred our clothes from the suitcases into the motel's closet when Elizabeth McKenzie, Mac's wife, called to ask me to come along to a coffee party where I could meet some of the other company wives. Her phone rang while I was there; it was Ted calling to tell me he'd been transferred to the district office at Jackson, Mississippi.

So we moved into the Alamo Plaza Motel in Jackson instead. (See? This is why I told you to remember the Alamo!) And there we stayed. It wasn't so bad, really. The motel had a swimming pool to retreat to through the heat of the afternoons that summer, and Ruthie started kindergarten, so I spent my days house-hunting.

Jackson was unlike any other community we had ever lived in. It was still a very Old South culture where life was lived in leisure and the old mimosa and magnolia trees provided a shady escape for ladies who still napped through the sultry afternoons. I found a church right away, of course, and introduced myself to everyone I met hoping to discover someone who might have a lead on houses that might be coming on the market. But what I was discovering was a far different environment than I'd ever experienced before.

When we arrived in Jackson in 1946, the white and African-American populations were of almost equal size, but the old social conventions of the antebellum South still hung on. There were laws firmly entrenched to prevent the integration of public schools, public facilities, churches, swimming pools, and recreation fields. Nor would that change anytime in the foreseeable future. The state constitution at that time included both literacy tests and poll taxes, which pretty much guaranteed that African-Americans wouldn't be permitted to vote as long as those old prejudices crippled any progress toward a better future.

By May, I found a house that could be ours to rent provided we bought all the furniture in it. That wouldn't be a problem, so we moved in and once again I started building a nest. The house had a lovely yard surrounded by honeysuckle bushes and a cute little garage that had been built into a play house so Ruthie was very happy. We nestled in for a long stay and, in September of 1947, our son Theodore Sidney was born.

In fact, we stayed such a long time in Jackson I was beginning to think we could get rid of the dynamite boxes. I not only volunteered to sing in the choir, I was even able to get to church on Sundays *and* on the evenings we had choir practice. And since the children and I walked to Ruthie's school every day, we'd introduced ourselves to the other families and very quickly we had a whole crew of neighbourhood friends along with those who worked with Ted at Shell. It was in Jackson that we met Wilf and Gerrie Baillie, who would become a very big part of our lives, but of course none of us knew that then. All I knew was that it was beginning to feel like we were sinking roots at long last.

But no. I should have realized that Ted's frequent business trips into New Orleans were happening too often to be a reasonable enough expense to get by Shell's accounting department and, sure enough, before little Sidney was even two months old, we were transferred again.

Ted was, by this time, the chief geophysicist in the New Orleans office so, since Mama was still with us in Jackson, having come to help out while I was in the hospital, she just stayed with us to help pack up the house. And, once she got the hang of the dynamite boxes, we were a pretty efficient team. Within a few days, the car was loaded and ready to go, so I put her on the train back to Texas and off we went to Louisiana. It was October of 1947. The war was over and, thankfully, the economic hardships of the Depression were too.

After Pearl Harbor in 1941, American contributions of money, industrial output, petroleum, technological innovation, food – and especially soldiers – turned the tide not only on the progress of the war, but also on the American economy itself. Unemployment was a thing of the past because so many people stepped up on the home front to move from low-productivity jobs to high efficiency occupations that were better managed through better technology. Everyone seemed to be working much harder and a lot smarter. And despite the fact that 40 per cent of the GDP was going overseas, Americans had accepted the necessity of higher taxes to pay for the war, whereas, before 1940, only about 10 per cent of employed people paid any income tax at all.

Personal income was at an all-time high. The hugely successful war bond drives convinced many Americans to invest their discretionary money in bonds that could be had at 75 per cent of the face value and expect to get their return when they matured at the close of the war, so personal saving was high, too. And wage and price controls were able to ensure that another recession wouldn't develop before post-war manufacturing could gear up to satisfy the demand for new products like cars and appliances and furniture for all the returning veterans and the coming baby boom.

Post-war America looked far different than it had before. There was a huge migration of farmers into urban centres through the Depression years and wartime, and that, combined with the thousands of returning servicemen, created a truly critical housing shortage.

Shell, by this time, had finally admitted that, with so many desperately looking for someplace to settle and get on with their lives, the company would have to start buying up what real estate they could find to house their employees. What they'd done in New Orleans was to buy an entire apartment block out in Metarie, near the airport.

This was our first sub-tropical climate, so we had to get used to the cockroaches and other assorted bugs, as well as the almost daily four-o'clock rain that made Metarie, sitting at about three feet above sea level, a permanent bog. Hot and humid in the summer and damp and drippy in the winter, we were all living in a constant state of dank.

But there *were* bonuses that made life in New Orleans really fun. Ted became the unofficial host assigned to schmooze the visiting firemen from Shell's head office, so we were enlisted to show them the best of the city, including the incredible restaurants in the French Quarter. I think we both gained about fifteen pounds in Antoine's alone!

Eventually, though, I learned to cook Cajun. For the uninitiated, I should let you in on its secret. All you need is a whole lot of scrap seafood and about a bushel of spices. We could go over to the fish market or to Lake Ponchartrain and, for practically nothing at all, buy washtubs full of fresh shrimp, oysters, and every other critter that happened to swim by. When you get home with your catch, take your cast iron skillet and make up a roux. Just fry up a little celery with some garlic and a couple onions along with whatever leftover pork you might have on hand, plus a little flour to thicken it, along with everything on your spice rack. This is key: *lots* of spice. Dump all that in your biggest pot with some tomatoes, a handful of okra, maybe a little chicken broth, and then add the shellfish. And if a few friends and neighbours happen by unexpectedly, just throw in some red beans and a little rice to the mix and voila! Be careful about the coffee, though. In New Orleans, the coffee's so strong your spoon stands up in the cup.

It wasn't *all* about the food, though. We'd inevitably waddle out of Antoine's or Brennan's or Galatoire's and head for the jazz and blues clubs to hear that incredible music, and that's when Ted started getting interested in learning more. He hadn't been raised in a musical home, but with me and my family all singing whether invited to or not, he had been fully immersed in music ever since we'd met. He bought us tickets to the New Orleans Symphony that first year and really became quite a serious student of classical music as time went on.

We were in New Orleans for the big hurricane of 1947, and, as I've said, Metarie is only about three feet above sea level so we were pounded by the storm as well as the storm surge from the gulf through the big canals. I'd been in more than a few tornados growing up but, as frightening as they were, they were over in just a few minutes. That wasn't the case with hurricanes. You knew they were coming and, when they got close, the noise alone was terrifying beyond belief. There were storm shutters on almost all the windows, so we sealed ourselves up in the middle of the apartment hoping that the banging and crashing wasn't a sign that the huge palms and live oaks were flying through the air. But of course that's exactly what was happening.

After the storm was over, the snakes that had been displaced by the sea water were littering the grounds around the apartment, and one afternoon I heard Ruthie outside shrieking her little head off. Before I could get to her, a neighbour who had been cleaning his shotgun ran to her rescue, shot the snake that had cornered her, and carried her home.

Ruthie was able to complete first grade as well as the first half of the second in one of the parish schools in New Orleans before we were transferred to Baton Rouge in February of 1949. I'm sure I wasn't thrilled about moving again, but I could do it practically in my sleep, and it barely created a ripple in our day-to-day lives. I found another school for Ruthie in Baton Rouge and offered up a silent prayer that she could stay there to at least finish her school year, but when Ted came home in April with that look in his eye, I knew we were at it again.

This time, he made me sit down before he'd tell me where we were going.

CHAPTER TEN

It'll Just Be a Year

"Calgary," I sighed. "Where's Calgary?"

"In Alberta." Ted looked a little frightened.

"Where's Alberta?" I could tell he was feeding me bite-size pieces of information.

"In Canada. Western Canada."

"There's oil in Canada?" Surely someone had made a mistake.

"We'll only be there a year. It's just a temporary thing. Shell pulled most of its operations out of there years ago, so they're just following up on something that happened up there recently. We will be back home in a year. It will be fun."

"What happened up there? You said something happened up there...."

"Imperial found something at a little place called Leduc, and another called Redwater. Shell just wants to have another look."

"But why us?" Surely there were geophysicists working closer to Canada than we were in Louisiana.

"Apparently, at Leduc they found the oil in a Devonian coral reef much like we've had experience with in the west Texas plays. They want to send us because we are familiar with the structures and we have the technology they need up there."

"A year. They *promised* a year?"

"Absolutely."

I looked him straight in the eye. "Are you *sure* they said only a year?"

"That's what they said. We will be home in a year." Ted was smiling to reassure me, and I really think he believed it, but all the reassurance in the world wasn't doing a thing to calm me down.

"Do we have to learn to speak another language?" I had barely had a chance to get used to Louisiana Cajun.

"No, they speak English in western Canada," Ted laughed, "but you might consider learning French in case we ever have a chance to go to Quebec."

What about Ruthie; were there schools? Where would we live? I was betting there wouldn't be an Alamo Plaza Motel, and I shuddered to think what we might have to live in. Canada, for heaven's sake! How would I ever break this to Mama? Papa had passed away just over a year before and I could scarcely bear to be a day's drive from her. After he died, she sent me the letter she found in his typewriter awaiting more news. It was addressed to me. I was still a long way from healing that terrible loss. How could I leave Mama so far behind to grieve alone? Where's the atlas? Had I unpacked the atlas yet? I'd better find out exactly where we'll be going before I call Mama. How would we get there?

"How will we get there? Do planes fly up there?"

"Sure, but I have a better idea," said Ted. "Let's buy a new car and drive up there with the kids. We will see the country on the way and it will be an adventure. I mean how often does anyone ever get a chance to do something like this? This will be something we will remember all our lives."

"You're *sure* it'll be just a year?"

"I'm sure; apparently there's some issue with Canadian currency. American employees can't be paid longer than one year in Canada. And Shell's also guaranteed they'll send us back to the States to jobs comparable to our current ones."

I could tell he'd been composing this speech for quite a while. His mind was definitely made up.

I called Mama. Her first response was, "Well! How nice. That's wonderful dear. You'll be close to Ted's parents in Michigan." Obviously her geography was as sketchy as mine.

"No, Mama, we're closer to them here than we'll be in Calgary. It looks like Calgary's a million miles from anywhere. How'd you like to come help me pack?"

After Papa died, my eldest sister, Lillian, the nurse, came back to Whitesboro and talked our mother into moving with her to Denton where the family had grown up with so many friends we had stayed close to through the years. The two of them moved into an apartment together but, since then, Nannie had been travelling all over Texas and Louisiana visiting all her new grandchildren. Of course she would come.

We hauled out the dynamite boxes yet again but, since Shell was moving so many people to Calgary, we found out that they would do all the packing and heavy lifting and we wouldn't have a thing to worry about until the truck arrived to move us into our new homes. Mama and I and the children could spend our time together visiting with my brothers and sisters while Ted went to Houston to get his instructions about immigrating to Canada.

Ted took advantage of a few days off to fly to Michigan, where he bought a brand new Buick fresh off the production line. It was electric blue and had three portholes along each side, so we turned lots of heads driving that car. New cars of any kind were still pretty scarce in those post-war years, and this one was so outrageously over the top that people couldn't resist looking into those portholes trying to figure out why in the world they were there.

I found out later that one of their designers – apparently still mourning the loss of his wartime fighter plane – built a prototype of a car he hoped Buick would put into production. He installed four yellow lights on the hood of the car wired to the distributor so they would flash on and off as the pistons fired – simulating the flames from the fighter planes. Evidently, Buick loved the idea but decided to dial it back a notch and bored portholes in the sides instead. Why portholes made more sense than exhaust jets I don't know. They were a design feature I never could understand.

It was definitely a comfortable ride, though, and certainly roomy enough for the five of us, so we dropped Nannie off in Denton, drove over to say goodbye to Ann and Ed in Olney, and then pointed its nose north. I knew about Denver, of course, and it was fun taking the kids to Custer's Last Stand in Montana, but with every mile it was getting bleaker and more barren. This was late April, so even though there wasn't much snow, spring had definitely not sprung on the northern plains. But there was a warm wind blowing like crazy. It *felt* like spring, but somehow it wasn't, and the brown and barren earth seemed to know that.

Eventually, way off on the horizon, I could see a tiny building with two giant flags flapping in the wind. We drove up wondering whether this was the right place; there wasn't another thing in sight. No people, no cars, no sign of human habitation at all. A few minutes went by, and then a man appeared out of the building, shambled over to the car, and leaned in the window. He looked into the back seat at the kids and said, "Where are you from, and where were you born, and where are you going?"

Ted answered, "I was born in Michigan, my wife was born in Oklahoma, my daughter was born in Texas, and my son was born in Mississippi. We have come from Louisiana. We are on our way to Calgary where I have a job waiting for me."

The customs officer was obviously confused. "Well how the hell did all of you ever get together?" And then, without another look, he waved us through with no further ado.

That was April 26, 1949. We were officially landed immigrants.

I didn't know it then, but the big oil companies had been very interested in Alberta at one time because of the gas that had been found through shallow drilling in the Turner Valley area southwest of Calgary, as well as down near Medicine Hat. In fact, as early as 1914, a great flurry of wildcatters and promoters flocked in after a discovery well produced natural gas along with a condensate called 'naphtha.' They stripped off this hydrocarbon mixture from the gas and found it was pure enough to burn in cars without even refining it. Because of its odour, they called it skunk gas. Huge excitement brought investors who practically threw their money at anyone willing to form an oil company and, within twenty-four hours, more than five hundred new companies were listed on the brand-new Calgary Stock Exchange.

Nothing much happened after that and most of the little oil companies disappeared, but one called Royalite eventually found a spectacular natural gas cap in Turner Valley and under it was enough oil to make Turner Valley Canada's first major oilfield.

Then the Depression intervened, which was arguably even worse in Alberta than it had been in the United States, so there was no more capital to invest to keep it going. Of course, once the war began, production started up again and peaked in Turner Valley in 1942, but then no one seemed interested in Alberta until 1946, when Imperial decided to take one last look before they, too, would abandon the search.

Rumour had it that Imperial had drilled 133 dry holes in Alberta and Saskatchewan up to that point, but some diehard geophysicist talked the company into one last play based on an anomaly he'd found after shooting some seismic logs on a farm owned by Mike Turta, just south of Edmonton. No drilling had taken place anywhere within a fifty-mile radius of that farm, but he had a hunch.

I've been told that, at first, the crew thought the well would be a gas discovery. But nothing was happening. However, at about five thousand feet, drilling sped up and the first bit samples showed free oil in the dolomite reservoir and, by continuing to drill another sixty feet, they found what they were looking for.

On February 13, 1947, Imperial invited all kinds of dignitaries to watch them bring in the well. Shivering in the bitter cold, the first thing they saw was a spectacular column of smoke and fire as the crew flared the first gas and oil. Then N. E. Tanner, Alberta's Minister of Mines and Minerals, turned the valve to start the oil flowing and the Canadian oil industry made a giant leap into the modern era with the discovery well that Imperial named Leduc #1.

Leduc #2 was drilled about a mile southwest of #1 and on May 10, at about the same depth, #2 struck an even bigger Devonian reef, which turned out to be the most prolific geological formation in Alberta, the Leduc Formation.

Exploration exploded! It seemed that every oil company in the world was racing to get to Alberta, and one major discovery followed another until a spectacular find in Redwater in 1948 finally got Shell's attention. The four lonely guys in Calgary, who'd been left all those years after the Turner Valley field basically closed down, were holding an office for Shell. They knew they'd better find a bigger space. They were about to be invaded.

But as we were making our way north from the border on April 26, 1949, all I was concerned about was where we were going to find a place to lay our heads. Apparently there *was* no Alamo Plaza Motel in Calgary. We were going to have to stay at some railroad hotel called the Palliser. I just hoped it was clean and had hot water.

Ted told me he'd found out there were about 100,000 people in Calgary, which was a very large city in my experience, and that it had some really big buildings, but he'd also heard that it was basically a dusty cow town. They had some kind of rodeo every year. It sounded pretty rough. I closed my eyes and mumbled a fervent prayer: please – just let there be hot water. When I opened them, we were pulling to the curb in front of a baronial castle that I swear must have been lifted straight out of the Scottish highlands.

And when I carried little Sidney up the staircase into the hotel, I was convinced they had moved the castle's entire contents along with it. Mahogany panelling everywhere, crystal chandeliers, rich tapestries hanging on the walls, heavy velvet drapes on all the windows, gorgeous oak furniture; I decided there would probably be hot water after all.

Early the next morning, after Ted slipped out to go to work, I lay in bed afraid to open my eyes in case I'd imagined it. But, sure enough Toto, we weren't in Kansas anymore! I could hardly wait to get the kids up and dressed so we could start exploring our new city.

The skeleton staff in the Shell office was frantically trying to find more office space, so Ted was conscripted by Sutton Metz, the exploration manager, to find a corner somewhere to set up the geophysicists and geologists. Shell was bringing in every available American employee who had had any exploration experience, along with an administrative staff that could maximize the minimal time they had to buy up leases on likely looking sites. I knew I was going to be a single parent, yet again.

The kids and I went downstairs to breakfast in the hotel's big dining room and were introduced to the fresh-from-the-brick-oven crusty bread that the Palliser was justly famous for. And, as soon as I introduced myself to the Scottish waitresses and housemaids, they practically fought over who would get to look after Sidney and Ruthie, so I could start house-hunting.

That first day, though, we just explored downtown Calgary. Stepping outside the hotel, we could see the Hudson's Bay building and just down the street was the big Calgary Herald building across from the Lougheed Building. Eighth Avenue was obviously the main downtown thoroughfare, but there were hardly any cars on the street. Obviously, manufacturing in Canada hadn't caught up yet, but there were plenty of people in Calgary who would be customers as soon as things started rolling off the production lines.

Business people on the street were dressed to the nines. The men wore wool suits, and fedoras, and some were still wearing spats on their shoes. The women were all gussied up too, with hats and gloves. That crazy wind was still blowing a gale so no one was wearing a coat, and I remember thinking we'd have a lovely long summer to get settled.

Sidney spied the trolley coming down the street and forever after wanted to "ride the bell car" the minute we'd leave the hotel for any reason. That first day, though, I was in a hurry to find a newspaper to find the house-for-rent ads. I needn't have been in a rush. There was nothing. The Canadian farm boys had come home from the war looking for places to live in the cities, and I realized we'd have to get on Shell's list and wait for a company house. It looked as though we'd be staying at the Palliser for quite a while.

I was told that Rideau Park School was relatively close to downtown so, within a few days, I left our little guy with the chambermaid who volunteered to look after him, so I could register Ruthie. She marched right in and took her place in the second grade as though she was a veteran, which I guess she was. By this time she had been in four different schools. What she remembers, though, was being shy because in the beginning the other children teased her for talking funny. But back at the hotel, it wasn't long before she made friends with everyone on the staff, and they would regularly take both the children to the kitchen for milk and cookies still warm from the oven as soon as she returned from school each day.

And it wasn't as though my children were a novelty at the Palliser. By the time we had been there for a month or so, the place was riddled with American oil company kids all chasing one another through the hallways and slamming doors and riding the elevators to hide from one another. You would have thought the staff, not to mention the other *guests*, would have gone berserk with all the commotion. To the contrary, everyone was amazingly understanding besides being so very helpful to all of us mothers, who were basically on our own trying to keep the children in school and on some kind of regular schedule.

At one point while we were there, Sidney came down with a cold, and after a few days the chambermaid, who looked after him while I took Ruthie to school every morning, said he was running a fever and she was worried about him. I realized I needed to find a doctor, and the hotel put me in touch with Dr. Prieur, from the Associate Clinic. He came over to see him right away and announced that he had developed pneumonia. Dr. Prieur came every evening to check on him until he recovered. I was so grateful for his kindness and for the concern of everyone at the hotel.

Ted worked long, long hours and was often out in some field or other on the weekends, so the children and I spent the next two months really exploring the lay of the land. One day we rode the streetcar all the way to Bowness Park, and on another we found Grace Presbyterian Church, so I enrolled the children in Sunday school and asked if I could join the choir. The church was fabulous, a huge sandstone sanctuary built in 1912 that included an upper balcony with gorgeous stained glass windows and lovely oak pews arranged in a semi-circle around the raised pulpit. Upstairs, behind the choir loft and the organ, there were Sunday school rooms and a nursery. And, in the basement, there was a big dining room with a kitchen along with a church hall. I was really looking forward to meeting some of the congregation.

Sunday morning dawned, I dressed the children and off we went to church. Dr. Frank Morley, the minister, started the service as I expected he would with the reading of the scriptures. After that, I was lost. The hymns were totally unfamiliar, and by the time he got into the sermon I had absolutely no idea what he was talking about. Maybe I'd made a mistake. Maybe this wasn't a Presbyterian church at all. I flipped through the hymnbook, and aside from a few Christmas carols and *Jesus Loves Me*, it might have been Greek. I looked around at the congregation to see whether they were as confused as I was, but apparently it was just me.

So, not to seem unfriendly, at the end of the service I joined the congregation in the church parlour for coffee, held out my hand to the closest person to me and said, "Hello, my name is Lola. My family has just joined the church and I'm so eager to get to know you all." Fortunately, it was Dr. Morley's wife, Mary. She would come to be one of my closest friends.

Mary welcomed me and introduced me to so many others that by the time Shell found us a little house on Westmount Boulevard, I was feeling right at home. And finally, at long last, the moving truck arrived from Baton Rouge. We were actually going to get our family settled for the duration of our year in Calgary.

Shell rig, 1938.

The Estes clan assembled around the old oak table at Thanksgiving, 1939.

Ted, Lola, and baby Ruthie with her paternal grandparents in Michigan.

Ted and Lola nightclubbing in Detroit.

Ted with his new 1949 Buick – complete with portholes!

CHAPTER ELEVEN

Acclimating to Calgary

Well, yes, the moving truck did arrive. But when they started un-loading, it was obvious that only part of our stuff was on it. It seems that the Robinson's furniture took precedence over ours, so not all of our belongings got loaded on this particular truck. Mr. Robinson was the new vice president of Shell Canada and his comfort and well-being were definitely more of a concern to the powers that be than ours. We were assured the rest would be along eventually – hopefully before our year was up.

At that point, it hardly mattered. We had a wonderful little house on Westmount Boulevard that had been abandoned when one of the geologists had to go back to Chicago, so Shell said we could move in there until they got their real estate sorted out. It was finally almost summer. After that spell of warm wind in late April, it got cold and even snowed once or twice in May, but now spring had arrived complete with dandelions and June was glorious.

As I was exploring our little bungalow, I stepped out into the backyard and was completely confused by the clothes line. It was much higher than I could reach; there seemed to be a little platform on one end with steps leading up to it, but how in the world was I supposed to reach the rest of the line? My next door neighbour was outside and saw me puzzling over this problem and rescued me. She came over, we introduced ourselves, and she explained that the line was on a pulley. "It has to be up high so that in the winter the sheets won't drag on the snow. You just stand on that platform and pin the sheets and clothes to the line, then yank on the pulley to make room for more."

She and I became great friends. She directed me to the closest grocery store where I could get meat and canned goods, and explained that a green horse-drawn cart would be by once a week with fresh produce, and that the milk man would deliver our milk every morning and leave it in that little box built into the house by the back door. And, if I didn't want to bake my own, a bread man would be by once a week to take my order. I couldn't imagine why the milk would require its own housing, but I thought it impolite to question what she seemed to think was perfectly obvious.

We arranged the bits and pieces of our furniture and unloaded our suitcases and, as the kids and I walked over to the little elementary school where Ruthie would complete the second grade, we introduced ourselves to everyone we met along the way. Before long, all the horse-drawn wagons started appearing at my door just as my neighbour promised. The kids and I were amazed that the horses knew exactly where to go and when to stop and start up again; the drivers never even had to hold their reins.

The Chinese man on the green-grocer's cart had lots of wonderful fresh greens and carrots and potatoes and other root vegetables. But unfortunately, I learned that, as delicious as the bread man's fresh loaves were, I was expected to slice them. However, that was nothing compared to the problem with the margarine. For some reason, the law said we couldn't have coloured margarine because the dairy farmers didn't want us to think we were eating butter. So the margarine came in a white slab – looking just like a hunk of lard – with a little packet of orange food-colouring that we could knead into it if we wanted it to turn an appetizing butter-yellow.

I don't want to sound ungrateful. After all, we had all just come through food rationing; so, believe me, these little oddities weren't enough to annoy me. They were just odd. It was summer, with neither stifling heat nor humidity, the evenings were long and gloriously cool, we were nestled snug in our little house and all of us were perfectly happy. I could hardly wait until Nannie could come for a visit.

Before long, that rodeo I'd heard about arrived with a huge parade that must have included every horse in the province. My neighbour told me to get everyone a cowboy hat, dress up the kids in western duds, and bring along a sleeping bag so they could sit on the curb and get up close to the whole spectacle. And it truly *was* a spectacle. There were cowboys and Indians and floats and marching bands, and big cars full of dignitaries, and little cars full of Shriners – sort of like the Fourth of July – only much better because it lasted a full week. It was the Calgary Stampede! We did the whole thing that July: the rodeo, the midway, the grandstand show, the fireworks. We square-danced in the streets and went to neighbourhood Stampede barbeques and Shell Stampede parties, and ate pancakes and sausages, and beef and beans for seven straight days ... and nights. By the time it was over, I was glad Nannie said she couldn't make it until November. I think Stampede might have killed her.

She had promised to come for Thanksgiving though, so we started going to the mountains to plot out some sightseeing trips for when she arrived, and Ted and I both fell instantly in love with the Rockies. We were so afraid that we wouldn't have a chance to see everything before our year was up that it seemed that we found a way to spend at least a part of every weekend on the road to Banff that summer. He was our resident geologist, of course, so the trips were a long lecture series on what had happened to fold and erode the mountains and what layers of rock were more interesting than others. In those days, before the Trans-Canada Highway, the old Banff road was often mired in mud so it took a whole day to get there. We'd take along a picnic supper and stay overnight at Becker's Bungalows on Tunnel Mountain where the chipmunks and deer were so tame the kids could feed them by hand.

Shell provided company cars for the guys who had to be out in the field, but they were not to be used for pleasure trips, and everyone who had a company car had to take a solemn pledge to abide by those rules. But all of us were excited about seeing every-thing there was to see in the Rocky Mountains, and the men, of course, could hardly wait to go fly-fishing, so if sometimes the rules were bent a little, there was an unspoken agreement that no one in Shell's administration office needed to know.

One glorious weekend that summer, a couple of the geologists who had heard about a mountain stream full of trout decided they'd get an early start and sneak up to Banff on their way out to the field. The company car was loaded with groceries for the crew so they parked it just off the access path to the stream under some pines to make sure the car didn't get too hot – as well as to provide some camouflage, I suspect – then took off up the path with their fishing tackle.

They spent the whole day fishing – and catching – and finally meandered back down the path just at dusk. As they rounded the bend to find where they'd hidden the car, they heard a terrible racket and took off running to see what the commotion was all about, then skidded to a halt at the hood of their car, which was shaking like it was about to explode.

Arming themselves with their fishing poles, they crept closer and realized that whatever was inside that car had entered through the trunk, slashed its way through the back seat, and was obviously dining on those groceries. And, at the very instant they figured out who the culprit was, the intruder decided dinner was over, pushed his way out the driver's side by ripping the door off the hinges, and shambled off into the brush.

When they told the story later on, they said at first they figured they could claim a horrible highway accident – maybe a scenario involving being rear-ended by a monster transport truck. But, after closer examination of the wreckage, they realized they weren't going to be able to account for the fact that most of the upholstery had been eaten, and the claw marks where the trunk had been gashed open were also a little suspicious. In the end, though, they knew they'd never get away with it; there was just no way in the world they could get rid of that very pungent and completely unmistakable smell.

Needless to say, the rules around the company cars got considerably more stringent, but then, out of the blue, in the middle of August, Ted got a call saying that Shell had just bought a house on 8A Street. Would we like to claim it? It was perfect for all kinds of reasons. It was an almost brand new bi-level with a big living room, dining room, kitchen, and three bedrooms with lots of room upstairs for little Sidney's crib and a playroom for Ruthie. She could walk to Elbow Park School, and at the bottom of the hill there was a huge park surrounded by giant poplars. There was a baseball diamond on it, and we were told there was a skating rink there in the winter. I think that's what cinched the deal for Ted because, of course, he had learned to skate as a boy in Michigan and was eager for the kids to learn while we lived in Calgary.

There was also a lovely little stone church across the street from the park and, since I still couldn't decipher Frank Morley's sermons, I toyed with the idea of switching churches. However, one Sunday at a high-church Anglican service convinced me I'd better stay with the Presbyterians.

We moved in just in time for Ruthie to start third grade at Elbow Park Elementary. That fall was spectacular with blue, blue skies against the yellowing leaves and the soft warm days lured all of us outside for long walks by the river nearby. Our neighbours, Roxy and Dick Shillington, became our instant best friends. He was a dentist and she had been a school teacher, and their little Barbara was just a year or so older than our Sidney, so we spent a lot of time together that fall.

Builders were working furiously to frame in as many houses as they could, but the land west of us was still mostly open prairie where the older boys in the neighbourhood took their BB guns to shoot gophers. One day, Roxy and I got so involved in the conversation we were having in the backyard that when we looked up, we realized suddenly that both Barbara and Sidney were missing.

Calling and threatening wasn't getting us anywhere, and we were both beginning to panic as it started getting dark. We couldn't imagine where they'd gone, but I was mighty afraid they'd toddled off down to the river. Finally though, with their backs to the setting sun, we could see three-year-old Barbara tightly clutching two-year-old Sidney's hand, dragging him back home across the prairie.

Sidney never *did* think common-sense rules applied to him. He was constantly wandering off and getting into mischief, but we soon figured out that he just needed to see how things worked. One afternoon that fall, Ted arrived home early, bringing along a visiting fireman from Shell. If I remember correctly, we were going to take him out for dinner, but Ted poured him a drink and we were having a nice visit in the living room. I should have realized that 'having a nice visit' *should* have rung a few warning bells. If we were having a nice visit, where was Sidney?

Almost before I had processed that thought, in toddled Sidney with the sprinkler, dragging the hose behind him. Before any of us could react, he lugged it all the way into the living room, set it carefully in the middle of the carpet, and let 'er rip. I went for Sidney, knowing that if Ted got to him first there wasn't going to be a happy outcome. With the visiting fireman collapsed in hysterics, Ted leaped out of his chair and threw the sprinkler and hose outside while I rescued Sidney and deposited him in his room so I could distribute towels.

Roxy invited us to share Canadian Thanksgiving with them that October. I couldn't understand why it would have been moved from November where it belonged, but I was polite enough not to question that one too closely either. As October drew on, however, I began to understand. Suddenly, it was dark. And cold. The yellow poplar leaves piling up in the gutters were frozen in the morning, and I had to buy long cotton stockings and woollen mitts and a hat for Ruthie to wear to school.

By mid-November, it was *seriously* cold. Giving thanks at that time of year would have been next to impossible! Nannie was on her way to celebrate American Thanksgiving with us, but my Canadian neighbours kept assuring me that the strange warm wind that had welcomed us to the border in April would be back several times throughout the winter, so there'd undoubtedly be a Chinook at some point while she was with us. "That's the best thing about Calgary," they said. "It never stays cold too long."

They lied.

It wasn't that I deliberately misinformed Mama, but I may have not told her the whole truth, so when she arrived she was truly alarmed. As I stood at the door every morning wrapping Ruthie up in her parka and snow pants, with yards of wool scarf around her face, stuffing her feet into her snow boots, her head in her toque and her mitts over her sleeves, Nannie was wringing her hands moaning, "I cannot *believe* that you would even *think* of sending that child out in weather like this!" I'd lift the scarf and shove a spoonful of cod liver oil into Ruthie's mouth and push her out into the dark of the morning so she could slide down the hill to school. She'd climb back up it at noon because there were no provisions for lunch at the schools in those days. Children walked home for lunch; that was just the way it was, no matter what the weather. And by the time she walked home in the afternoon, it was dark again.

And no, it wasn't just the shock of our first Canadian winter. It *was* seriously cold! Even the Canadians admitted that. Planeload after planeload of American wives and children arriving from Oklahoma and Texas and Louisiana were landing daily at the Quonset hut they called the Calgary airport, and some of those women took one look out the window and refused to get off. Those that did deplane were sorry they hadn't asked what the temperature was before it was too late. That winter it bounced between 30 and 45 below Fahrenheit and stayed there for months … and months … and months. From our vantage point on the top of that hill, every morning I could see the smoke rising from the chimneys – straight up – not a breath of wind – icy, bitter, brutal cold.

But life went on, even for those of us from the hot-house tropics. Everyone learned to let their cars idle while they ran errands or went shopping to keep them from freezing up. (Yes, I too can hear all the environmentalists groaning.) There was one woman who ran into a drugstore to pick up a prescription, leaving her baby in the car to stay warm. From his perch on the front seat, he could just reach the gear shift. And pull it out of park. Unfortunately, the car was idling so fast that it drove itself right into a bus coming down 4th Street. There was no damage to the baby, but I was told his mother never recovered.

The men used to take the batteries out of their cars and bring them inside overnight to keep warm. We women were smarter. We learned that both Jenkins Groceteria and the Hudson's Bay Company stocked groceries and would take our orders over the phone and deliver them for a price ... which we were glad to pay.

And that little cubicle for the milk next to the back door? It may have helped keep the milk from freezing on most winter mornings, but that year the bottles came off the wagon with the cream already sitting two inches above their rims. They were frozen solid before they could even make it to the protection of the milk chute.

Most of us had grown up in the Deep South, and we wanted so much to experience everything we possibly could that winter. We knew we weren't likely to have another chance once our year was up, so almost every Friday evening we'd drive out to Bowness Lagoon or trudge down to the community rink with our first pairs of skates, determined to learn how it was done. Of course, all the kids picked it up pretty quickly and were mortified to be seen with their parents, who were gamely pushing around kitchen chairs like rickety old folk pushing their walkers.

Fortunately, I had Michigan-born Ted who could hold me up for at least one turn around the ice accompanied by *The Tennessee Waltz*, which was apparently the only recorded music the community owned. It was probably a very good thing because, by the time Patti Page warbled through the whole tragedy of her lost love, I had frozen solid and needed to escape back to the shack to warm up. There was always a circle of frozen wool mittens sizzling on the lid of the pot-bellied wood stove, and I discovered that if I took off my skates and held them close to the flames for a few minutes they might stay warm enough to thaw out my feet once I put them back on.

We should have picked up on the clue that *our* families were the only ones out there that winter. One of my friends found out why that was. She was determined that her children would learn to skate while they were in Canada, so every afternoon, as soon as she got the boys back to school after lunch, she would bundle up her three-year-old and off they'd go to the rink. She'd stuff her little girl into her parka and snow pants over layers of long johns and sweaters, packing her in so tight she could barely bend her knees much less pick herself up off the ice when she fell. And that was a problem because my friend was equally stuffed and equally inflexible. Finally, after about a week of this torture, her next door neighbour peeked her head out of her front door as they were leaving for the rink and hollered, "Mary Ann, I think you should know that not even *Canadians* make our children go skating when it's 40 below!"

Unfortunately, Ted had to spend much of his time in the field with the seismic crews that winter and their trucks and machinery constantly froze solid. Worse yet, there was no escape from the cold, and he was seriously afraid that the guys might freeze to death if they were left there overnight. He started sketching out plans for a transportable trailer that could serve as an office during the daytime and sleeping quarters at night. He looked up a Mr. S. D. Southern, who had started a little trailer company a couple of years prior, and talked him in to building a prototype based on his design. Before long, Mr. Southern's company could barely keep up with the demand. That company became ATCO Trailers.

We were neither mad dogs nor Englishmen, and there was definitely no heat in the midday sun, but we all liked to party, so not even *that* winter could discourage us from throwing together a bridge game or a pot luck supper whenever the mood struck. Frankly, there was a little bit of self-defence in our flash-mob socializing because, as much as we loved most of our neighbours, there were *some* Calgarians who resented the invasion of 1949.

Understandably so; we *were* a mob, and we *did* talk funny. Worse yet, most of us were finding places to live during a time of an extreme housing shortage thanks to the largess of the American oil companies. And those of us *without* company houses had large enough salaries to afford what homes that did come onto the market. To make matters even more uncomfortable all around, the companies – whose business, after all, wasn't actually real estate – were buying up as many houses as they could assemble, and they all seemed to be clustered in and around Mount Royal and Elbow Park, probably for reasons of management efficiency. But what they were creating was an American enclave in the southwest quadrant of the city that grew larger day by day.

This meant that all our kids were going to the same schools, we all seemed to attend the same Presbyterian and Baptist churches, and let's not forget the old resentment about the late arrival of the Americans into the war. But we invited our Canadian neighbours to join us for casual suppers and discovered they kind of enjoyed being introduced to jambalaya and cornbread. Then, of course, they happily reciprocated so we could try steak and kidney pie and prime rib with Yorkshire pudding.

But, more to the point, the fact was that in this relationship it was Canada supplying the raw materials and the U.S. corporations supplying the industrial capacity. We were there for a year to introduce the Canadian employees to the newest exploration technology. Then we'd leave. But it was made clear in many ways that some people thought that, once we were through pillaging their resources, we'd take the money and run.

Well, I figured, the only defence is to kill them with kindness. I volunteered to help out with any project that needed doing. I sang in the choir, of course, and quite literally got in up to my elbows in the annual Grace Church Christmas cake bazaar. (I hasten to clarify that this was an old and well-established tradition at Grace Church; I was just naïve enough to offer to help out.) I know you're going to think I'm exaggerating, but there's no hyperbole expansive enough to convey what actually happened that November.

The women of the church assembled in the basement kitchen every weekday morning. (Henry Ford would have been proud.) One woman was assigned to crack dozens of eggs as fast as she could, and another measured the bulk fruit. That poor soul had to pick through all the raisins to remove their stems. Another divided the fifty-pound flour sacks into manageable portions, and so on until we all manned the huge spatulas to pour the batter into individual loaf pans that we'd take home to bake in our own ovens. We'd bring them back to the church the next morning to wrap for the sale, and then start the whole production line again. Those Christmas cakes had become so popular over the years that they were almost all sold before we even started buying the ingredients. The bazaar was a significant fundraiser for the church and, as I say, it was an outstanding success. But I promise you, it was definitely a job of work.

Maybe I was just so busy through November and December that it simply didn't register on me that the American invasion wasn't slackening off. One newspaper columnist wrote that, on average, twelve babies were born every single day that year. More astonishing, thirty-one *new* people immigrated to Calgary each day – young people like us – at least in part responsible for launching that baby boom.

Yes, it's true that Ted was still working very long hours. And it's also true that he was up north very frequently checking on likely looking plays. But Nannie was there and we were keeping one another company, so I suppose I just didn't notice that there was no talk at all about our next assignment. We spent our Christmas together and there were lots of Shell parties to celebrate New Year's Eve. We invited all the Texans to our house on New Year's Day and Nannie fixed black-eyed peas to bring us good luck in the new decade. Maybe I just didn't hear the men talking among themselves about the fact that the company hadn't started making plans to send us home in the spring.

By mid-January, though, even I knew that Shell had discovered that Leduc and Redwater represented only the tip of a very, very large iceberg as far as the potential for Alberta oil was measured. Send people home? Not a chance. Shell needed *more* people; there would be no transfers. If an employee insisted on going back to the States, the company wouldn't guarantee him a comparable job. Everybody was needed in Alberta. Currency controls were a thing of the past. American corporations were on a massive hunt to locate and develop these resources; the Canadian economy would be fused even *more* closely with that of the United States.

Ted came home from the field one afternoon in late January. We still hadn't had a Chinook. He said we needed to talk. I felt sure I knew what was coming and I steeled myself to hear it.

CHAPTER TWELVE

The New Frontier

… and here *I* was thinking he was just going to tell me we'd have to stay a little longer … maybe until next fall. I never expected *this* bombshell!

"You want to leave the company? You want to leave Shell, but you want to stay in *Canada*?" Ted was talking fast and I was trying to stay composed enough to decipher what it was he was trying to tell me. "You're saying you want to leave Shell, start your own seismic company, and then contract your services *back* to Shell?"

I kept looking through the frost on the window as we sat together at the kitchen table, his voice now drowned out by the noise in my head. What in the world was he thinking? Didn't he know how lucky we were? He had a secure job with a great future. If he wanted to start his own company, why wouldn't we just go back to Texas to do that? And how could he start his own company anyhow? Even I knew how expensive a proposition *that* would be. And even if he could, who would he hire? Everybody he knew was tied up with the big oil companies. This was crazy!

Maybe if I was perfectly calm I could get through to him. "Won't Shell want this house back if you leave the company?"

"Yes."

I thought so. Not only would we be penniless, we'd be sleeping on the street. I glanced at the thermometer hanging outside on the window frame; if I was reading it correctly through the frost, it was 35 below.

It was like *I* was the one teetering on the top of the building threatening to jump and *Ted* was the rational one trying to talk me down. Very slowly he started listing off the steps it would take. We could cash in his Shell pension for the down payment on a house. He could put the house up as collateral on a business loan to finance the new company, and then buy whatever equipment he couldn't lease. And there were plenty of new graduates who'd taken advantage of free tuitions after they'd come back from the war; he could start recruiting geologists and geophysicists straight out of university. Exploration was going full bore in Alberta. All the big companies needed all the seismic data they could possibly assemble. The work he had done in the months since we'd arrived in Calgary gave him the first look at the potential that was out there – and that potential was virtually limitless. Being a part of this boom was giving him far greater experience and education than he would ever get by going back to Texas. Yes, this would be a risk, but it was a calculated risk. The worst that could happen was that it wouldn't work. If that happened he could always get another job.

I glanced again at the thermometer. It read 37 below.

January, 1950, is still the only January in recorded history that never had a single Chinook. I honestly don't remember what I did after listening to Ted's plans; I suspect I took to my bed. I'd like to think it was just to get warm, but most likely I headed there for a good cry.

In all our years together, I'd never once dug in my heels about a move, but this time we'd been *promised* that we'd get to go home after a year. This time, however, Ted didn't even want to wait until the year was up. He not only wanted to jump ship, he wanted to stay in this god-forsaken deep freeze and risk everything we had on a gamble that he could go it alone.

I guess I had to decide whether *I* could do it. It would mean far fewer chances to see my family back in Texas. We'd have to live on pretty slim pickin's; there'd be no money to spend on vacations back home to Texas. Would we lose contact with all our Shell friends? We'd have to move away from our wonderful neighbours on 8A Street. Would we even be able to find a house we could afford? All that new construction we'd seen in the spring had frozen to a complete stop, but that hadn't meant that the planes full of incoming Americans had. Ruthie would have to change schools ... again. And, let's face it, if he had to hire new graduates, we'd be right back to where we'd been ten years before. Ted would be spending the bulk of his time on a seismic crew again – at least until he got the new guys up to speed. I'd be a single parent with two small children isolated on the back of beyond.

I don't want to imply that Ted had made this a unilateral decision. He wanted me to sign on because he saw this as a joint effort between the two of us. And I knew he believed that's what it was; this was *our* decision. But that didn't make it any easier.

It would be nice to think I pulled myself together with a whither-thou-goest-I-will-go speech, but I doubt I was that selfless through that frigid, soul-destroying January. This was something Ted really wanted to do and, when push came to shove, I guess I knew he could. Count me in.

And no, it definitely wasn't that easy. What you have to remember is that people simply didn't jump from one job to another in those days. We had all come through the Depression, then through the war years into a very uncertain economy. If you were lucky enough to have a good job, you stayed there until you got your gold watch forty years later. You wonder why the '50s was such a conservative decade? Everyone had had their fill of uncertainty over the previous twenty years; all anyone wanted was a little peace and quiet.

Well, everyone but the Rozsas, I guess.

The bulk of Canadian oil and gas sits in the Western Canadian Sedimentary Basin, which stretches from southwestern Manitoba to northeastern British Columbia, and it covers most of Alberta. This wasn't news in 1950. Everyone knew about the big natural gas finds around Medicine Hat as early as 1890 and, in 1912, Eugene Coste had built the first important gas pipeline from Bow Island to consumers in Calgary. After Leduc, though, everyone in the petroleum world knew that Alberta's future would be all about oil.

Ted knew very well where the oil was; his job would be to prove that to clients he had yet to acquire.

He wasn't the first geophysicist in Calgary to reach a similar decision, however. John Galloway, who had been with Standard Oil, was transferred to Calgary from California in 1938 to open a local office. Five years later, he, too, resigned to start his own petroleum consulting firm. Others followed and in April, the month we arrived in Calgary, John assembled eleven others like him to talk about forming a Calgary chapter of the Society of Exploration Geophysicists. In June, fifty additional people gathered at the Palliser Hotel for an inaugural meeting where the Canadian Society of Exploration Geophysicists was born, and Ted paid his two-dollar membership fee.

I've learned over my many years that the only way to heal any loss, whether it's the death of a loved one or simply a disappointment, is to put your feet on the floor every morning and get to work. And half the work is just getting your feet on the floor.

Once I'd done that, the rest came along just as Ted had outlined it for me.

Well, sort of. By June he had his ducks in a row and was ready to announce his intentions to Shell, but they were so busy they begged him to start work immediately. They would sign the contract if he would stay on for another few months as a consultant. Nowadays, I'm told that if an exploration employee resigns, he or she is ushered out the door with a security guard to ensure no maps or confidential documents leave the premises. In those days, though, a man's handshake was his word, and, in Calgary's business community, a man's character defined whether or not he could be trusted. In Ted's case, he continued to work for Shell from June through November until finally he withdrew his pension and struck out on his own.

He named his new company Frontier Geophysical.

I found us a little house way out on the far western outskirts of Calgary in a brand new development that would come to be known as Marda Loop. Beyond us was nothing but prairie, foothills, and the Rocky Mountains, but Richmond Elementary School was close by and that was the only essential requirement. The house wasn't nearly as nice as the one we'd had to give back to Shell, but we had certainly lived in far worse. It would be fine.

That miserable first winter was finally over. Ted set up his first office at the house wearing the three hats of land man, geologist, and geophysicist. He had worked for Shell for fourteen years, and they knew what he could do. He was smart, honest, he knew the lay of the land in Alberta, and they knew he could be counted on. Shell agreed to be Frontier's first client.

In fact, within very short order he got a phone call from Joe Little, who was working for Shell, suggesting that if he was looking for a field crew, he had the perfect guy. His name was Sandy McDonald. He had a degree in engineering physics and wartime experience in artillery. He knew everything there was to know about explosives along with a healthy respect for them and was now interested in getting into seismic work. By the end of that week, Sandy and Ted were in our driveway building Frontier's first dog house, with little Sidney handing them tools as ordered.

The dog house is designed to hold the geophysical recording instruments and it's mounted on a truck. And once the ink was dry on the contract with Shell, they could buy a shooting truck and a water truck besides.

Ted found his crew of interpreters just as he'd predicted. He had been working at Shell with Wilf Baillie since our days in Jackson, Mississippi, and at his suggestion he hired Wilf's brother Dick to join Sandy on the crew. And over the next few months they brought on Ed Rutledge, Gerry Sykes, Ted Pattinson, and Bob James to complete their crew. Two years later, Wilf joined them as a partial owner.

Armed with a folding table and two chairs, Ted moved into two bare rooms he'd found in the back of the Uptown Theatre on 8th Avenue. For a while, when I could find a sitter for the kids, I'd go down there to woman the phone and keep some order, but very quickly Frontier got so busy they needed full-time office staff.

However, we still weren't eating very high off the hog. It was hot dogs and beans and peanut butter sandwiches for me and the kids, but it was definitely worse for Ted. He took his first crew north to the Peace River and Grande Prairie and worked very long hours. Money was so tight in the beginning that the crews had to use hand augers to drill the shot holes, but that first winter when the ground was as hard as cement, Sandy told me they'd just drop in a little dynamite and blast them open.

Then, quite quickly, it all began to pay off. Within a year Frontier grew to five crews.

Dick Baillie always said it was a dream job for a young guy trying to get a foothold on a career. He told me that since they did all the interpretation out in the field, he had a chance to learn everything from the guys who were basically pioneering the industry in Alberta. "Ted hired me as a computer, and then I was a surveyor, then party manager and, within a year and a half, I was party chief. Every time I got moved up a notch in the company I got a pay raise, so it was a pretty heady time. There was just so much opportunity out there!" Indeed, by the mid-'50s, there were about 175 crews operating in western Canada.

I had a hard time understanding why these big companies wouldn't just grow their own seismic operations in house, but Ted explained that the corporations were so hogtied by corporate regulations and policies that if ever they had to lay off a jug hustler for any non-performance issues, it would end up costing them far more than the employee was ever worth. On the other hand, if the employee belonged to the contractor, then it was up to the contractor to deal with the issues. And the contractor, if he was smart, made sure he didn't hire anyone who couldn't, or wouldn't, carry his weight.

The guys Ted hired were outstanding and we saw a lot of them socially as well as on the job. It felt very much like being back on those dusty, isolated plays back in Texas and Oklahoma with our big seismic crew family. They knew we had lived the life, so we understood what they were going through when they had to be away from their wives and girlfriends for weeks and months at a time. And we understood, probably better than most of the big corporate employers, how important it was to take care of those crews out on the job.

In the summer, the crew worked on jobs out on the plains, but in the winter they moved north near High Prairie close to the Swan Hills field. Ted bought the first half dozen trailers that ATCO produced for one of his very first camps. The trailers were on wheels, rather than skids, they were about twenty-five feet long and most had double-decker bunks as well as living space. That first winter, it went to 50 below, so the crew was pretty grateful for shelter. But in the beginning, the trailers only had little Duotherm heaters, so the guys on the top bunks nearly suffocated from the heat, while those on the bottom about perished from the cold. However, there was also an office trailer, a kitchen trailer, and a utility trailer with washrooms. Unquestionably, it was the utility trailer that was most appreciated; until that time, all the field crews, no matter who their employers were, had had to use outhouses. I take that back; it was actually the cook that was most appreciated. Everybody took *very* good care of the cook.

Dick Baillie used to say it might have been pretty chilly on those bottom bunks, but it was a far sight better than being outside trying to get the wheels on the trucks to turn. At 50 below, the rear differentials would freeze solid. "We'd drag trucks all over the compound trying to get the wheels to turn over because the grease in there was so stiff that the tires would just skid around on the snow before they warmed up enough to actually turn."

Ted, though, seemed to love being out there. He'd happily ensconce himself in one of the two rooms of the office trailer and work away on the interpretations late into the night. Dick said that one miserably cold night he and Sandy were in the other room trying to stay warm and they began hearing some strange noise they couldn't quite identify. Maybe, they thought, it's the almost musical sound they say you can sometimes hear with the northern lights. They stuck their heads out the trailer door, but no, the sound was coming from the other office. Dick said they pressed their ears to the wall and, sure enough, it was Ted contentedly singing to himself. He still chuckles remembering that time. "It was just so out of character for Ted," laughed Dick. "He was a great guy and he was extremely intelligent, but he was always so very reserved with people. This was an entirely new Ted!"

The kids on the crews were mostly young guys straight from the war or right off the family farm back in Saskatchewan or rural Alberta. They'd had no education in seismology, of course, so Ted and Wilf wrote a little textbook in order to help everyone understand how their on-the-job training actually related to the science of the discipline.

Hearing their stories now, I'm sure most people would cast a dubious eye at any of those jug hustler tales from the '50s. I wasn't actually there, of course, but I certainly heard enough to know they were real. Ted set the pace and everyone worked very hard, long hours. But when they had a chance, they played hard too. They were expected to actually record a certain number of hours every month, but those hours didn't include the time it took to service the equipment or even the time they had to stand down because of inclement weather. So, if they *did* get time off, they were ready to drink beer in whatever small town was closest to the site.

The bars opened at 11 o'clock in the morning and shut down for an hour at suppertime. Evidently, it was the courteous thing to do in the saloon culture to leave the crew's beer untouched on the table until the required hour was up, so they could resume drinking until closing time at 11 at night. In those days, beer parlours were segregated. Women without escorts were excluded, so these places definitely weren't meant for social drinking. There are veterans of some of those early seismic companies still bragging about staying awake and drinking beer through three straight days off, and then going back to work on the fourth, bright-eyed and bushy-tailed.

By the end of 1952, Frontier was well-established, and we had assembled seven outstanding crews plus two slim-hole rigs simply because word spread that it was a company well-regarded in the industry that treated its employees fairly. Ted never had to recruit new people; they came to him. Jean Donnelly, who replaced me in the office, stayed with the company for years and made sure everyone was supportive of all the people who worked there *and* in the field. My kids still talk about going down to the office with Ted, knowing where Jean kept the candy jar, and being genuinely welcomed by everyone. It really was a family, complete with company picnics every summer on the banks of the Elbow River.

And speaking of family, before too long there was enough money for me to take the kids back to Texas to visit all my brothers and sisters. In those days, boarding a flight was a dress-up occasion even though we had fly the milk run from Calgary to Lethbridge, to Cut Bank, to Great Falls, to Billings, to Sheridan, to Casper, to Denver, then finally transfer to an American flight into Dallas. That Calgary to Dallas flight was always packed with kids, most of them throwing up with every bumpy descent along the way, so by the time we at last made it to Denton, I'm afraid those dress-up clothes were more than a little the worse for wear.

My brother Charlie was a teacher, so he invited nine-year-old Ruthie to visit his class. He took her by the hand and introduced her to the children saying that she could tell them all about what it was like to live in Canada. She promptly launched into a lecture about living in an igloo and riding the dog sled to school. Evidently, though, she was an equal-opportunity prevaricator because her teacher told me that when she got back to Calgary and was invited to tell her classmates about her trip to Texas, she told them we were attacked by Indians and had to retreat to the fort for protection.

Things were going so well out in the field that I could afford a sitter occasionally, and I had a chance to get more involved with the American Woman's Club. It had actually started back in 1912 as a social club to encourage philanthropic and civic improvement activities, and it even had its own clubhouse on 14th Avenue and 10th Street. As you can well imagine, it got its second wind in 1949.

Between 1950 and 1960, it's estimated that 30,000 Americans arrived in Calgary and made it home. It wouldn't surprise me if 15,000 of them actually added their names to the membership list. We collected all our Southern recipes and published a cookbook to raise money for local charities and produced talent shows to take to the old folks' homes, and had bridge parties and book discussion groups and dances to entertain ourselves. We were a tenacious lot; the club wasn't finally dissolved until 2007.

Ted was even able to carve out a little time for recreation. He played in the Oilmen's Golf Tournament at the Banff Springs in 1951 but realized he'd only had that opportunity because he happened to be in town when the notice went out to all the big oil companies. The guys out in the field missed their chance since, by the time they heard about it, the draw was filled. Ted felt badly about that and started lobbying for a way to let them get involved too.

The next summer, he joined the Earl Grey Golf Club and played as often as he could, and he bought us tickets to the Calgary Symphony. The orchestra in those days was composed of enthusiastic amateurs playing to a small audience of even more enthusiastic listeners who assembled faithfully for every concert in the Grand Theatre downtown. Ted was determined to support it and to help it grow, and he continued to study the music as they introduced it to him.

Calgary had very quickly transitioned from dusty cow town to big-city status. It was truly a metropolis on the move, so it's almost impossible to exaggerate the frantic pace of the early '50s. The planeloads of Americans kept coming. As fast as you could say suburbia, the builders slapped up subdivisions of little houses made of ticky-tacky, and the city just kept mushrooming. Grace Presbyterian Church reported that the membership and the annual giving both doubled in the first half of that decade. Frontier Geophysical was thriving right along with Alberta's burgeoning economy. We barely had time to look around and smell the roses.

≫ CHAPTER THIRTEEN ≪

Two Cars in Every Garage

Well, on second thought, maybe we *did* have time to smell a few roses. I found out I was pregnant again the winter of 1953.

The little house on the prairie was no longer going to be big enough for us, so I went house-hunting. Actually, I didn't need to hunt at all. I knew *exactly* where I wanted to be. And that was right back in the neighbourhood with all the friends we had left in 1950.

Don and Mary Harvie were selling their house on the corner of 10th Street and Council Way, just two blocks or so from our former Shell house. Ruthie could go to junior high at Rideau Park and Sidney could start first grade at Elbow Park. I would again be close enough to the church to make it to evening choir practice and to the morning meetings of the women's fellowship. Wo-Shi-Lo (abbreviated from Work-Shine-Love) had just been organized by the American women of Grace Church who all lived in the Mount Royal/Elbow Park enclave, and it was really thriving, so I was eager to be even more active in the life of the church. The friendships I made in Wo-Shi-Lo with Gerry Brinkerhoff and Jean Dunlap during the early '50s, after we all arrived in Calgary from points south, have lasted to this day. And besides all that, I loved any chance I could get to take part in the musicals being produced at the American Woman's Club. This house was situated at the epicentre of my social life.

Just as an aside, Don Harvie's father, Eric, was the lawyer who presciently bought the mineral rights from the British Dominions Land Settlement Company, which had owned the former CPR property in central Alberta where the phenomenal Leduc discovery was made. He invested the great fortune that fell into *his* lap in the priceless collection that has made the Glenbow Museum the world-class museum and art gallery that it is today. And, following his example, Don and Mary have also been enormously generous to Calgary.

Anyway, they had outgrown their house too, so it came onto the market at the perfect time and we grabbed it. It wasn't a pretentious house in any way – really just a lovely little four-bedroom bungalow, but the minute we moved in I announced that the only way Ted would get me out of there would be feet-first. I loved it from that moment on. And so did Ted.

There was a green apple tree in the backyard, and I picked apples every fall to make pies and applesauce and baked apples. Our neighbours, Beryl and Leon Libin, started calling Ted the happy hooker because he invented a coat hanger contraption that could snag the apples from the top branches, but they didn't want to discourage him because they were getting some of that harvest simply because we couldn't possibly eat it all. In trade, though, they gave us jars and jars of delicious home-made kosher dills.

I realize now that not many of our granddaughters still do that sort of thing. Canning and pickling and preserving seem to be skills of the past, and if apple trees are still being planted, they're usually the ornamental variety that doesn't bear edible fruit. I suppose it's simply a matter of available time. When we were raising young families, most of us didn't work outside our homes. And besides, there was no such thing as prepared food in those days, so there was both the necessity and the time to spend on canning and cooking.

Those were also the days of the rumpus room, long before the family room was invented. The rumpus room was always in the basement, primarily because it was intended to be the children's playroom. Most often, it was an unfinished concrete dungeon with a washing machine in one corner and maybe a utility sink, but Wilf and Ted decided they could decorate ours, so they painted western scenes on all the walls to brighten it up for the kids.

Ruthie and Sidney were both in school by this time so I had the luxury of waiting through this pregnancy in relative leisure. These were the halcyon days before TV, so evenings were spent together as a family. We always had music playing on the record player. Broadway show tunes, jazz, classical, it really didn't matter. The kids and I sang and danced to it all. We had finally acclimated to the winters and knew better how to take them in stride, so the weather no longer got in the way of having a good time. Ted had bought us skis the winter before, so he and the kids went to Sunshine whenever possible, and I took them to all their activities at the church. Ted was able to be in town much of the time now that Frontier was booming along, so I had the chance to fix big Sunday dinners after church just the way Mama always did. We never found a table that would seat thirty, but I was always happy to accommodate who ever happened to show up, and I loved hosting the crew parties and hearing all their stories and watching their kids grow up. All of my children still say this was the best of times, when we were all together in this big extended family.

By spring, though, I was glad to get outside again and see about digging in a few flower beds close to the house. However, there was a little cotoneaster hedge around the front yard that became an issue. I'd always suspected that Ted was a touch obsessive and I'm afraid he proved me right that first summer. Mowing the lawn on a weekly basis was never enough. He'd do it twice week; first east–west, then north–south, and occasionally a third time diagonally. But that hedge had to be manicured, too. *No* one else was allowed to touch it. *THE HEDGE* belonged to him. Every weekend he'd throw on the ratty old grease-spattered coveralls he wore out in the field and, armed with hedge clippers and a carpenter's level, he'd confront his masterpiece. Seriously, he actually used a level.

The problem was, the house sat on kind of a treacherous corner. If you took it too fast there was good chance you could run into Ted's hedge, and, believe me, you didn't want to do that. He took an inordinate amount of pride in it, so we all learned to treat it with great respect.

Gossip got back to me that some woman driving through the neighbourhood saw grease-spattered Ted working on the hedge and stopped to question him about whether he'd consider taking care of her yard, too. She reportedly asked, "What do these people pay you?"

"Oh," said Ted, "this guy doesn't pay much. But once in a while he lets me sleep with his wife."

Needless to say, from that point forward, I tried to encourage him to play more golf on the weekends. He had first joined the Calgary Golf and Country Club and, about a year later, he joined the Earl Grey Golf Club, but several of the Earl Grey members were talking seriously about building a new course out at Canyon Meadows – waaay out south of the city – and Ted was intrigued by the idea. At that point, he was playing within a couple of strokes of par and he liked the idea of building a course that could meet championship specifications. So, on those long summer evenings, we'd drive out in the country to walk the fairways, pick out the rocks and the dandelions, and plant the trees. Eventually, he was on the first board of directors with Glen Watson and Sam Moss and, together with Otto Anderson, their first golf pro and course designer, they helped build the Canyon Meadows Clubhouse.

Then, at about the same time Ted decided that if the guys out in the field couldn't play in the Oilmen's Tournaments he'd help assemble a draw for a Doodlebug Tournament.(I love that name! Back in the day when diviners roamed the frontier offering to find water for the farmers and ranchers, they called their magical divining rods 'doodlebugs.' The name stuck, and, forever after, anyone looking for whatever might reside in the subsurface geology became known as a doodlebug.)

The kids like to say that Ted's priorities were family, work, and golf, but not necessarily in that order. I was never willing to pin him down on that list, but I certainly conceded that golf was as essential to him as the air he breathed. That summer he was, of course, signed up to play the first Doodlebug at Banff Springs, but there was serious doubt whether I'd be able to go along simply because, by the first of September, I was definitely great with child. However, Nannie and my sister Lillian were visiting at the time and Lillian checked me over and declared that, from her perspective as a nurse, I was safe for travel. So we left the kids with Nannie in Calgary, and off we went for a grown-ups' weekend at the Banff Springs Hotel.

While Ted played golf, Lillian and I walked the hiking paths around the golf course and found a bench to rest on by the river at Bow Falls. We knew that Marilyn Monroe and Robert Mitchum were in the area somewhere because they were filming *River of No Return*, and there was lots of activity going on with cameras and people busily doing whatever it is that filmmakers do. And suddenly, without any warning, there were Marilyn and her co-star dragging themselves out of the river right in front of us, both soaked to their skins. Their minions came running with blankets and off they all scurried to the warmth of their nearby trailer.

Now I can't say this for sure because I didn't actually see them go over Bow Falls, and frankly I can't imagine that any Hollywood lawyer would ever be crazy enough to let those two mega-stars do their own stunts, but it sure looked to us as though they had. They got by us so fast that I barely had time to recognize either of them so, when we went to dinner later that night and saw them huddled over a little table in a dark corner of the dining room, it was abundantly clear that I would have to apologize for my prior rudeness.

Much to Ted's embarrassment, I got up from our table and made my way over to Marilyn and Robert, held out my hand and said, "Hello, my name is Lola and I want to welcome you to Canada." Marilyn was very sweet and she patted my belly and said she hoped

I'd have a beautiful baby girl. Her dinner companion never so much as looked up from his plate.

Golf in those days was a sport for men. To be fair, most women realized it would take four or five hours out of the day and childcare was hard to come by, so there wasn't a big demand coming from younger women. But if there were women who *did* play golf, they most certainly weren't welcome to play in any of the tournaments. Harriet Watson, Glen's wife, had been a champion lady golfer in Oklahoma, and, when they moved to Calgary and joined Canyon Meadows, she started teaching some of us to play. But what the tournament organizers did in the '50s was find a few of the wives who could dream up some kind of entertainment for the women as well as plan the evening banquets and dances. It was *years* before they'd even consider scheduling a parallel tournament for the wives.

From my perspective now, I can hardly believe how conservative and staid we were in those days. None of us thought to object to being excluded from the tournaments. I'm pretty sure we thought we were incredibly lucky to be permitted to tag along to applaud the men.

In fact, we were *all* pretty fortunate in those days. President Hoover had promised a chicken in every pot in the '40s. In the '50s, Prime Minister St. Laurent could very well have promised two cars in every garage. The general sentiment was that, if government would stay out of the way, the demands of the marketplace would make sure we could *all* prosper.

The United States was still providing the overwhelming bulk of Canada's imported goods, but by the early '50s we were exporting twice as much to the States as we had before the war, and the demands of the post-war American military/industrial complex fuelled that growth. In ten years, American investment in Canada would represent fully three-quarters of all foreign investment, and most of that investment was in manufacturing, oil, and mining and smelting.

And yes, there was a dark side to that imbalance. American culture flooded into Canada right along with American currency. Few

Canadians were objecting in 1953, but it was an issue that would grow with time, and the American presence in Calgary walked a fine line between identities. On the one hand, we were ex-pats making our living in Canada but, during the '50s, all of us assumed we'd be headed back to the States any day, so we walked that line with one foot in each country. Every time any of us returned from trips home to visit our extended families, we hoarded the U.S. cash we brought back, so if any of us had an emergency we could pool our stashes of American currency for whoever needed it. We registered our Canadian-born babies with the American Consulate to ensure they had dual citizenship, and we flocked to the 4th of July parties they hosted ever year. In fact, I've been to so many of those 4th of July picnics, they've started seating me up front so I can schmooze the visiting dignitaries.

Eisenhower, the war hero, was elected president of the United States in 1952, and Louis St. Laurent was still prime minister of Canada so it was as if everyone in North America had agreed that all we needed during that post-war decade was a sane and sober father figure to keep the ship on course and out of the squalls. The Korean War ended that year, thankfully. The Cold War was heating up, but in 1953 we weren't really aware of what was going on. At the beginning, there was just a vaguely defined anxiety about what the Communists might do if they got hold of the nuclear technology that had been unleashed at the end of World War II. The difference in the early '50s was that we didn't have non-stop news coverage the way we do now. We were tired of the news. The further it stayed away, the more grateful we were to just get on with our lives and raise our families.

For those of us who were stay-at-home mothers, and most of us were, it was an era when child-rearing was a full-time job. Dr. Spock told us to relax, that we knew more than we thought we did. If the baby was crying, he was probably either hungry or wet, and, if neither, he likely just wanted some cuddling, so I suspect that we were all more heavily invested in our children in those days. By that time, penicillin and vaccinations had made most of the really terrifying diseases of childhood a thing of the past, so when the polio epidemic flared up in 1953 our anxiety about the unknown made us hyper-vigilant. That September, at the height of the epidemic, schools were closed, swimming pools were shut down, and we quarantined our children within the perimeters of our own backyards. In truth, the incidence of polio in Alberta was only about 1,500 cases, but one in ten died and others were left permanently disabled or encased in iron lungs. Actual numbers meant nothing; no one was willing to expose her child to possible contagion.

Within two years, Jonas Salk developed a vaccine that literally wiped polio from the face of the earth. Science could do that. Nothing was impossible.

1950 was obviously a very different decade for many reasons. The advances in science and technology were funded by the prosperity resulting from all the wartime manufacturing. So, science and technology, combined with the huge demand for post-war production and new housing, made the '50s the decade of consumerism.

That decade belonged to the young people. Those who survived the war years took advantage of free tuitions to get them started on careers of their choosing and they moved into the cities to prosper. No one was interested in the past. New homes weren't the cozy little cottages of our parents; what most of us wanted was sleek and modern. We were looking to the future. Ironically, we were setting ourselves up for a rude awakening in the next decade but, in Canada at least, we were pretty well insulated during the 1950s.

I suspect we were just as politically conservative as our Canadian neighbours, but we were considerably less formal. In Calgary, the ex-pat wives learned that you 'dressed' for dinner and if you left the house, winter or summer, you wore gloves and a hat. Hemlines were pegged at mid-calf. I knew older women who had been friends for years who called one another by their married names, as in 'Mrs. Jones' and 'Mrs. Smith.' Worse, there were specific social rules about who poured at afternoon tea parties and what end of the table she poured from. The society editor from the *Calgary Herald* had two columns assigned to cover every female event in town, and she referred to the women as 'Mrs. Robert Jones' or 'Mrs. Stanley Smith.' We women apparently had no names of our own. And there was a particularly officious young woman who wrote a column specifically directed at teenage girls where she harped at them endlessly about the expected rules of deportment.

Oh yes, I'm willing to concede that I was expected to follow Preacher's rules, but truly, this was different. This seemed to be a holdover from the old British class hierarchy, which had far less to do with morality than with keeping everyone in her rightful place. And I hasten to say that it didn't last all that long, but it was definitely there when we arrived and all of us commented on it.

Maybe, though, it was because the royalists were so thrilled about the coronation of Elizabeth II that year that they led the push to whip us all into a frenzy about the etiquette and protocol that was expected for an event of this magnitude. I certainly didn't expect an invitation, but eight thousand people were invited to the event from all over the colonies, including several people from Calgary. Those that went had a chance to buy the chairs that had been reserved for them in Westminster Abbey and ship them home. They were quite a keepsake.

I don't want to sound blasé because the kids and I had been in Texas when King George VI died and I watched the funeral procession on TV with great interest, so I knew the coronation was going to be a grand spectacle. It would be a once-in-a-lifetime opportunity to see the ancient pageantry of the English aristocracy at its best, and it was very exciting to hear all about the planning for it. It was the one time I was really sorry that TV hadn't yet made it to Calgary because I would have loved to watch the whole thing, but I'm afraid we all had to settle for newspaper photos.

However, as exciting as all that pomp and pageantry was, it couldn't compare to the *best* event of 1953. On September 12, our daughter Mary Lillian was born. And just as Marilyn Monroe had predicted, she was indeed a beautiful little girl.

However, the doctor whisked her away before I could even count her fingers and toes to check her over thoroughly. With this pregnancy I found out why I had had the previous miscarriages. I was Rh negative. Ted was Rh positive. Because of this incompatibility of blood types, the babies weren't able to survive because they unfortunately inherited Ted's blood type. And because of the blood exchange through the placenta, my antibodies were recognizing the different blood types of the babies so they were attacking them as a foreign substance. Despite the army of Estes kin who surrounded me with each pregnancy, no amount of tender love and care could overcome what my own body was doing to the babies *in utero*.

When she was born, Mary Lil hadn't had to fight this process because our blood types were compatible. And fortunately, by this time, medical science had figured out what was happening, so the doctors were able to ensure no incompatibility could occur. By the time they handed her back to me, she was pink and glowing with heath. Unfortunately though, I had some post-partum difficulties, which ultimately resulted in a medical pronouncement that this should be our last child.

Mary Lil was a beautiful, happy baby. Her older sister was soon to be twelve; her big brother was six. Frontier Geophysical was thriving. Life was very, very good for the Rozsa family.

CHAPTER FOURTEEN

And Now We Are Five

We brought Mary Lil home and introduced her to her big sister, who became like her second mother, and to her brother who I'm sure instantly recognized that eventually she would interfere with his toys, so she'd better keep her distance. I've often thought what a luxury it was to have such widely spaced children. It gave me a chance to devote my full attention to them one at a time and to savour their baby years. But of course it also meant they had nothing in common with one another until they grew up. Compared to my family of six siblings in ten years, my three children had a very different experience. I suppose there are advantages to each kind of family. On that day, however, I thought ours was perfect. The baby and I settled in to get to know one another through a long, cozy winter and she grew happy and healthy.

By the time she was close to two years old, I found a wonderful woman who could look after Mary Lil and the other two children occasionally so I could join Ted on the golf course out at Canyon Meadows. I had never played golf, but Ted loved the game and was a fabulous teacher, so that made it easy for me to gain enough confidence to sign up to play with the ladies on Tuesday mornings. And slowly, with a little extra coaching from Harriet Watson, I discovered I could play well enough not to embarrass myself too often.

They say there's no such thing as a casual golfer. They're right. It's probably the most frustrating – and addictive - sport ever invented.

The problem is, in eighteen holes *every* golfer can hit at least one perfect shot. Perfect. Obviously that shot is in there somewhere – you pulled it out this one time. Why shouldn't you be able to pull it out again? String a few of those together and you could play the tour. But, of course, you can't. It's gone. Never to be repeated.

The next day, you hit a *different* perfect shot. The same thought goes through your head. But no, it too vanished the moment it left your club.

I have a friend who's a tennis player. She says that if you hit 10,000 forehands and 10,000 backhands and 10,000 lobs, and 10,000 drop shots, eventually you can play a pretty decent set of tennis. But in golf you *never* hit the same shot twice. The ball is always on a different slope or in a different rough, or the pin is in a different position, or the distance between you and the green requires you to use a different club, or the wind is blowing a different direction, or your socks don't match the colour of your tees. (I threw that last one in there to see if you're paying attention.)

The point is, golf is not an easy game. The Scots invented it, as you know, and, being good Calvinists, I suspect their motive was to make it a test of character. I quickly learned that my only opponent was myself and one of me was likely to lose. If I couldn't have fun just being in the moment enjoying the day and the company of my golfing partner, then maybe this wasn't going to be the sport for me. Worst case scenario: I could always play tennis. Tennis is far less expensive and it seldom takes four hours to play. Unfortunately, however, I loved to play golf from the moment Ted handed me my first five iron. I was instantly addicted.

That summer drew too quickly to a close, but I was happy to get back to some of the things I liked to do in the community. Ted and I had remained very faithful to the Calgary Symphony Orchestra while they were playing downtown at the Grand Theatre. So, when it was announced that Alberta would be celebrating the fiftieth anniversary of the province by constructing state-of-the-art performing arts theatres in both Calgary and Edmonton, we were both very supportive of the movement to upgrade the Symphony's musical professionalism to match that of their new home.

Contrary to Calgary's prevailing image as a cow town, the city had had an enthusiastic arts community almost from the day the North-West Mounted Police built Fort Calgary in 1875. The Mounties' primary duty was to establish friendly relations with the people of the First Nations, but, to do that, their first two priorities were to push the whiskey traders back into Montana and then to maintain law and order. They made friends with the ranchers scattered in the area, many of whom had ventured west directly from the sophisticated cities of the east where they were accustomed to the finer things of civilized society, so the officers occasionally hosted receptions and welcomed any visiting musicians. Rumour has it that these soirees at the fort were well lubricated by the evidence seized from the whiskey traders, but this was undoubtedly very helpful in encouraging an appreciation of many things.

The first Calgary Symphony Orchestra was founded in 1910 by violinist A. P. Howell and, in 1947, the New Calgary Symphony was assembled by Clayton Hare, who combined the old orchestra, comprised largely of community volunteers, with members from the Mount Royal College Orchestra. They performed about ten times a year in the old Grand Theatre on 1st Street West to loyal and enthusiastic audiences.

By 1955, however, their audience decided that Calgary deserved a professional Philharmonic Orchestra. The Dutch conductor, Henry Plukker, was approached to find out whether he might be willing to come to Calgary and oversee the considerably complex transition from amateur to professional musicians. He agreed. For a price. The transition had begun. This would take more than enthusiasm; it would take development funds.

Shortly thereafter, Percy Smith who owned another seismic service company, approached Ted one day with his hand outstretched. Ted knew Percy, of course, but he was caught flat-footed when, instead of greeting him as a fellow oilman, Percy said he was on a mission on behalf of the new Philharmonic Orchestra. Would Ted write them a cheque for $1,000?

In hindsight, that first $1,000 seems like an easy ask. And, in truth, it was. Ted loved the music and Percy knew that if he could get Ted and others like him on board, they would become far more than season-ticket subscribers, they would be development partners for life. It was an excellent strategy on Percy's part because it was frankly a win/win proposition. The orchestra provided Ted with the immeasurable pleasure of their music, and he, in turn, offered them his services throughout the years as a board director and frequent contributor, and throughout the years he happily immersed himself in his study of classical music. And 'immersion' is definitely not an exaggeration. Anything worth doing, according to that man I lived with, was worth doing to excess. He built himself a fabulous stereo system so he could listen to the recordings of the music the orchestra was planning for the current season, and then compare the different interpretations of the compositions after he heard the orchestra's performances. Unfortunately, he expected the rest of the family to appreciate those subtle differences, too. But to his credit, the musicians in the orchestra recognized that Ted, even though he wasn't a trained musician himself, was extraordinarily well informed about their art. In fact, at one point many years later, they invited Ted to select the music for the upcoming season.

Within two years, the Calgary Philharmonic Orchestra under the baton of Henry Plukker moved out of the Grand Theatre and into the newly completed Jubilee Auditorium, where audiences of a thousand or more came to hear each new concert, growing their own appreciation of the music accompanied by the growing strength of musicians' performances.

At about the same time, I was hoping to get more involved with music because I loved singing in my church choir and, through Ted's interest I had also learned to appreciate classical music and thought I might be able to help with some of the fundraising too.

The Women's League of the Philharmonic was launched in 1955 to raise money for the orchestra and to help grow an appreciation for classical music through the schools and eventually to offer music scholarships too. Molly Mooney was the first president of the League and I volunteered to help – along with others, of course – so for the first several years we brainstormed all kinds of wild schemes to raise money.

But then someone brought in a great idea. What would we think about holding a used book sale? Just between you and me, I'll admit I was perhaps a little dismissive of the effort it would take. I thought, how hard can this be? I'm a veteran of the Grace Presbyterian Church Christmas Cake Bazaar marathons after all. A few phone calls, a day selling books … no problem.

Before I go any further, I think I should explain the truly awesome phenomenon of voluntarism in Calgary. There must have been something in the water in those days because I've never seen the equal of it anywhere else. It was as though Calgarians were absolutely helpless when approached for assistance with whatever cause was being peddled at the moment. They seemed physically unable to say no. I don't mean that they were just quick to write a cheque. They wrote the cheque *and* they stepped up to the plate to help make it happen.

And it wasn't a new phenomenon. Nor was it peculiar only to the male half of the population. I suppose it might have started with the homesteaders who came to the Prairies and realized they'd better help one another raise their barns and get their wheat in before the frost just so they could all survive the winter. But then, as early as 1912, they decided that Calgary needed an exhibition to advertise the limitless possibilities that awaited new immigrants to the west, and the Calgary Exhibition and Stampede was born. I'm told by the historians that the very first parade was attended by an estimated 80,000 people – a number made even more impressive when you know that the population at that time was only 60,000!

This monumental annual effort has always required the incredibly intense labour of literally thousands of volunteers. But then at about the same time, the Calgary Local Council of Women was organized and started raising funds and providing the womanpower to address the needs of the community's less-advantaged people. Unlike most communities I had been familiar with in the South, voluntarism in Calgary didn't necessarily restrict itself to the churches and the Rotary clubs. *Every*one did their part, including the unchurched. The Women's Christian Temperance Union, the Mothers' Milk Fund, the Library Society, the Children's Hospital Society, the Calgary Horticultural Society, the Lions Club, the Calgary Humane Society, the United Way, and, yes, the American Woman's Club. More and more and more charitable organizations sprang up to do good works, raise funds, and provide services where necessary. By 1955, it was obvious that the progeny of those early volunteers were still drinking the magic water.

I may be getting ahead of myself here, but just to prove my point, I'll add one thing. The 1988 Winter Olympics in Calgary was run *entirely* by volunteers; 10,000 volunteers. That had never been done before. Or *since*, for that matter.

As you can see, I wasn't joining a bunch of amateurs. The idea had been proposed by one of the American women who had seen it done in her hometown back in the States, but these women of the Philharmonic knew what it would take and how to get it done. Calgary's Benny the Bookworm Sale was officially launched and Nadine Blake, the new president of the Philharmonic Women's League, mobilized the troops.

Who knew Calgarians were such voracious readers? As I recall, this was the first used book sale conceived in Calgary, so we thought our most difficult hurdle would be in explaining the concept to potential donors. Not so. People fell on us practically weeping in gratitude the minute they found out we'd be relieving them of their old books. That first year, we offered to pick up books all over town, and the donors welcomed us with open arms. Open, but not empty.

Grocery bags, cardboard boxes, suitcases and trunks – all full to the brim with books. We should have gone armed with dollies to move the haul out to our cars, but none of us expected such a bounty of riches.

We stored our collected trove in our basements until the day prior to the sale and then lugged the books downtown for sorting. There was a little store across the street from the Hudson's Bay that permitted us to use their premises for three days: Thursday for sorting and assigning to tables, Friday morning for the finishing touches, Friday afternoon and Saturday morning for the sale.

So, on the assigned Thursday, we sorted and priced everything – in those days that even included *National Geographic* magazines – and then opened the door promptly at noon on Friday. However, it was quickly obvious that book lovers are closet hoarders too, because as soon as we opened for business, there were our donors … buying more books.

We should have realized we were creating a monster, but I suppose we were giddy with our success. At the end of the day, we counted our money and we were just short of $1,000. We looked at each other and then, without a word, all of us opened our purses and added enough change to make it an even thousand. We could hardly wait to schedule it on our calendars the next year. We proudly presented our cheque to the board of the Philharmonic and told them there was more where that came from.

What we didn't expect, though, was that all those voracious readers scheduled it on *their* calendars, too! And they told their friends. They were waiting for us, armed with books and dangerously overstocked. We had unwittingly created a Rube Goldberg perpetual motion machine we'd never be able to stop. Benny was a flow-through supplier for book junkies.

The next year remains a bit of a blur. The original twenty of us obviously weren't going to be enough to handle the onslaught. We expanded. We knew we couldn't manage the pick-up-and-delivery system we had started with, so we made our phone calls and launched a little advertising campaign to invite donors to bring their cache of unwanted books down to the Philharmonic's office. The staff would store them. (Needless to say, *that* didn't work a second time.)

The next year, we made a giant bookworm out of papier mâché. It was about twelve feet long and three feet around, and we painted it such a garish shade of yellow-green that we were afraid it might frighten small children. But what the heck, it was terrific advertising and we lugged Benny around everywhere we went.

A store across from Eaton's donated their space, and the same hours were advertised, but this time we had people lined up down the street waiting to get in. Joyce Matthews and I thought to bring in a record player so the customers could hear the music of the Philharmonic as they shopped, and that seemed to be another magic ingredient. We made *more* than a thousand dollars and, even before we hustled the last customer out the door, our new president, Jean Funnell, whose husband was the manager of the Bay, suggested that we move the sale there the next year. Suggested is probably not quite the right word. She insisted.

Sure enough, the Bay turned out to be the perfect venue. They could receive and store the books for us and, on the expanded two and a half days of the sale, people were lined up before the store opened. Those that couldn't squeeze into the area reserved for the book sale were forced to shop through the department store until the previous buyers made room. It was a licence to print money. We made so much profit that we weren't even resentful of the few books left unsold at the end of the day. Those were sent to the correctional institution just out of town.

We kept the sale at the Bay for several years then moved out to the new Chinook Shopping Mall following the suburbanites as the city grew. There used to be a party game that everyone played during those expansionist times. Someone would look around at a room crowded with guests and ask, "Is there anyone here who's actually a native of Calgary?" Invariably, there would be only be a scattered few. Everyone seemed to be from somewhere else. But Calgary was the perfect place for that to happen because it meant that there weren't social barriers that excluded anyone. In the decade between 1950 and 1960, the city's population *more* than doubled. With all the immigration of the previous ten years, Calgary had reached its tipping point and had become a city that took pride in its ability to absorb its newcomers. Strangers were welcomed and invited to get involved. The Philharmonic thrived and continued to accommodate those people who were new to classical music and in fact jumped at the opportunity to introduce their music to the uninitiated.

The Women's League arranged for all the junior high students in the city to have a morning at a live Philharmonic concert, thanks to the generosity of the bus companies, the Calgary Public School Board, and the city Police Services. And, before long, we even had enough money to award two music scholarships each year. Benny the Bookworm made all that possible.

Benny gave me a chance to be a small part of that success, and I remain grateful to this day for everything those experiences taught me. I found out how to inspire others to get involved, and how a successful advertising plan is launched, and how to engage the media and business leaders in a civic project, and how to leverage one donated gift to enable three others to follow. I realized that if I really listened to people, they were invariably telling me what they hoped could happen. All that remained was for me to help that process along. Most people are genuinely happy to help; sometimes they just need to know *how* to do that.

You know the old saying about it taking a village to raise a child? Well, it also takes the whole village to build a healthy community. Never think that a few people can do it all; it truly takes all of us contributing whatever time and talent we can share. I loved being a small part of Benny's success, but I also saw so many other community projects going on at the same time that I was – and remain – truly humbled by the generosity of thousands of others, so many of whom were *new* Calgarians. These were people who had only recently arrived and yet they wholeheartedly poured their support into making this city one that we are all so proud of. I remember being at a party one time when, once again, the familiar question was asked. "Is anyone here actually a Calgarian?" There was a pause, and then a man stood up and said, "Yes, I'm a Calgarian. By choice."

Me too.

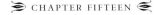

CHAPTER FIFTEEN

Home Again, Home Again

Yes, me too.

But no matter how strong our ties to Calgary, I still missed my family, and I always made a priority of taking the kids back to Texas to visit. In the summer of 1958, we went for a reunion with the Estes clan at a lodge on a huge lake in north Texas. In fact, we had a minor claim to fame as far as that lake was concerned because it was my father, the Preacher, who named it.

Thirty or so years prior, probably as another of President Roosevelt's public works projects, the Dennison Dam had been authorized for construction to control flooding and to generate hydro-electric power on the border between Texas and Oklahoma. During World War II, German prisoners of war were put to work helping to finish it, and in 1944 all was ready for its official opening. Sam Rayburn, my father's good friend who was speaker of the United States House of Representatives, was sent to officiate on behalf of the U.S. Government. Sam came to call on Preacher to ask his assistance at the dedication. He said the lake was going to need a name but that he hadn't been able to think of anything that would be acceptable to the Oklahomans as well as to the Texans, who both wanted to claim it. "Well," said Preacher, "why not call it Lake Texoma?"

Lake Texoma it became and so it still remains, a beautiful recreational lake with more than a thousand miles of shoreline. In the summer of 1958, we were all headed to the Lake Texoma Lodge and were looking forward to learning how to water-ski. Ann and Ed brought their new boat – attached to their brand new turquoise Impala convertible – and the kids fell all over one another trying to be the first to get up on the skis.

Finally it was the grown-ups' turn, so Ruthie was the assigned spotter with my nephew Eddie driving the boat. I had watched all the kids gradually lift up out of the water onto the skis, so, following instructions, I centred myself over the skis, yelled to Ruthie that I was ready, and the boat took off. Well, I'm not sure what went wrong, but I simply couldn't stand up on those skis. I was hanging on to the rope for dear life, bouncing down the length of that lake on my bottom too terrified to let go, and Ruthie was laughing so hard she couldn't tell Eddie to stop. I don't think I've forgiven her yet.

By 1959, though, the kids were growing up and trips home were getting harder to orchestrate. Mary Lil had started school and Sidney was involved with his friends in all their junior high's activities. After Ruthie graduated from Central High School in June, she and I decided we'd drive down to the University of Colorado together to get her settled in her dorm room.

In those days, college kids didn't load up their backpacks with a couple of pairs of jeans and a few tee-shirts and call it a wardrobe. We spent *weeks* shopping: outfits appropriate to wear to class, outfits for weekend wear, party outfits, and formals both long and calf-length for dressy events. I still shudder remembering the number of pairs of shoes required to match all that! There were linens for her dorm room, her record player, her radio, and whatever keepsakes she felt she couldn't survive without. It took all summer to assemble all that paraphernalia, and it took most of the morning that early September day to load up the trunk and back seat of our current car. It was a coral and sand Oldsmobile that seemed about a block long, and I figured that even though we got kind of a late start, we could make up some time once we got to the highway. As we finally lumbered off toward the border, I was confident that if we had to we could find a place to stay overnight somewhere in Montana.

There's nothing more fun than a road trip with your daughter. We yattered our way through southern Alberta, made a stop at every potentially interesting roadside junk sale, and only noticed that it was starting to get dark after we crossed the border and realized that any evidence of human habitation was becoming more and more sparse. Then, the dusk became dark night. Oh yes, there were definitely stars in the sky, and for that matter we even had a sliver of moon. We knew that because our headlights were pointing straight up, like search-lights illuminating the heavens. We had so overloaded the car that the rear end was practically dragging on the pavement. However, that meant we couldn't see a thing *other* than the sky. The road ahead was in the pitch black of deep night. If there *had* been a sign directing us to a motel, we couldn't have seen it, and, besides, I was trying to drive using Braille – weaving between the rumble strips on the right shoulder and the rumble strips on the left shoulder to keep me centred on the road. It was a very long trip.

My solo journey back home in an empty car was much less eventful but, further to the wardrobe issues, I had some planning to do. Friends in Calgary had floated the idea that Ruthie might like to be a part of the Calgary Highlanders' Debutante Ball in the coming June, and Ted and I were delighted. We knew it would be fun for her to take part, and she would have a glimpse at a centuries-old British tradition that had made its way to the colonies around the world. Originally, the whole idea behind debutante balls was to provide an occasion where one might present his marriageable young daughter to suitable suitors of a certain similar social circle. (She sells sea shells by the seashore!) It was all rather anachronistic by 1960, and Ruthie certainly had no inclination to consider any suitors we might choose for her, but she *did* love a good party. However, this would require another wardrobe – for *all* of us.

When she arrived home from university in the spring, Ruthie was immediately swept up in all the pre-Ball festivities. There were brunches and afternoon tea parties hosted by all the girls' families, fittings for the white ball gown she would wear, and armpit-length white kid gloves to purchase to wear with it. She learned to walk down the elegant Palliser staircase in her voluminous ball gown by feeling the back edge of each step before actually committing to it, so she wouldn't plummet into the girl ahead of her and topple them all like dominoes. There were curtsey lessons so none of the girls would wobble when they were presented to all the attending dignitaries, and dance classes with the Highlander cadets and young officers who would be the girls' escorts for the occasion.

The Calgary Highlanders are a light infantry battalion of the Canadian Expeditionary Force, and the young men in their scarlet dress jackets and Black Watch kilts seemed right at home in the baronial ballroom of the Palliser Hotel that night. And when the pipers and drummers led the sixteen girls and their escorts in for their presentation and introduction to Georges Vanier, the Governor General of Canada, and the Lieutenant Governor of Alberta, Percy Page, I have to tell you it was magical moment … anachronistic or not.

Back in real life, Mary Lil and Sidney were happily engaged with school and their friends. It wasn't going to be as easy to break free from all that as it had once been, and our trips back to Texas became fewer and shorter. Besides, after ten years in Calgary I discovered I was feeling more and more at home. We had built close friendships with everyone on Ted's crew and from Canyon Meadows, and my church choir, and a great many from our volunteer work with the Philharmonic. I can't say we had learned to love the climate, but we most certainly loved the people.

We had met Beryl and Leon Libin over the back fence when we first moved to 10th Street, and they in turn introduced us to many of their friends and our other neighbours. And since I was about ten years older than Beryl, I became the go-to big sister in matters of emotional crisis. When Beryl turned thirty and was totally inconsolable, grieving over her lost youth, I grabbed Leon and told him to take all the kids for ice cream so I could comfort Beryl. He clamped his ever-present cigar between his teeth, piled the kids into the back seat of his car and took off, leaving Beryl and me to work through this crisis over a slice of cheesecake. From that point forward, the kids adopted him as their surrogate father and invented every possible problem that might require an ice cream solution.

Frontier Geophysical had moved out to a new building on Acadia Boulevard in 1955 and by 1956 they were using the new playback technology, so Ted and the other interpreters were spending the majority of their time at the office in Calgary rather than out in the field. It seemed like we had finally sunk roots. Thankfully, we had planted them in what was rapidly becoming inner city.

Calgary was oozing beyond its borders so quickly that new subdivisions had to wait for paved roads long after the new home buyers moved in. I was always commiserating with friends who looked forward to winter freeze-up because, once spring arrived, out came the gumboots. But the pace of construction in those days was unbelievably frenzied; no one could keep up. That was the year that McMahon Stadium was built in only a hundred days. And the University of Alberta's Calgary Campus, next door to the stadium, opened to its first students that fall. It would take a few years before it finally seceded from the University of Alberta, but that political process certainly didn't get in the way of all the new buildings that shot up all over the campus. I remember thinking how nice it would be if the U of C was well-established by the time Sidney was ready for college.

You're probably thinking that anyone with *my* history of hopscotching through multiple homes would know better than to talk about sinking roots. I'd never stayed *any*where longer than ten years. Maybe I was getting so rooted that I'd forgotten that the geophysical industry *has* no fixed address. So even though we had recently been to a cluster of farewell parties for oil-industry friends who were being transferred back to the States, when Ted came home one day and announced that Frontier was going to have to make some pretty drastic changes, he completely took me by surprise.

Until the late '50s, geophysical contracts were awarded on a yearly basis despite the fact that the Alberta government prohibited any activity during the month of April until mid-May because of road conditions into the back country. This meant that Frontier, along with all the other crews, had to stand down for that six-week period and the companies who had contracted their services were paying them despite that hiatus because there was just so much work they couldn't afford not to.

By 1961, however, the big companies started pulling in their oars and ceasing to out-source their work. They announced to the geophysical industry that contracts offered in the future would be short-term, if at all. At the time, Frontier had seven crews and one slim-hole rig. Sadly, some of the crew would have to be let go.

It was a very tough time. The guys at Frontier really were like an extension of our family, and Ted agonized over each one of them. Some wanted to find different jobs in the industry and others decided that the timing was right to go back to school to back up their on-the-job training with university degrees or technical diplomas. Ted was able to help with those transitions. But some of the office crew had been with him since the beginning, and they felt like they were losing the company they, too, had built. And justifiably so.

Ted had a lot of sleepless nights trying to figure out a way that would permit the fellows that had stayed with Frontier through all its transitions to keep the company and hopefully hang onto it through this rough patch in the economy. He approached Sandy McDonald, Ed Rutledge, and Dick Baillie with a proposition. Would they be interested in keeping Frontier if he could arrange financing that would enable them to buy it with no money down? He would keep 50 per cent of the company; they could buy the other half and pay him for it through their future profits. It would mean they would have to strip it to its bare bones for a while, but it would be their company. Ted would be the major shareholder, but he would be a silent partner. The company would be theirs to operate as they saw fit.

Dick Baillie still says that when that deal was offered to them, none of them could believe their good fortune. "It was incredibly generous. Anyone else would have just sold the company outright, but Ted gave us a chance even though he knew we had no way to buy it from him. All of us were raising families in those days and were mortgaged to the hilt, so we had no capital to invest at all. And he had no way of knowing whether we could make a go of it. He simply trusted that we could. But there was even icing on *that* cake: he gave us the company membership to Canyon Meadows too!"

Ted wasn't a workaholic by any means, but what really drove him was an insatiable curiosity about new technology. The kids used to say, "Never ask Dad to tell you the time. He'll try to tell you how to build a watch." All kidding aside though, he really did need to know how things worked, and nothing made him happier than trying to improve a new invention. So, when the guys agreed to take over Frontier, he kept a little office in their building and started researching options for his own future. He had always been the first to try out whatever was being touted as the latest and best equipment, so when some fellows arrived from Houston with a new idea for a seismic machine that would do the work of the subsurface reverberations without using explosives, Ted was very interested in what they had to say.

He asked them to leave their prototype with him so he could study it a little further and he found some pretty significant flaws that he thought could be addressed in the next iteration of the model. When he called them back, they immediately offered him a partnership. They needed him in Houston. Major investors, they said, were committed and lined up to move forward, and the seismic industry in the States was sold on the product. What they needed from him was his technical expertise to fine-tune the prototype along with his access to the very lucrative market in western Canada.

When he came home to tell me about the offer, all I heard was Houston. We could finally go back to Texas and be near my family once again! "But couldn't we live in Dallas instead?" Nannie and Lillian were still living in Denton in north Texas, and in Dallas I would be practically on their doorstep. And besides, I really didn't know Houston at all.

But so what! In Houston I'd be a whole lot closer to everyone, and the timing was perfect. Ruth Ann had decided to transfer to Michigan State in the fall in order to take Radio and TV Journalism, and Mary Lil was still little enough that changing schools in the third grade wouldn't be an issue for her. But most important, this would be a perfect transition year for Sidney. Like most adolescent boys, he was slacking off in junior high school, and I'd been talking about his difficulties with my sister Eleanor and her husband Mac. Mac was principal of the high school in Conroe, Texas, and Eleanor was an English teacher, so we'd been considering the possibility of Sidney spending a year with them to get him back on track scholastically. We could put him in school in September in Conroe then, when we moved to Houston in December, he could join us. This was almost too good to be true!

It's hard to explain how I was feeling about all this. Ten years before, when Ted announced we wouldn't be going back to Texas, I was devastated. But then I had only been in Calgary a matter of a few months, a few wretchedly *cold* months. This time was far different. This time I would be leaving close friends and connections to projects in which I was deeply invested. This time I would be leaving a city I loved.

I wasn't alone, of course. Many of the Americans we had arrived with in 1949 and 1950 were being transferred back to the States, so we were all being feted with going away parties and there were many tearful farewells. One of my friends who was on her way back to Midland moaned, "I can't believe this! Shell kept saying we'd only be here a year, and then another year, and then another. Finally, after eleven years, I decided I wouldn't spend one more winter without a fur coat, so I bought one just six months ago. Now I'll never be able to wear it again!"

We put Sidney on the plane in September in time for him to start the ninth grade in Conroe and then called the real estate agent about listing our house. This was the house I promised I would only leave in a pine box, and in many ways I felt that I was leaving the best years of my life behind. We knew that our wonderful neighbours, the Libins and Roxy and Dick Shillington and the Tavenders, all of whom were so welcoming when we first arrived, could never be replaced.

It was with very mixed emotions that I wound up all my commitments to Grace Church and the choir, Wo-Shi-Lo, the Women's League of the Philharmonic, and the American Woman's Club. Would I ever again have a chance to be involved in such a meaningful way with women I had learned to admire so much? We played our last golf game with our friends from Canyon Meadows and Ted resigned from the Doodlebug Tournament Committee. Saying goodbye was very hard for both of us.

Along with the slump in the oil industry, the real estate market suddenly skidded to a dead stop and not much was moving in the housing market. This was unfortunate because Ted had promised to meet his new partners in Houston the first of January to finalize the deal and start to work. Like it or not, we'd have to pack up the furniture and leave the house in the hands of the real estate agent despite the fact that the winter months were bound to get even slower.

I'll admit that as time passed and we drew closer to Christmas, I was so looking forward to spending the holidays with all my family back in Denton that not even this hiccup in the housing market was worrying me. We had decided that Ted would fly to Michigan as soon as Ruth Ann's first semester at Michigan State was over, pick her up, and they would both drive to Grand Rapids to have a little visit with his parents. Then they would go to Detroit, buy a new car, and drive down to Texas to meet the rest of us in Houston. For the first time in a very long time, the whole Estes family would gather in Denton for Christmas. The only thing missing would be that old oak table. Nannie would have her children, their spouses, the grandchildren, and the great-grandchildren assembled to give thanks for the bounty that God had provided us. I was so grateful to know that all of us would be there to give thanks too.

As soon as Mary Lil was dismissed from school for the Christmas holiday, the moving truck arrived to load our furniture. They drove away with promises they would meet us in Houston, and Mary Lil and I boarded a plane for Texas.

Christmas in Denton was everything I'd hoped and, despite my sadness at having to leave good friends back in Calgary, I was so happy that we would be close enough to do this often, particularly because Nannie was beginning to age and I wanted to spend as much time as possible with her in the next few years. However, when everyone started back to their own homes, I was eager to get going. Ted loaded all of us into the brand new purple Chrysler, and we headed straight for Houston and – you guessed it – the Alamo Plaza Motel.

I found a wonderful new home in Hunters' Creek, a subdivision of Houston that was growing almost as fast as Calgary had. We all loved the house even though it was considerably grander than our 10th Street house, but I was pretty sure I could make it homey enough to suit us. There was an elementary school not far from the house, so I registered Mary Lil in the third grade and off I went to choose carpeting and tiles and plumbing fixtures and all those other little details that go with moving into a new place.

Every afternoon, I would meet Ted back at the Alamo Plaza at the end of his day at the office with all my plans for the new house. I guess I had so much on my mind with the rush to complete the purchase of the house and get it ready before the moving truck arrived, that I didn't notice that Ted wasn't having much to say. So, when another few days went by and he said we needed to talk, I was truly blindsided.

The whole deal, he said, was smoke and mirrors. The new technology was worthless. Basically this was a fraudulent scheme they'd tried to sell to Ted. We would be going back to Calgary. He would start a new company. This time he would get into the exploration and production side. Logistically and financially, it would only work if we went back to Calgary. We couldn't stay in Texas.

I can talk about it now, but at the time I doubt I could even form the words to express my disappointment. From the perspective of hindsight, though, maybe it's easier to explain why it was such a blow. I was forty-one. Ted was forty-six. I say that because, when I reflect back on what happened, I realize that it took place at a very vulnerable time in both our lives. I suspect that most of us look back at our forties remembering how we seemed to be flying apart at the seams with so many big transitions. It seems to be that decade when the kids start taking flight. And, if you'll forgive a golf metaphor, we all begin realizing that we've rounded the corner of our lives. We'd started the back nine. It was a time of reassessment.

I had just come from a perfect Hallmark-card kind of Christmas with my family, the family who had raised me believing that the very core of my being was nurtured by the values shared among us. Within that family, I was the youngest, and as such I undoubtedly felt the most loved and protected. At nineteen, I was the last to fly from that nest. I just happened to be the one that flew the farthest. For the past ten years, deep inside I had carried that longing to return. During that idyllic Christmas week with all my siblings, each one of them wrapped *my* little family in that circle of love. I was almost home. I know this is hard to understand, but it was maybe the first time that I had had to face the fact that it was long past time for me to move on. My own first child had flown the nest; my second would follow in a few more years. As much as I might have wanted to gather my children to me and stay in Texas sheltered by my extended family, that choice was absolutely unthinkable. I was no longer that youngest sibling. I had my own family; it was time. My home was with them.

This sounds like I had no idea how Ted must have felt. But I did. He would have given anything to make me happy. In fact, that's probably the reason he misjudged the people from Houston who brought him the partnership proposition in the first place. It *was* too good to be true, and I know that if he hadn't wanted so desperately to make me happy, he would have recognized that far earlier. All he could do was to try to make amends. However, like many men, all Ted knew was to work harder to make up for my disappointment.

We came back to Calgary, took the house off the market, and waited for our truckload of furniture to arrive back from Texas. Ted built himself an office in our basement and worked sixteen hours a day, determined to fight his way out of the mess he blamed himself for making.

On that first morning back, I admit, it was very, very hard to put my feet on the floor.

Mary Lil went back to her third grade classroom and when her teacher asked the children to tell one another what they did for their Christmas holiday, she stood up and said, "We went to Texas and we took all our furniture along!"

Home again, home again, jiggity jog.

UPPER MOUNT ROYAL, 1949.

RUTHIE AND SIDNEY STUFFED INTO THEIR NEW PARKAS ... AND IT WAS ONLY OCTOBER!

TED WITH WILF AND GERRIE BAILLIE SHOWING OFF FRONTIER'S NEWEST TRUCK.

IN SUMMER, AT LEAST, THE WHEELS WOULD TURN ... UNLESS THEY WERE SUNK
IN THE MUD.

THE GUYS ON FRONTIER'S CREW.

A Frontier picnic.

Just to prove
that once upon
a time *I* baked
Mary Lil's
birthday cakes!

THE KIDS WERE GROWING UP FASTER THAN THE FOLIAGE IN FRONT OF OUR
HOUSE.

Ruthie's debut.

SKIING AT SUNSHINE.

TED WITH THE MARTINSONS AND THE BAILLIES AT ONE OF FRONTIER'S SKI
SYMPOSIUMS.

CHAPTER SIXTEEN

Shifting Gears

Remember that blatant foreshadowing back in Chapter 13 when I mentioned that we'd rue the day when all that 1950s conformity and complacency would come back to bite us? Well, welcome to the '60s.

There have been volumes written about the causes of the societal transformation that happened in that decade. I can't pretend to add anything to the weighty scholarship of that enormous library of recorded history. All I can do is tell you how those times played out in our particular family, in our particular time and place, from my particular perspective. I wish I could say this will be a story you can learn from, but probably the most important thing history teaches is that every generation is faced with its own distinct challenges. How we meet them will determine what we leave to our children to fix.

These things always sneak up on you. No one ever announces that you should prepare yourself for an assault on everything you've always taken for granted, so you trundle along day by day not really noticing the vague ripples in the air way out on the horizon. We felt pretty secure in our snug little house in Calgary.

In our case, the decade had already opened with enough turbulence to keep us fully engaged in getting our feet back under us. We came back to Calgary from Houston in January of 1962 minus our two oldest children, Ted was completely absorbed in creating a new exploration/production company he called Rozsa Oils, and I was busy returning all our farewell gifts. I went back to church and the choir and the women's organizations desperately hoping they'd never noticed I'd been away.

The best part of those first few months back was that, with Ruth Ann and Sidney away, it was a chance for Mary Lil to be an only child. She and I both looked forward to the afternoons she'd run home from school and we'd curl up on the couch together to read endless storybooks through the long winter evenings.

We'd left Sidney in Conroe with my sister and brother-in-law to finish the ninth grade and, when he came back to Calgary in the spring, ironically he was the one who brought the news up close and personal to the Rozsa family.

We were living in Jackson, Mississippi in 1947 when Sidney was born and as much as we loved the languid, old-fashioned pace of life in the Deep South, we were both taken aback by the rigid antebellum social restrictions that still existed there. Despite the war years of the early '40s that brought soaring cotton prices and manufacturing to Mississippi, Jim Crow laws still supported staunchly segregated public education, public transportation, restrooms, restaurants, and drinking fountains. Poll taxes and literacy requirements meant that most African-Americans were de facto non-citizens. And, even worse, the Mississippi Klan was still alive and well in those days.

We weren't in Mississippi very long, however. Sidney was still a baby when we left, and really just a toddler when we moved to Calgary. I hasten to concede that most of us in that first wave of oil industry immigration were from the American South, so none of us were so naïve as to protest we were unaware of the realities of racism. Of course we knew. But now that we were all comfortably ensconced in western Canada, we never imagined that any of our children would ever have to confront that reality.

And yes, I *do* see the irony in a statement like that. That's what I meant when I said our children ultimately have to fix the issues their parents fail to deal with. Sidney came home from Conroe in the spring of 1962. We had left him there as a Canadian-raised fourteen-year-old, blissfully unaware of Southern racism, totally unequipped with any prior experience in dealing with those ancient prejudices.

It's now a suburb of the huge Houston metroplex, but in 1961 Conroe was still just a quiet little Texas town that had seen its own boom and bust economy level out to a nice even pace. Its population was middling prosperous and overwhelmingly white, but about 30 per cent of the people were still marginalized by the separate-but-equal legislation that supported segregation. And despite the Brown v. the Board of Education U.S. Supreme Court ruling in 1954 that said separate education for black and white children is inherently unequal, Conroe public schools remained segregated by Texas law.

Sidney arrived into that culture in 1961 and, as a big strong kid, was approached by the football coach who invited him to try out for the team. He was a freshman; it was a great way to meet the other kids in the high school, and Sidney loved football, so the invitation was very much welcomed. However, it didn't take long before he saw what was happening to the black kids in that community and heard the other kids' racist slurs.

He discovered that the black population literally lived on the other side of the railroad tracks and that there was a side door off the alley at the only movie theatre in town. Inside that door were stairs that led directly up to the 'reserved' balcony. When he went to the Dairy Queen he saw two water fountains, one labelled 'Colored,' the other 'Whites Only.' So, in class one day, unable to choke it down any longer, he took emphatic exception to a blatantly racist discussion. When the class ended, selected members of the football team grabbed him and ushered him out behind the gym where they gave him an education.

I doubt any of us ever prepared for that moment. Most of us – at least those of us who were born and raised in the South – had lived these facts since childhood. My parents had simply included everyone in their ministry, black, white, or brown. They modelled the best in human decency, and each of us learned to do the same. But of course too many Southerners didn't. No one had ever asked us to defend the system. But very few had really thought to challenge it either. However, I think I speak for all of us when I say we most sincerely hoped that loving hearts and wiser heads would override racial discrimination in the South before any of our children would have to deal with it. I suspect that most of us decided the less we said to them about the situation, the better. But in 1962, our fifteen-year-old son was asking, "Why?"

Two years prior, black college students in North Carolina sat down at a lunch counter in a Woolworth's store, asked to be served, and were denied. In response, 70,000 students waged their own sit-ins across the nation. In Arkansas, the Governor called out the National Guard to prevent nine black students from entering Little Rock High School. In October of '62, James Meredith, a black student, tried to enter the University of Mississippi and needed three thousand federal marshals to get him through the door. In August of '63, 200,000 people marched into Washington, D.C., demanding jobs and freedom and, at the culmination of the march, we heard Dr. Martin Luther King Jr. deliver his *I Have a Dream* speech from the steps of the Lincoln Memorial. And in the same year, we listened to Alabama Governor George Wallace's inaugural address in which he infamously ranted, "Segregation now, segregation tomorrow, segregation forever!" We watched the police turn the fire hoses and dogs onto women and children, and listened in shock as the news came in about the bombing of the 16th Street Church in Birmingham. Four little girls were killed in that bombing.

Why?

How could I possibly explain to a fifteen-year-old raised in Canada what slavery had meant to 350 years of American history? Slavery was a cancer that had consumed the humanity of ten generations of white Americans, and its resulting social chaos continued through four generations of Southerners after post-war Reconstruction. We could only hope that Martin Luther King's voice for non-violence could bring some degree of sanity to this agonizing march toward justice.

Ironically though, after Sidney came home it wasn't long before we got a call from his Calgary high school principal reporting that he had objected to certain remarks by his English teacher concerning racial discrimination in the American South. Evidently he stood up in class and accused the teacher of simplifying an issue that was obviously beyond her limited knowledge and walked out declaring he wouldn't return to her class. In the end, I suppose what he really learned was that nothing that really matters is ever easy to change, particularly when it involves who we believe ourselves to be. As long as any of us imagines himself to be innately superior to any 'other,' there will be discrimination – whether it's racial, religious, cultural, or national.

Dinner table conversations got louder and more contentious as the decade advanced. In November, President Ngo Dinh Diem was executed during a coup in South Vietnam. A few weeks later, we watched in horror as President Kennedy was assassinated in Dallas. Mary Lil arrived home for lunch just as Walter Cronkite made that awful announcement on TV, and all I could think to do was to draw the drapes and gather my family to mourn our loss through the long, sad days that followed – just as we had mourned the death of Franklin D. Roosevelt in 1945. In many ways, I think we all understood that this time we were grieving our loss of innocence. The American community in Calgary felt very far from home, and we withdrew into isolation and pain, our church once again a refuge.

After she graduated from Michigan State in 1963, Ruth Ann decided to apply for a job in communications with Pan American Airlines. It was a glamorous opportunity, but during her interview they explained they were desperate for stewardesses. If she would agree to work as a stewardess for a year, they'd guarantee her a communications job.

We weren't thrilled about it, but Ruth Ann saw it as a first step toward the job she really wanted. She donned her blue uniform and perky little hat, passed inspection by the rather stern head stewardess who checked to make sure the girls were all tightly cinched in girdles. And then she marched them off for their month-long training course.

In those days, because Pan Am flew only international flights, all the girls had to learn another language. Ruth Ann had taken high school French, of course, but could hardly be described as bilingual, so the language instructor decided she would use her native tongue which, from looking at her name, he declared was Hungarian.

Not only had she never heard the language spoken, Ruth Ann couldn't even say her name with the rolling *R* it required in Hungarian. (She, and the rest of us for that matter, *always* have to explain that 'Rozsa' is pronounced 'Rose–ay' with the accent on the last syllable.) She promised the language instructor that she'd *definitely* study up on her French.

Then, much to her surprise, she found she really enjoyed the work. She was able to visit the fabulous cities of Europe and Africa and, because she had frequent layovers at many of them, she had the good fortune to visit beyond their city limits as well. And since she was assigned to the first-class cabin, she had some great opportunities to meet people she never would have otherwise, so it was a very good experience for her during her early twenties.

Ruth Ann was headquartered in New York and shared an apartment at the south end of Manhattan, thoroughly enjoying a very glamorous life. One morning in Chicago as she was eating breakfast in the hotel dining room before leaving for the airport, she noticed a couple of businessmen eyeing her from across the room. She looked away to discourage them, but moments later they were at her table introducing themselves. They were account representatives from the Thompson Advertising Agency who were creating a campaign for Dentyne. They were looking for a model with a terrific smile. Would she be interested in having her picture taken posing in the engine well of a new Pan Am jet? It was too bad she didn't ask for residuals because that ad got a lot of play through the years. Ruth Ann still describes it as her fifteen minutes of fame.

In December of 1965, Ruth Ann married a young American Air Force officer. They were stationed first in Del Rio, Texas, and because Reed was on the career fast track, he was away frequently on training exercises. They moved from Del Rio to Fairchild Air Force Base in Spokane to Merced, California, so Reed could train on the new KC 135 tanker jets. And when he was scheduled for the three-month courses, Ruth Ann would come back to Calgary to visit and the conversation would inevitably go to the escalating war in Vietnam.

The American military advisors in Vietnam had been given permission to return fire on the enemy if fired upon. After the 1964 Gulf of Tonkin destruction of two American destroyers, Congress authorized President Johnson to take action against the North Vietnamese, and less than six months later the president ordered the continuous bombing of North Vietnam below the twentieth parallel. Eight months after that, the first draft cards were burned.

Sidney turned eighteen in 1965. He was an American citizen living in Canada. He would have to register for the draft. Reed was on active duty with the U.S. Air Force. Can you imagine the tension around our dining room table?

Remember too, the war in Vietnam wasn't happening on a clean slate. The Cold War was in full deep freeze. An American U-2 reconnaissance plane had been shot down over Soviet territory. Children in American elementary schools were having regular Soviet attack drills as though hiding under their desks was going to save them from nuclear annihilation. Mary Lil was just old enough to hear about the Cold War on the news but not quite old enough to understand the context, so she was frightened to death and secretly packed a suitcase full of canned goods and emergency supplies in case she couldn't locate us and had to find a nuclear fall-out shelter on her own. The Berlin Wall was raised in 1961. The Bay of Pigs disaster in Cuba continued to be an embarrassment for Americans.

Ted and I were on a three-week Chamber of Commerce trip to the Orient with a number of Calgary business people in October of 1962. Sam and Olga Nickel, Webster and Sheila MacDonald, Wilbur Griffith, Gordon Love and his wife; we were a mixed bag of Calgarians on a mission to learn more about Hong Kong and Japan, and we were most warmly welcomed and feted throughout the trip. However, we were cautioned to stay close to our guides as we approached a fence separating us from Communist China. We could see that people were living in squalor just steps away from that fence. One of our group moved toward them with his camera poised, but, within seconds, armed soldiers confronted him, and it was obvious they felt no hesitation about firing should he fail to respond to their orders. We were scurried away and strongly reprimanded by our guide.

Later that evening, we were having a lovely dinner with members of the Hong Kong Chamber of Commerce when we heard the news about the Kennedy–Khrushchev stand-off in Cuba. Wilbur Griffith was so alarmed by what had happened to us earlier in the day that he decided those of us in the group who carried American passports had better be ready to board the American battleship anchored in Hong Kong Harbour. From that time on, I don't think any of us had any illusions about the Communist threat. After those thirteen days of terror, we figured we had been within a blink of World War III.

In defence of my own generation, I tried to remind my kids that during the so-called complacent '50s we were recovering from a Depression and a World War and working hard to manage our own social upheaval as the face of North America rapidly changed from rural to urban and from agriculture to manufacturing. We were proud of the future we were building for the next generation, but it's true – there *were* serious crises looming that they had now been swept up in. Communism would have to be stopped in its tracks in Southeast Asia. Ted and I believed it was the right thing to do.

Sidney graduated from Western Canada High School in 1965 and registered for his first year at Michigan State just shortly after the first American combat troops arrived in Vietnam. Now that he was grown up and about to venture out on his own, he decided to use his first name, reserving his middle initial. Young Ted, as a student, was safe at least for the time being. By the end of June, American warplanes were bombing Hanoi and Haiphong, and by December more than 385,000 troops were stationed in South Vietnam.

With each trip home, Ted grimly reported that students he knew in Michigan were talking about how they could take action to stop the war. One, the son of a Dow Chemical executive, was radicalized to the point he was seriously plotting to blow up Dow's headquarters where the napalm was manufactured and stored. Ted said he and another friend spent several late nights casing the office of the local draft board to find out whether it was feasible to prop the basement window open, slip through it, and set fire to the files. They didn't, but obviously student protest against the war wasn't restricted to colleges on the east and west coasts. We constantly worried. Did young Ted have the wisdom to know when legitimate dissent turns to reckless disregard for life and property? Dinner table conversations continued to escalate.

When he went back to school after the holidays, it was almost too quiet. Ted felt so sorry for Mary Lil that one day he brought her a little Basset Hound puppy. He was all long floppy ears and sad eyes, and we instantly bonded. We were his to do with as he liked. Not that he ever indicated that he *shared* our affection, mind you, but little Tex was the new baby of our family and we all loved him to death.

Mary Lil and I read all the books about Basset Hounds and decided we should take him to obedience school. To this day, I can't swear that Tex was actually the one being trained. All I know for sure is, by the end of that experience he had *us* whipped into shape.

In fact, we were *so* compliant that, when someone suggested we enter him in a dog show, we jumped at the chance.

Only one of us could actually *show* him, so while Tex pranced Mary Lil around the ring, I sat with the other competing owners nervously chewing our nails in the bleachers. I don't want to sound prideful, but Tex really was a good-looking dog, so I was sure he could hold his own against any dog in the ring. Unfortunately, though, part of the competition actually involved obedience. The dog's obedience, that is. Not Mary Lil's.

As I've said, we weren't very confident that Tex actually understood this concept. Mary Lil was extremely well-trained, as I'm sure Tex would attest, but neither of us knew whether or not he might decide to humour us with *his* cooperation.

The instructions were that Mary Lil was to walk Tex around the ring one time. Then she was to release him from his leash at the judges' end of the ring and tell him to lie down and stay put while she went to the other end. On her command, Tex was to stand up and walk to her where she would replace his leash and walk him back to the judges.

The first part was easy. Tex was born tired. The minute Mary Lil suggested a nice rest, he took advantage and lay prone – as if dead. However, when it became apparent that he was to walk all the way to the other end of the ring for no particular reason, he sort of cocked one eyebrow. We could tell he was irritated. Then, with profound distaste, very, *very* slowly – one – vertebra – at – a – time – he deigned to rise to a sitting position.

He could tell that Mary Lil was desperate; everyone in the room felt sorry for her. Tex, I think, was just embarrassed for her. But finally he decided to put her out of her misery. Inch by agonizing inch, he made his way to Mary, sat down next to her, sighed, and looked up from those reproachful brown eyes as if to say, "Really? *This* is what you're reduced to? Have you no shame at all?"

He won a ribbon. He was one of only three Basset Hounds in Canada to get an obedience certificate. We were ecstatic! We went on the dog show circuit … and Tex came along for the ride. (Umm, in the interest of full disclosure I should probably note that we had started introducing him to a couple of lady friends hoping we might one day have a litter of little Texes, so maybe he only came along for the ride anticipating a date with one of his girlfriends.)

Like I say, Tex was born tired and he took full advantage of Ruth Ann's visits home with baby Howard. Every afternoon at nap time, I'd spread out a baby blanket on the floor of the living room, lay Howard on one side and Tex on the other, and the two of them would instantly start snoring, each of them drooling on the other. And when Howie woke up, Tex would come find me, no doubt because the baby had so rudely awakened him. As nannies go, Tex may not have won any prizes for encouraging parallel play, but he could sure teach those babies to sleep. I often thought I might make a little pin money renting him out to all my friends with visiting grandchildren, and one time suggested as much to him. Tex gave me his most withering look … again.

Tex and the dog shows were the comic relief during that decade. Every single day seemed to present another tragedy. Thursdays were always the worst; they announced the body counts on the Thursday evening news. The worst year was 1968. In March, President Johnson announced, "I will not seek and shall not accept the nomination for a second term as president of the United States," knowing that there was so much opposition to the war in Vietnam he could no longer provide the leadership to proceed. In April of that year, Martin Luther King was assassinated in Memphis. In June, Robert F. Kennedy was shot and killed after a campaign victory celebration in Los Angeles. In August, the Chicago police took on the protestors outside the Democratic National Convention and caused a riot between the 10,000 anti-war demonstrators and 23,000 police and National Guardsmen.

Friends Ted had known in university were delivered home from Vietnam in metal caskets. He was aggressively working the system and twice changed his place of registration for the draft from the Foreign Residents' Draft Board to the local Michigan Board and back again to reset his priority on the record. Ultimately, though, he was issued a draft notice and ordered to report to Detroit for his pre-induction physical in the spring of 1969, and, despite the fact he had severe back problems, it was determined that he was fit, so he was classified 1-A.

On the first of December, he and a group of friends gathered to watch the first draft lottery on TV. All physically able young men, without other deferments, who were born between 1944 and 1950, were eligible. Should his birthdate be drawn, he would be called to serve. He told us that one in three ground soldiers in Vietnam weren't surviving their first ninety days. The first number drawn was September 14; Ted's birthday is September 16.

Ted was lucky. His friend Eric Farkas wasn't. He was watching the lottery that day with Ted; September 14 was Eric's birthday. Eight hundred and fifty thousand young men aged nineteen to twenty-six were included in that lottery. The 1970 draft was the highest of the Vietnam era; more than 450,000 were called. Ted missed by a headcount of less than 30,000. Thousands of potential draftees illegally fled to Canada. Ted never found out whether his friend Eric survived the war.

Reed was flying tankers between Guam and Southeast Asia. By the time Woodstock and the Summer of Love was over, Mary Lil was decked out in full hippy garb. In our family, around the dinner table at least, we finally had to agree to disagree.

CHAPTER SEVENTEEN

Give Me a Song and a Stage

Throughout the '60s, my involvement with the American Woman's Club grew primarily through the singing group that produced shows for the old folks' homes. One time when we did an Easter routine, a sweet little old lady followed me around all afternoon trying to buy the Easter bonnet I'd concocted out of all the feathers and boas and flowers I'd expropriated from Mary Lil's dress-up trunk. But we got to do more interesting things too, and the group let me have a recital one time. I sang *Smoke Gets in Your Eyes* in my most sultry voice and was so convincing, at least to myself, that I decided I'd audition for an upcoming theatre production of *Showboat*.

I didn't get the lead, they imported a professional for that role, but I was able to be a part of the supporting singers and the theatre bug bit me hard. The show played for a week. The rest of the cast, which included Mort van Ostrand, Jack Goth, and Les Kimber, were all volunteers, so I suspect we all thought our primary goal was to have fun, and we certainly did! I'd always loved to sing, but acting was pretty new to me and I discovered I enjoyed being on stage even more. One night, the director of the MAC 14 Theatre overheard me talking with some of the cast of *Showboat*, and he approached me with a proposition. He was casting roles for Tennessee Williams' *Cat on a Hot Tin Roof* and said his actors were sorely short on Southern accents. Would I consider coming down to the theatre as dialogue coach?

The Musicians and Actors Club (MAC 14) had evolved from the theatre troop Betty Mitchell had originally assembled back in the '40s with her drama students in Room #14 at Western Canada High School. In 1964, they converted the old Isis movie theatre downtown on 1st Street West to a live stage theatre and started with a pretty ambitious line-up of plays. In their very first season, they produced eight plays, the next year ten, including *Cat on a Hot Tin Roof*. I was there almost before he'd finished propositioning me.

We spent a couple of hours learnin' to drop our g's and drawl lazy-Deep-South, and I went home thinking I'd be sure to buy tickets when the play opened. But the next morning I woke to a ringing telephone. Would I be interested in coming down to audition for the role of Big Mama?

You bet I would! Mort van Ostrand had been chosen for the role of Big Daddy and Arnie Dvorkin was to play Brick and, once they padded me up in a plump suit to look like a Southern matriarch, we were a pretty imposing cast. Mort really didn't have much of a presence in the play; he was supposed to be returning from the hospital where he'd been diagnosed with a terminal illness, so the play started with the rest of us talking about him and how his avaricious passel of heirs would divide up his estate. My first line was, "Brick! Brick! Big Daddy's home an' he's gonna git betta!" It was easy as shoofly pie.

The show played for two weeks and every performance was sold out. Mary Lil wanted to come see the play because she had been helping me memorize my lines (even though I wouldn't let her read the cuss words), but I thought it was little too risqué for a twelve-year-old. Jamie Portman wrote such a glowing review in the *Calgary Herald* that I told him I'd better retire at the top of my game. In 1968, MAC 14 became Theatre Calgary, and we finally had a truly professional theatre.

I still had lots of opportunity to keep singing. Grace Church had hired John Searchfield as choir director in 1958, and the very first thing he did was talk us into learning the Bach *Christmas Oratorio*.

No Calgary choir had tackled anything as big and difficult as this, but the choir had grown to sixty members so we were excited to try it. It was such a success that we jumped right in to learn Handel's *The Passion of Christ*, then the Bach cantata *Christ Lay in Death's Dark Prison*. Then we did a Festival Chorus presentation of Bach's *St. John's Passion* as well as an annual *Messiah* at Christmas time. We had fabulous soloists and John introduced us to wonderful new anthems too, so with the major choral concerts in addition to our Sunday services, we were really challenged musically. Often he had us up in the dusty old attic above the balcony doing echo effects. We were so good that Dr. Morley ordered special ceiling tiles in the sanctuary to improve the acoustics. All of us were so enthusiastic about the music that we became great friends and started having family picnics in addition to all our choir practices.

The music offerings at Grace Church kept expanding over the years to include two junior choirs and the teenage Gateway Singers as well as a hand bell choir. The junior choir was always a top competitor at the Kiwanis Music Festival, and in the mid-'60s the joint choirs staged a huge production of *Noah's Flood* where I think every child in the congregation took part dressed in some kind of animal costume.

Each Sunday morning, we arrived at church as the bells in the tower sang out a welcome, and when they finally succumbed to old age sometime during the '80s, all of us mourned their passing. From that time forward, we all complained about missing the bells, but the economy had again fallen on hard times and the repair of the bells wasn't high on the church's to-do list. I don't know why it took me so long to do something about that, but finally I decided *some*body would have to step up and take action. And very kindly, in thanks for my offering, the church elders arranged for me to hear them as they rang for the first time in more than thirty years – on my ninety-second birthday.

Back in the '60s, as one of a captive audience up in the choir loft, I was beginning to understand Dr. Morley's sermons. Well, maybe that's a stretch, but I did finally figure out that Dr. Morley was less a pastoral preacher and far more a social justice advocate who passionately believed that, if you could rally enough people behind the ideas taught through the lessons of Christianity, you could change the world. His PhD was in Constitutional Law and History so he undoubtedly knew where he wanted to lead the congregation. And he had certainly convinced members like Max Bell who offered Dr. Morley a bully pulpit through his newspaper, *The Albertan*.

There were more than a few Conservatives in the crowd who I'm sure listened to some of his sermons with a raised eyebrow, but they too were faithful in their attendance and very generous with their financial support. The Mannix family was loyal to Grace Church through several generations, and I'm pretty sure most of those American oilmen never voted for the Liberal Party, but that never stopped their support of the church. I suppose it was a given that eventually Frank Morley would toss his hat into the electoral ring, but when he and Mary left Grace Church after twenty very successful years, I had a feeling that down deep he was disappointed in all of us.

However, the great majority of congregants at Grace Church stayed on to welcome new ministers throughout the years and it has continued to thrive. For twenty-five wonderful years, I sang in the choir, but when I finally made the transition to a congregational pew in the sanctuary, I was thrilled to hear them from a new perspective.

It's a shame that Dr. Morley didn't live to see how it has evolved, because Grace Presbyterian has now become an inner-city church, and its congregation today is far more involved in issues concerning social justice than ever before. I'm also proud to say that Mary Lil has served as an elder of the church for the last fifteen years as well as chairing the music committee. I hope that my father, who never had a chance to meet her, and Dr. Morley, who baptized her, are both cheering her on.

Mary Lil was growing up quickly, so as she entered her teens, Ted and I were able to play golf together occasionally whenever I could drag him away from his work. Rozsa Oils was unfortunately launched just as the economy slumped in the early '60s and those early years were incredibly tough. From '64 to '68, he never took a nickel in salary and he ran a one-man office in our basement where he was everything from bookkeeper to on-site geologist, so he was very, very busy. Somehow, though, we also both found time to spend on our ongoing development work with the Philharmonic, too.

But, as it always does, the slump in the economy had affected the arts community first, so it was a difficult start for the newly assembled professional orchestra and we had a number of conductors after Henry Plukker moved on. Haymo Taeuber took over in 1963, and, despite the economic uncertainty, by 1968, he had almost tripled the size of the audience. Following his tenure, José Iturbi, the noted pianist, became our conductor for one year, and then we had a series of guest conductors in hope that we would find a perfect fit. Maurice Handford really moved the orchestra along during his five years at the helm, providing stability and professionalism and bringing several players from England with him who are still members of the orchestra. Franz-Paul Decker and Arpad Joó had their terms at the helm, but I think my favourite during this period of time was Richard Hayman, who brought us a pops series straight from Boston.

Richard was the consummate showman. His jackets were louder than Don Cherry's, (although in far better taste), and he always carried two or three harmonicas in his pocket, which he'd play whether anyone requested him to or not. He was so engaging and effervescent in his pre-concert conversations with the audience that he started a whole new trend, which Calgarians have come to expect from all their conductors. He definitely took the stuffing out of the stuffed-shirt music and ushered in a whole new era of appreciation for all kinds of music from pops tunes to the classics.

Unfortunately, though, Richard's first love was always the Boston Pops Orchestra, and he couldn't be lured away except for occasional guest appearances, so our first priority was to find a first-rate principal conductor who could fine-tune our excellent musicians. Second on that list was the search for development funds to make that possible.

Ted had joined the board of the Philharmonic and, in the mid-'60s, I served as president of the Women's League for a couple of years, so fundraising was our first order of business. Benny the Bookworm continued to work his magic, and our annual book sale proceeds had quadrupled by this point but we were getting pretty blasé about them. Book junkies were way too easy. Was there other low-hanging fruit out there waiting to be introduced to the Philharmonic? Of course there was. We just had to figure out what might draw them in.

*Every*body loves music of some kind; the only trick is discovering which music appeals to which audience. We would make sure everyone could be included, even those who hated the thought of having to rent a tux. And since any social gathering could be tailored to fit its appropriate music, we hosted everything from the Symphony Balls to fashion shows, teas, a Grey Cup Warm-Up Party and a Boston Pops Party featuring Arthur Fiedler himself.

We hosted the Symphony Ball in 1966 at the Palliser Hotel complete with a fanfare of trumpets to welcome our distinguished guests, served them an all-French menu (followed, believe it or not, with cigarettes and coffee), danced them off their feet, and bid them adieu after picking the lucky winner of two Air Canada tickets to Vienna. I can't tell you what our guests paid for that evening. From this distance, not even I can believe it.

I *can* tell you the price for our Boston Pops Party featuring Arthur Fiedler conducting the Calgary Philharmonic at the Stampede Corral. Guests were seated at tables throughout the Corral so that a non-stop selection of European and domestic wines and hors d'oeuvres could be served throughout the concert. Tickets for those premium tables went for $4.50 a head. Should you not be able to afford that, the cheap seats went for a buck and a half.

Still too hoity-toity for you? How about that Grey Cup Party? Dancing, drinking, dinner, games, and singing could be yours for $2.50. *And* you were instructed to wear your hometown colours!

If you happened to be of the female persuasion, there were endless teas and fashion shows, which may not have raised as much money, but they made fast friends of women who had not had much prior exposure to classical music. And many of those women – and their husbands – signed on for life.

The Symphony Balls though, from that time on, were the signature events of the Women's League of the Philharmonic. Women especially loved getting dressed up at the holiday season, and very often these events sold out practically as soon as the tickets left the presses. I remember laughing decades later when the first invitations were issued for a No-Show Ball. The privilege of *not* having to get dressed up and *not* going to a fancy-schmancy hotel ballroom and *not* eating a gourmet dinner, and *not* dancing until the wee-small-hours-until-your-feet-are-destroyed-by-the-new-shoes-you-had-to-buy-for-the-occasion would cost you a whopping one hundred dollars. We may have danced them completely off their feet, but that didn't mean they quit giving. *Those* tickets sold faster than ever before!

In the summers, the work of the Women's League slowed down, but that didn't mean it was all-golf-all-the-time. Sometimes the women were called upon to produce the entertainment for the golfing season, and those of us at Canyon Meadows were in hot demand. We put on fashion shows and entertainment for parties, as well as song and dance routines. Gertrude Dimple, who I'd first met through the American Woman's Club, also joined Canyon Meadows and brought along her theatre talents. She wrote, produced, and choreographed a golf-related song and dance version of *My Fair Lady* that brought down the house. One time, at a show we put on at the Country Club, I was one of the Andrews Sisters along with two others, and I'm proud to say that our rendition of *Boogie Woogie Bugle Boy* is still considered a classic by Country Club oldtimers.

But that didn't mean I wasn't playing golf, too. With Ted's coaching and the regular play I was getting on Ladies' Day, I had my handicap down to about eighteen and was winning the occasional ladies' long-ball competitions and feeling pretty comfortable playing social golf. I admit I never had much of a competitive streak, but Ted was an excellent teacher who from the beginning taught me the rules of golf as I'd get myself into trouble along the fairway. I hadn't really played any casual pick-up golf before, so learning the rules from the beginning seemed natural to me and, once I started helping out with the women's tournament golf, it came in handy if there were any disputes.

Ted, as I've mentioned before, was a stickler for precision, so I think he kind of enjoyed some of the rather arcane rules of golf, and eventually the men's committee invited him to give a seminar for anyone interested in officiating at the tournaments. I think he decided it would work better if we'd do these sessions together; he could be the straight man of the act and I could be the comic sidekick. As it turned out, we made quite a tag team.

Let's get one thing out of the way: there's no such thing as a gimmie, a mulligan, or a do-over. Nor is there any limit to the number of strokes it takes you to get into that cursed hole. However, if you're out there on a hot July afternoon playing social golf, you'd better know when to concede the hole and put your ball in your pocket so your friends will invite you back to try again another day. Still, there is *some* good news. Although you can't replace the club you smashed against that offending tree, should you be using your club as a cane, and it breaks, you *are* allowed to replace that one. Remember this rule; I guarantee the time will come when you'll need it.

Like I say, the Scots invented this game and I suspect that, as much as they pontificated about character-building, they really doubted that any of us could be trusted to compete in a game where there were no umpires to keep the players honest. Hence, *The Rules of Golf*, a tome only slightly less dense than *Finnegan's Wake* yet equally punishing to the despairing reader. However, once you fight your way through all the verbiage, essentially all it says is that when your ball inevitably lands in water, behind a tree, in the rough, in quicksand, or within the coils of a poisonous snake, you can move it. But you can't move it any closer to the pin.

Despite their Calvinist streak, the Scots do concede that there are lucky breaks in life. If your ball bounces off a tree deep in the woods back onto the green, it's an act of God and thus quite acceptable in the *Rules of Golf*. Alas, it's also acceptable if your ball, smartly struck with your four iron, ricochets off the skull of your opponent and onto the green. Do this too often though and your friends may stop returning your phone calls, never mind the *Rules of Golf*.

We played golf, talked golf, organized golf tournaments, vacationed at tropical golf courses, and hung around with other golfers. Ted won a set of steak knives every year for playing the most rounds in the season. We had a *lot* of steak knives. Did our children play golf? Of course not. They were all completely uninterested. Ruth Ann still says she was permanently scarred by the time I decided to introduce her to golf and bought her an outfit that matched one of mine. (In retrospect, perhaps the orange polyester was an unfortunate choice.) Young Ted played football in high school, as did his friends, and aside from occasionally caddying for his father at the Oilmen's or the Doodlebug, he had no interest in playing the game at all until much later in life.

Only Mary Lil has happy memories of golf season. She likes to tell about the time Ted and I were away on late summer back-to-back golf tournaments. Since Ruth Ann hadn't left to go back to university, she had been charged with manning the home-front for her younger brother and sister for the two weeks we'd be away. I had stocked the larder with everything the kids would ever need or want but had forgotten to stop the egg delivery. Apparently this had become an issue because Ted wasn't around to eat his usual two-eggs-a-day breakfast.

The eggs were piling up and the kids figured they were going bad so Ruth Ann, priding herself on her household management skills, decided that they'd use them up before we arrived home. Mary Lil says that for the week prior to our return, the daily menu consisted of scrambled eggs for breakfast, omelettes and egg salad sandwiches for lunch, quiche for dinner, angel food cake for dessert, and eggnogs for bedtime snacks. Good thing nobody knew about cholesterol in those days; child welfare would have been after me for sure.

Mary Lil always looked forward to summer because it meant that she could go to camp for the first month, and then to visit Ruth Ann wherever she and Reed were posted for the second month, so Ted and I could play as much golf as we wanted. However she then insists on telling my friends that since her birthday fell a few days after school started in the fall, smack dab in the middle of tournament season, she was always left at home alone to bake her own cake. Any kind but angel food cake.

How's that for a little zinger?

CHAPTER EIGHTEEN

Call Me 'Mammaw'

Mary Lil's little jab to my conscience was undoubtedly meant to remind me that, despite the fact I'd become a grandmother when she was only thirteen, I was still expected to attend to all the motherly details, too. Truthfully, it *was* kind of discombobulating to become a grandmother at forty-six, especially since I thought I was still a long way from launching my two remaining children.

Reed was stationed at Fairchild Air Force Base in Spokane, Washington shortly after Howard was born in 1966, so I felt very lucky that Ruth Ann and the baby were able to come home so frequently during those first few years. The kids had decided upon Howard's birth, since Nannie had become 'Nannaw' once she became a grandmother, I would have to be 'Mammaw,' and that's the way it stuck. And I'm happy to say it's stayed that way through seven grandchildren and four great-grandchildren.

Ted's new company, Basset Oil, was incorporated in 1969 and was growing rapidly. Baby Karen joined Ruth Ann's family that same year and the children were even more accessible, so we got to see them often, but Ted and I both pined for even more time with these precious grandchildren. Following them around the United States and then to Guam when they were posted there during the Vietnam War from 1971 to the fall of Saigon in '73 wasn't enough for either of us. But that was the career Reed had chosen and Ruth Ann discovered she really enjoyed life in the military. She developed a very successful home business that contributed substantially to their family's income so she didn't need to spend time away from the children when they were little, and I think she adapted to that life very happily.

Young Ted, meanwhile, was still at Michigan State and had been dating Sandy, whom he married before he graduated. They moved off campus to start their married life and their two boys, Scott and T.J., were born in Michigan, followed by Stacy, who came along after their family relocated to Texas. By the time Stacy was born in 1973, Ted and I had welcomed five grandchildren in the span of seven years.

I remember thinking how Nannie would have wrapped those little ones close to her heart, and how perfect it would have been for them to hear her stories about their extended family. Sadly, though, we had just lost Nannie to the infirmities of old age and I grieved for her still. She had lived a long and generous life and left a legacy of loving gifts with whomever she had touched. And yet, as I moved beyond her, I came to realize that her life was so very confined by her circumstances of time and place. I could see why all of us siblings were drawn back to our *first* family. It was a simpler time when the lessons she and Preacher taught us made sense in that smaller, less-complicated world. Ours was infinitely bigger and more complex, and I knew very well that the world our grandchildren would inherit was as yet incomprehensible to any of us.

All the Estes siblings had gathered in Denton in 1970, and we celebrated Nannie's last birthday along with Karen's first. I think Nannie would have appreciated the symbolic closure of her life as she left her newest great-grandchild to carry on.

I wish I could say we survived to see the end of the domestic fallout from Vietnam during the '60s, but the '70s opened to escalated violence in reaction to President Nixon's so-called peace-with-honour invasion of Cambodia. A month later, we watched in horror as the Ohio National Guard fired on protesting anti-war students at Kent State University killing four and injuring nine others.

It would take another three years before the United States finally pulled out of Vietnam. By that time, even Canadian students had joined the anti-war movement, and when Mary Lil became a hippie we knew we had misjudged this generation. Somewhere along the way, they had lost respect for the people leading the country. They were faced with a choice none of them wanted to make. They didn't see themselves as anti-American; they were anti-war. Would they go to Vietnam to fight in what they saw as an unjust war if they were drafted, or would they refuse? Should they stay in school to keep their deferments, especially knowing that it would be the high-school dropouts who would take their places – the kids who didn't have their advantages?

In defence of the older generation, I can say that the actions of the students on the militant left overshadowed the vast majority of those who only sat in at peace-and-love demonstrations. But the very fact that the SDS and the Weathermen were populated by some of those bright, middle-class college kids was truly frightening. If we lost that generation, what would become of the society we'd worked so hard to rebuild after World War II?

Within three years, the United States pulled out of Vietnam, Vice President Agnew resigned from office following his plea of no contest to charges of bribery, extortion, and tax fraud, and President Nixon's gang of thieves was on trial for the Watergate robberies. It was a time that profoundly informed the values of those young people.

In Canada, we were somewhat insulated from all of that con-flict, but our children felt very much a part of it. And of course we in Canada had problems of our own in 1970. In Montreal, the FLQ kidnapped British Trade Commissioner James Cross and Quebec's Labour Minister Pierre Laporte. Their demands were for the release of twenty-three political prisoners, half a million dollars, and the broadcast and publication of the FLQ manifesto, along with an air-plane to take them to Cuba.

In response, Prime Minister Trudeau invoked the War Measures Act and called in armed federal forces to assist the Quebec police. In relatively short order, the separatist terrorists were either in residence in Cuba, rounded up, or tried and convicted in court. However, the movement toward a separate Quebec continued to escalate.

And, as predicted, the cultural imbalance as a result of the huge American immigration and investment-capital invasion beginning in the early '50s finally caused the Canadian arts community to take action.

Canada, despite the perception of many in the United States, is *not* a northern American state. Our culture in Canada is really quite different. Canada has a different history, different traditions, and a public policy that is emphatically salad bowl rather than melting pot. Canada's settlement history wasn't entirely without conflict, but those early interactions with both Inuit and First Nations people didn't involve the kind of carnage that took place south of the border. Slavery did exist in Canada, but not widely and not for long. We have two official first languages and we are religiously diverse. We have publicly funded health care, and our tax dollars help support educational institutions from elementary schools through universities. Canadians believe that every citizen should expect equal access to excellent health care and education, and we are particularly proud that our students attending public schools in Alberta currently test among the highest in the world. We are governed by the Parliamentary system inherited from Great Britain, we follow English Common Law, we don't permit capital punishment in Canada, and we have progressive social legislation.

If I sound like I'm delivering a lecture, I apologize, but it's a speech I got used to delivering to my Texas clan. There never seemed to be any Canadian news coverage in the States. As Pierre Trudeau once famously said, "Living next to you is in some ways like sleeping with an elephant. No matter how friendly and even-tempered the beast, one is affected by every twitch and grunt."

He was right then as well as now. We are truly inundated by American culture in all its forms. Understandably so; Canada shares a very porous border with the United States that permits unlimited access by every American television network, plus countless cable channels, radio broadcasts, and print publications. American music, dance, theatre, literature, and art dominate simply because we share a common language, and its cultural export is ten times larger than our own population of artists can produce in Canada. By 1970, Canadian culture was being pushed to the margins and risked disappearing altogether.

In defence, the CRTC finally dictated that a certain percentage of a domestic broadcaster's transmission time had to include content produced by Canadians. AM radio music programming had to include Canadian-produced songs, there was a federal policy to provide financial assistance to Canadian book publishing, and the Canada Council was formed to promote the production and enjoyment of the arts in Canada. By the end of the decade, the cultural pendulum began adjusting slowly toward the centre.

We began to see more and more Canadian artists being featured at the Calgary Philharmonic concerts including pianists like Marc-André Hamelin, Angela Hewitt, Anton Kuerti, Jon Kimura Parker, and Louis Lortie. James Ehnes, the Canadian violinist, is arguably the best in the world right now, as is Ben Heppner, the Canadian tenor. But perhaps most definitively Canadian are composers like R. Murray Shafer and Harry Somers. To hear their music is to understand how very much our culture is influenced by our unique geography. They are to the ear, what the Group of Seven painters are to visual art. Undoubtedly, the decisions made back in the '70s have nurtured those talents and have brought Canadian music and musicians to the front of the world stage.

Mary Lil, our Canadian-born child, had benefited most by this shift in cultural perception. She knew that Canada offered her experiences she could find nowhere else in the world. Every summer, she'd been going off to Pioneer Ranch Camp at Rocky Mountain

House both as a camper and then as a leader. She was a strong skier and an experienced hiker and had spent a lot of time in the mountains, so wilderness adventure was a big part of her life.

After she graduated from high school in 1971, she heard from Reed that a Whitworth College prof was launching an expedition across the Northwest Territories from Yellowknife to Baker Lake to do a mapping project in cooperation with the Canadian government. Reed had met this fellow at a survival training course and was impressed by his plans. For two months, he and eighteen students would travel the Arctic river systems in canoes and portage where they couldn't get through by water.

Ted and I were flabbergasted when Mary Lil announced that she wanted to go along. She didn't know anyone on the expedition, and she would be the youngest of the group. But there were a couple of other women, so I guess we thought she could probably handle it too. "In case of emergency," she said, "we'll be carrying some sort of walkie-talkie arrangement. There's a NORAD plane that flies over this river system once a week so if we get into trouble they can help us." (You can imagine how much *that* information reassured me.) "Besides," she said, "if I go I can earn three credits toward my university degree." She knew which buttons to push. Since she was looking toward including this trip in her long range college plans, this was one of those once-in-a-lifetime experiences we weren't going to deny her.

Mary Lil met the group at Whitworth to take part in their training exercises. They flew to Yellowknife, rented eight Grumman canoes, loaded them up with food and provisions to last eight weeks, and pushed off on a trip of 1,100 miles through herds of musk oxen and caribou. She said it was a slow start, however, because by the end of the first day on the water they realized they were so heavy they were barely floating. Provisions would have to be jettisoned. But, since only the food was expendable, this meant they'd *really* have to live off the land.

She described how they would camp close to the water overnight and watch the sky turn a hazy rose as the sun dipped toward the horizon, paused, and started its slow ascent once again. At night, herds of migrating caribou would come so close to their camp they seemed to be curious about them, yet too cautious to come closer. Someone suggested they crouch down like rocks scattered across the muskeg. Evidently the caribou had the same idea so there they were in an Arctic Mexican standoff, neither species willing to make the first move.

Mary Lil still talks about the musk oxen. She said they looked like stout British gentlemen gliding across the barrens, long heavy hair smooth as silk. And when they circled protecting their young, she knew better than to approach. They found a wolf's den and waited to see whether the pups were in residence and, sure enough, Farley Mowat was right. The mother came back to move each one of them away from the prying eyes of the strangers who had invaded her territory. There were wolverines and arctic loons, and one time they climbed a thirty-foot rock wall to see a nest with four peregrine falcon chicks.

At that time of year, the surface of the permafrost softens to spongy muskeg and, although they had tents for protection, when they were off the water, they were fodder for the ravenous Arctic black flies. She said they coated themselves and their tents in repellent imported directly from the jungles of Vietnam and strained their food through their mosquito net headgear, but that didn't discourage the giant mosquitoes. They were slow and easy to kill but there were so many hovering and whining around their heads all night, the torture was unrelenting.

After about a month, the food they hadn't dumped overboard on the first day of the trip was getting pretty sparse in addition to downright tedious, so they started fishing for grayling and Arctic char and agreed that dumping all that dried pasta and meat-like gorp was the smartest thing they ever did. But even though they were eating well, they were more than thrilled to find that the Hudson's Bay boat had just arrived when they pulled their canoes out of the water at Baker Lake. They celebrated the end of their adventure with fresh produce.

I was enormously proud of her for taking that opportunity. She and the other girls on the trip were the first white women to make that trek, and she was first in line to sign up for the next trip the following summer. I can't say I ever quit worrying about her safety, but since she was smart enough never to tell me any of the *really* scary details, it got easier as she gained more experience.

At the same time Mary Lil was trekking the Arctic, I was trekking the golf course with the ladies from the Country Club. One day, obviously when I was distracted by other issues, a woman from the Calgary Ladies Golf Association approached me asking if I'd let my name fill a spot on the nominations slate for their executive election. And almost before I figured out I had actually volunteered to be the sacrificial lamb, I was elected vice president.

In truth, though, I discovered I really enjoyed helping to arrange the city championship tournaments and, in 1974, I also served with the provincial association as the Calgary zone chairman. As teams chairman, I had to attend all the provincial tournaments to identify the female golfers who would compete at the national tournaments, and that's how I got to know so many of the very young golfers who were playing during the '70s and into the middle 1980s.

When I first met them, I couldn't understand how, with such a casual attitude toward the game, they could be so talented. Some of them would wander into the tournaments with mismatched clubs, and some played in their sneakers because they didn't own golf shoes. They chatted amongst themselves down the fairway seemingly without a care in the world. But the minute they stood up to address the ball, you could see the raw talent that would be honed as they matured. What they brought to their game was a genuine love for golf combined with a huge desire to do their best.

Judy Medlicott, Linda Rankin, Jackie Twamley, Marilyn Karch, Dawne Kortgaard, Lauren Rouse, Trish Murphy, Paula Imeson; there were so many talented young golfers in that era. We'd celebrate their good games, and I'd comfort them if they played poorly, and I thoroughly enjoyed every minute of my time with them. Now, of course, those young women are senior champions and they've been kind enough to stay in touch through all these years. Judy was totally irreverent about the game and always had a trick or two to play on me during the tournaments, so when she instigated my nomination to the Alberta Golf Hall of Fame in 2008, she made sure all the girls were on hand to accompany the ceremony with their cheer. "Lo – La! Lo – La! Lo – La!" rang out as I went to the podium to receive that wonderful honour. I think Judy paid me the greatest compliment ever: "Lola always had the right thing to say when she was chaperoning all of us to those tournaments. It was never all about golf. Lola's focus was always on fun. She made sure we got to see the ocean when we were out in the Atlantic provinces and that we could go sightseeing in the cities."

Judy (Medlicott) Forshner is now head pro at the Glencoe Golf and Country Club, and she's never lost that irreverent streak. She said that one day she was teaching the little kids' clinic to a gaggle of five-year-olds fresh from kindergarten where they had had a visiting fireman tell them all about fire safety. Obviously the fireman was a great teacher because they all came away knowing exactly what to do in case their clothing ever started on fire.

Judy, however, was trying to divert their attention back to her own lesson on the etiquette of the golf game. She had them all lined up at the driving range smacking range balls as far they could, and interrupted them to ask, "Now what do you yell if you accidentally hit your ball toward someone else?" Instantly, one eager little boy threw his club in the air and yelled, "Stop, Drop and Roll!"

Be warned. If you're ever golfing ahead of Judy, should you hear her yell, "Stop Drop and Roll," duck and cover.

I stayed with the Alberta Ladies Golf Association as vice-president in 1982 and '83, and as president in 1984 and '85, and accompanied the national team to Nova Scotia, London, Ontario, and the Canadian Open in Newfoundland and Saskatchewan. But a real highlight of my career in golf was when I was with the Canadian Ladies Golf Association in 1986, serving as a rules official, and was able to take a week-long rules course from the USGA in New Jersey.

However, I eventually knew I was in the wrong place when I was chastised by one of the women on the executive of the Canadian national association for loaning a skirt to one of the golfers on the American team. I was told in no uncertain terms that it was inappropriate to offer assistance to competitors on other teams, even if it was only wardrobe assistance. And then, in that condescending tone reserved only for the extremely self-important, she said, "Lola dear, you have a Southern accent. Tell me, where are you from?"

I smiled sweetly and said, "I'm from south Calgary."

Life's too short; I went back to play golf with the women who know it's only a game and the object is to have fun, and became president of the ladies golf section of the Country Club.

Besides, there were other attractions back home in Calgary.

Ted's company, Basset Oil, had caught the wave created by OPEC in the early 1970s and was riding high and flourishing, producing more than 6,500 barrels a day from forty-one wells. OPEC had been founded to coordinate petroleum policies among international members of oil-producing nations, and it rose to international prominence as member countries took control of their domestic petroleum industries and acquired a major say in the pricing of crude oil on world markets. Oil prices rose steeply, triggered by the Arab oil embargo in 1973 and the outbreak of the Iranian Revolution in 1979. So, despite the fact that Canada wasn't a member of OPEC, the Alberta economy was booming again, thanks to high oil prices.

The company was so busy that Ted and I discussed the possibility of inviting both young Ted and Reed to join Basset, and it seemed to be the right time to initiate that proposal. Ted was working in Texas but had told me that if he could ever be of help in his dad's company, he'd like to do that. Reed was still in the Air Force and on a direct career path toward becoming a major, but when the invitation was issued, he was immediately interested, even though

Ruth Ann discouraged it. She knew he was exceptionally good at his job, she and the kids enjoyed military life, and he was about to reap the benefits of a significant promotion.

Ted tells me, however, that when he and Sandy and the kids arrived at the Canadian border, they stopped for a long second thought. He had essentially been on his own since he left high school, so joining his father's company demanded some pretty intensive soul-searching. His father had sweetened the offer and tied it to an opportunity for the kids to buy homes in the newly developed subdivision of Lake Bonaventure. Ted would be making a good living, which would compensate him for having to be out in the field so much of his time, and the three children would have many of the advantages he couldn't have promised them if he'd stayed in Texas.

Mary Lil laughs when she remembers this time in our lives because it was so obvious to her that I had always hoped to gather our family together again, and now Ted had the wherewithal to make that happen. Ted and Sandy crossed the border in 1974 and settled into their new house and Ted's new job with Basset. Reed resigned his commission from the Air Force, and he and Ruth Ann, along with their two children, arrived from Ohio a year later and moved into a house not far from Ted and Sandy on Lake Bonaventure.

And, despite my oath about hell freezing over before I'd leave the wonderful bungalow where we'd raised our family, Ted finally convinced me in 1976 to move into a much larger house directly across the lake from our two children and five grandchildren. Mary Lil was a student at Trinity University in San Antonio by this time, and after graduation she would be back and forth as she established her career, but her fixed address was still with us.

The house was certainly large enough to house all the visiting Estes clan, and we were able to convince most of them to come-stay-awhile those summers. One time Ruth Ann dropped by with her friends Mike and Deb O'Connor. Mike was on his motorcycle and I was admiring it, so he thought he'd tease me a little by inviting me to hop on for a ride. I'm sure he never expected me to jump on the back but, practically before he finished the invitation, I had the extra helmet on my head and was yelling, "Let's go!" We took off down the cul de sac and blasted down Macleod Trail laughing insanely the whole way. Ruth Ann said I had bugs in my teeth when I got back.

The lake was a four-season playground for all the grandchildren. There were wind surfers and paddleboats docked against our deck all summer, and the kids could head for our house to warm up after tobogganing on the island or playing hockey on the lake in the winter. Within a few years, all five grandchildren would be in the same school together.

Best of all, the twelve of us could assemble around our dinner table every Sunday evening for Southern fried chicken with all the trimmin's. By the time the kids had wolfed down the green beans seasoned in bacon drippings and the mashed potatoes smothered in chicken-fried gravy, and the still-warm-from-the-oven cornbread, I had carbo-loaded them enough for a solid week and they could go home to fresh fruit and veggies. But I think you should know, it's that Southern fried chicken they all remember best.

CHAPTER NINETEEN

Giving Back

I suppose as much as any of us can set the stage exactly as we'd like, none of us can predict how the players will interpret the script. However, as the twelve of us gathered around our table for the first time, I was blissfully content. Impossible as it may have seemed thirty-six years prior when I drove away from my family to start our married life, I felt that I at last had come full circle. Life was playing out as it should.

In the oil patch, every indication was that we were in an economy that would give our now-adult children opportunities to build their careers and perhaps to realize dreams far beyond any of our expectations. Ted and Reed landed in Calgary at exactly the right moment; it was perfect timing. However, the roller coaster reality of the province's boom and bust cycles was something neither of them had experienced before.

When we arrived in Calgary in 1949, we jumped on at the crest of that ride, and ten years later we rode it down to its crash over the rocky cliffs of the '60s. But compared to what was happening to the oil industry in the mid-'70s, the post-Leduc boom seemed hardly more than a bump. I think Ted and I both knew we were in for a wild ride. Fortunately, we were old enough and experienced enough to hang on and make it through. I'm afraid the younger generation, who hadn't had that experience, came out of it with considerable bruising.

By the 1970s, Alberta was taking on a far more sophisticated and worldly demeanour. It would no longer be Central Canada's country cousin. In 1971, Peter Lougheed wrested control of the provincial legislature from the Social Credit party, which had been in power since Premier William Aberhart's voodoo economic theories fooled Alberta farmers into thinking he knew how to end the Depression. However, even though Aberhart's disciple, Ernest Manning, had been a hands-off friend to the growing oil industry, he was hardly equal to representing such a volatile issue as oil on a national, let alone a world, stage. And, make no mistake. *Every*one knew that Alberta was sitting on an almost unlimited supply of what the world needed now more than ever before.

Peter Lougheed personified the *new* Alberta. His grandfather, Senator James Lougheed, was one of the province's very first movers and shakers back in 1883 when it was still technically part of the Northwest Territories. But Peter belonged to *our* generation; he had lived through the Depression and watched his own father lose the considerable fortune the family had amassed during his grandfather's stewardship. It wouldn't happen under his watch. Those close to him saw him tick off the steps it would take to place him in a position where he could call the plays.

In high school, he lobbied for a students' union and became its first president. At the University of Alberta, he was awarded both a bachelor's and a law degree while serving as president of the students' union, and writing for the student newspaper. At the same time, he played football for the university's Golden Bears as well as professionally for the Edmonton Eskimos, and then he retired from sports so he could go to Boston for an MBA from the Harvard Business School.

Peter was a young man who knew where he was going and how to get there. He came back to Alberta to lay the foundation for a political career beginning with a management position in Fred Mannix's construction business, then moved along to establish a law practice in Edmonton and finally, in the mid-'60s, he got political.

In scarcely more than five years, he was the leader of the Progressive Conservative party and elected premier of the province.

Under Premier Manning's administration, the oil companies had been left alone to explore and develop to their hearts' content, and Alberta prospered from royalties collected from their profits. However, with the arrival of OPEC onto the world's stage in 1969, the price of oil skyrocketed and Peter Lougheed recognized what this windfall could do for the province. It was shaping up to be the mother of all booms. Like the rest of his generation, he was weary of being buffeted about by the stormy climate of the oil industry, so he upped the royalties on oil and gas and established the Heritage Trust Fund to sock away the profits for a rainy day and to encourage a little economic diversification. Understandably, Alberta oilmen grumbled as they watched their profits being diverted into the provincial coffers.

Calgary, of course, was at the eye of that storm. And to make matters worse, this was all taking place during the disco era, arguably the tackiest decade of the twentieth century. Four thousand people a month flooded into the province during the boom, and the vacancy rate for both apartments and office space plummeted to zero. The real estate market went crazy. Oil prices made millionaires of people who stumbled into the economy of the '70s with only limited business experience and even less judgment. Everyone seemed to be speculating in real estate or experimenting in oil ventures. Sadly though, as the Texans like to say, many of them were all hat and no cattle. There were stories about four-martini lunches at the Petroleum Club, and cocaine replaced marijuana as the drug of choice among a smattering of young people who couldn't think of anywhere else to spend their money. Apparently, Las Vegas casinos were sending planes to Calgary to collect the high rollers, and building cranes sprouted like weeds throughout downtown Calgary knocking down '50s-era office towers to replace them with '70s-era office towers. Another story – perhaps apocryphal – reported an ongoing underground Monopoly game that required a buy-in of a million and a half dollars because the players used real currency to buy and sell *real* houses and hotels sitting on Calgary's Park Places and Boardwalks. The decade's favourite expression was, "He who dies with the most toys wins."

However, when Prime Minister Trudeau marched into the maelstrom with the hand of the *federal* government outstretched, it was the last straw. From that point forward, the relationship between Alberta and the national government spiralled out of control, a hurricane wreaking havoc as it swept over those of us caught up in it.

By the time Mr. Trudeau's National Energy Program brought it all to an end in the early '80s, the damage suffered by the young families who had been swept up in that short-lived culture of excess was a terrible thing to see. Unemployment in Alberta rose to 10 per cent. For the first time ever, more people were leaving the province than arriving to settle, and Alberta led the nation in housing foreclosures, bankruptcies, divorces, and suicides. Those of us who survived that decade reeled into the '80s older and much wiser about the stewardship of our lifetimes' rewards.

However, Ted had decided in 1979 that, since his family was well and truly launched, and he was at an age where a little more time on the golf course wouldn't be out of line, he would sell Basset Oil to Dallas Hawkins' company, Oakwood Petroleum. Considering the timing of the sale, it turned out to be a prescient decision, so we were left in a position where we could thank all our neighbours, friends, and business associates who'd offered their friendship and support over the years. Ted owned a farm just south of town so we decided we'd throw a yell-yahoo!-and-have-a-boot-scootin'-good-time Stampede party. Young Ted took on the project, and it turned out to be such a barn burner that we knew we'd have to make it an annual event, so the next year we included practically everyone in the phone book plus all their visiting relatives – along with all of the kissin' kin imported from points south. I decided Ted and I needed matching cowboy shirts with matching, embroidered Texas roses, and from that point forward the whole production just got bigger.

Ruth Ann was a seasoned veteran of the Stampede Board's Caravan Committee, so she definitely knew how to marshal the forces for a major feeding frenzy and entertainment spectacular and, within a very few years, the Rozsa Roundup took on a life of its own.

But we also decided we could offer our appreciation to Calgary in a more substantial way. Both of us were still very much involved with the Philharmonic, and by the mid-'80s, Ruth Ann had followed in our footsteps and was active in the annual Gala and Dream Auction that was sponsored by the Women's League. Unfortunately, Reed had discovered he wasn't cut out for life in the oil industry, and he was unhappy living in Calgary, so he prevailed upon Ruth Ann to take the family back to California in '81. It was short-lived, however, and they were divorced a year later, so Ruth Ann and the children came back home in '82. It was, of course, a terrible blow – one that was unthinkable from my perspective – but so many young marriages didn't survive the '70s. I was grateful that the children were back in the arms of their Rozsa family though, and I know both Karen and Howie felt well-loved and secure in our support.

The string of guest conductors at the Calgary Philharmonic continued throughout the '70s to the mid-'80s, and the board was more committed than ever to finding a resident music director. When they heard rumours that Mario Bernardi might consider stepping away from the National Arts Centre Orchestra, provided the financial incentive was available of course, four of the CPO directors took Ted out to lunch.

Would he consider paying Mario Bernardi's salary and endowing a Maestro's Chair to ensure its sustainability? It would require a cheque with six zeros.

Ted always joked about that day. He said, "Beware of four lawyers who offer to take you to lunch. You'll be outnumbered and there are enough of them to pin down all four limbs until you give in." In 1984, Maestro Bernardi became the Music Director of the CPO and held that position until 1992. In 1985, the orchestra moved into the Jack Singer Concert Hall in the Performing Arts Centre and, during Mario's tenure, the Calgary orchestra was considered to be among the top two or three in Canada. Ted was delighted that he could help bring this kind of talent to Calgary, and, in return, the CPO gave *him* countless hours of superb music.

Following each of the concerts, the board took turns entertaining Mario and the visiting soloists at our homes and we got to know one another very well. We often invited the kids in the orchestra to come out to skate on the lake and join us for weekend afternoon drinks and nibblies, and Hy and Jenny Belzberg offered their home for many of the receptions following the concerts. The Belzbergs were so generous toward the Philharmonic and we adored them both. Jenny came up through the ranks of community volunteers much as I did, so we had many experiences in common, but I think I most admired her for her whole-hearted support of the small initiatives she championed as they gained a foothold in Calgary's non-profit sector. Many of those organizations were arts-related, but others were in support of the development of new community leaders. She saw that the face of voluntarism was changing. Younger men and women had full-time careers, but less time to offer to the organizations that could profit by their help. Jenny gave her support and mentorship to their leadership development, knowing that the next generation would soon be called upon to take our places in Calgary's community board rooms.

Ted gave an additional seven figure cheque to the Philharmonic a year after his first to bump up the endowment fund, and throughout the following years he continued to help as needed, especially where music was involved. He gave to the Honens International Piano Competition and the Calgary Opera, but he was also very generous to the Foothills Hospital, the Banff School of Fine Arts, the Centre for Performing Arts, Theatre Calgary, the Glenbow Museum (where he was a director of the board for a time), and Grace Presbyterian Church. Very few of those donations were made public until finally someone convinced him that his philanthropy might provide a model for others to get involved.

In the early '80s, we finally figured out we could escape the worst of the cold weather by taking our golf clubs to Hawaii for a few weeks in the winter, so while we were there I talked him into buying a place in Maui, which we were able to share with friends and family. But Ted's retirement didn't last long, I'm afraid. By the time we got back from a two-week vacation after he sold Basset, he was back at work putting together another company he called Rozsa Petroleum.

I could see it wasn't going to be easy to get him to slow down; his idea of a vacation was to take his golf clubs to a new golf course. It didn't much matter where it was. We had tried a few sightseeing trips that anyone else would have loved, but I'm afraid all that interesting culture and beautiful scenery was wasted on Ted. Luckily, though, I had raised adventurous children who loved to travel so I had the chance to visit Ruth Ann in some of the exotic places she went with Pan Am and where they were stationed with the Air Force. And once Mary Lil was bit by the adventure bug during her trip across the Arctic, she was first in line for a chance to go along the following two summers. They further whetted her appetite for more remote excursions, and it wasn't long before she started asking me to join her.

One time, Mary Lil won a trip for two to Australia, so she asked me to come along. The prize, evidently, was limited to the flight alone, so she would have to take care of the food and shelter part. It didn't faze her at all. She would be perfectly happy in a youth hostel, so, of course, assumed that I would be too. We went to Papua New Guinea and travelled in dug-out canoes and hiked up into the highlands where white women had never been before. While we were observing a dowry being negotiated before a wedding, I realized Mary Lil and I were the only women wearing tops, except for one tiny, toothless old woman who had an American flag tie wrapped around her neck, fashionably draped in her cleavage.

The next time she invited me to join her, she was biking across Europe and suggested we meet in Milan to celebrate American

Thanksgiving in Italy. She booked us into the Hilton and promised to meet me at the train station near the hotel. You can imagine how thrilled I was! No more youth hostels, no more dug-out canoes. I had visions of sightseeing through the high-fashion capital of the world and seeing every Leonardo da Vinci painting I'd ever read about. At last, I thought, Mary Lil has finally discovered the good life.

As promised, she was there as I arrived, although suspiciously burdened with a very large backpack. "Why didn't you just leave that at the hotel?" I asked in my most reasonable voice, knowing full well I really didn't want to hear the answer. But before I could stop myself, Mary Lil brightly answered, "Oh I just slept here in the train station last night. No sense paying for a hotel room when I've got a perfectly good sleeping bag."

Okay, I thought, I won't make that mistake again. If I don't want to hear the answer, I have to learn not to ask the question. No matter, the Hilton was just a block or so away so we could both shower and change our clothes and, by the time we were ushered into our lovely room overlooking the fabulous Milan cityscape, I was ready to drop. She could see that I was exhausted by the long overnight flight and very sweetly asked, "Mom, would you like a cup of tea?"

Thank heaven for room service. "Yes, that would be perfect. Thank you. I'll just jump into the shower first." I stepped out of the bathroom a few minutes later wrapped in a fluffy white robe – courtesy of the Hilton – and found Mary Lil surrounded by the entire contents of her pack and bicycle panniers, squatted over her camping stove boiling water for our tea. I was wise enough to just shut up and be grateful.

Mary Lil, between adventures, finished her undergraduate degree at Trinity and took an Education degree at the University of Calgary, where she would eventually receive an Honorary Doctor of Laws. During one hiatus though, she worked briefly at the Rozsa Petroleum office and wandered across the hall to introduce herself to a fellow who was at that time buying and selling diamonds. He was the quintessential '70s-era entrepreneur, always open to exploring new deals. Gary and Mary Lil became great friends and scuba diving partners, and eventually she invested in some land in Mexico that he had introduced her to. She built a condo development on the property and, since there was a ratty little golf course nearby, she decided she'd introduce her friends to it by hosting a golf tournament. And who better to organize it than her very own mother, a veteran of many tournaments. I can't say it would have passed muster by the PGA, but we had commemorative tee-shirts made and I can guarantee we all had more fun than any tournament before or since.

Back home in Calgary, though, it was generally tough sledding after the economic meltdown of the early '80s. Those who survived the National Energy Program had to batten the hatches and prepare for rough weather yet again. Those who didn't, either through financial mismanagement or personal recklessness, watched their businesses dissolve and their marriages fail. The only bright note on the horizon was that we had been awarded the winter Olympics for 1988, so almost everyone we knew was involved in those preparations in some way or another.

Politically though, Albertans licked their wounds and muttered about separating from the Dark Side. Peter Lougheed, although he had fought the good fight against Central Canada's claim on Alberta's resources and ultimately ensured that Alberta would never retreat to its former protectionist position, resigned his position as premier. Albertans remained steadfastly loyal to the Conservative Party. But the most astounding political change during the '80s was Calgary's civic election of 1980 when Ralph Klein was elected mayor.

I think even Ralph was stunned when he won that election. He was a high school drop-out, a TV reporter whose favourite beat was the seedy St. Louis Hotel pub, where he could multi-task his interviews with the more colourful populous. He was Alberta's version of a good ol' boy and, in a city that takes a certain pride in its reputation as the most highly educated in the country, he was not expected to be a viable candidate.

It was a landslide victory. I never could find anyone who actually admitted to voting for him, but obviously plenty of people did. Those that did were proud to; they *loved* him! Ralph played to their animosity against the "eastern creeps and bums" who had caused all their financial misery, and I was lucky enough to have an insider's ear on all the civic gossip about the mayor's excesses because the most famous 'alderbroad' on City Council and I shared a hairdresser.

Sue Higgins was truly a character, and the press loved her because she never minced words with anyone – including me. So, as we sat under our side-by-side hair dryers every week, she'd give me the lowdown on uptown Calgary. She was hilarious and we became good buddies throughout her long tenure on City Council, and I rooted for her all the way when she launched her campaign to unseat Mayor Ralph. She lost that one but was handily re-elected to Council and she continued her fight for fiscal restraint for many years. It was because of Sue that I had an opportunity to serve on a civic committee to renovate City Hall, and I came away from that experience with huge respect for so many ordinary Calgarians who volunteer their time on behalf of the community. As I've gotten older, I've found I have less and less patience with people who gripe about civic issues yet refuse to step up and take action when action needs taking. I'm likely to interrupt their litany of complaints with, "And what are *you* doing about that?"

Ralph continued riding a wave of civic popularity. He was nothing if not a party guy, and the Olympic Games were shaping up to be the biggest party of the century. And by the time that was over, Ralph was poised for a promotion to premier of Alberta.

I'm afraid that for those of us in the oil business, however, the party was *really* over by that time. Unfortunately, those too young or too inexperienced to ride out the storm suffered. In the years since, I still haven't been able to understand why all those young marriages were victims in that collapse. Ted and I saw ourselves as more than mates and best friends; we were life partners. We had been through repeated boom and bust cycles since the day we left Whitesboro for

Stroud, Oklahoma. There were times when I know I gave serious thought to bolting but, as my friend Mary Ann often said, "I've considered murder on more than a few occasions, but never divorce!" Divorce was absolutely unthinkable. I suppose that the Depression years had taught most of us that we needed one another to survive; it was better to face life together than to try to go it alone.

The values my parents had taken from their forbears had been absorbed like the air we breathed in an era where multiple generations lived in close proximity to one another. Those forebears knew that life was precarious. Illness, weather, crop failure, anything could decimate small families. Extended families stepped in to help young couples through childbirth and illness, and to help old people through their final days. We needed one another to survive the hard times, so we shared the bounty of the good times with others, all the while knowing very well our own time of need would inevitably come. We toughed it out and did unto others as we would have others do unto us, not because Nannie and Preacher said so; we did it because that's what works best for all of us.

I spent many hours on the telephone with my Estes siblings during the '80s trying to understand all the upheaval of that decade. Actually, if truth be told, we had *always* spent many hours on the phone together, but we had grown up very much involved in each other's lives and had learned to seek one another's advice when difficulties arose. In the Preacher's family, living cheek-by-jowl with the small town congregations, there were definitely no secrets between us, nor from anyone else in town, I'm afraid. I suppose I realized that, as the youngest, I would have the advantage of their experiences or at least the assurance that this too would pass, so the once-a-week calls to each of them was the best therapy going.

But I must say I was more than a little miffed when all *our* children decided they'd have a cousins' reunion. And that it wouldn't include their parents. Worse yet, the whole thing was instigated by Ruth Ann and my nephew Eddie Hart, who conspired to gather up all the cousins and whichever second-cousins that could assemble for a weekend in Dallas. Fourteen of the younger Estes clan attended, and I'm told it was a huge success. Of course it was. Who better to turn to than extended family, those who love you in spite of your shortcomings? Who better to help you process your thinking through difficult times? Extended family will always assure you that eventually the cream will rise and that everything will look better in the morning. Who better to urge you to pick yourself up, brush yourself off and get back at it? We taught them well; I suppose I was just a little jealous about not being invited along to see how those values extended into the next generation.

My guess is that the meltdown of the '80s caught many in our children's generation at that very vulnerable time when they were old enough to profit by the boom, but not yet wise enough to have found a framework of values to replace those they had distanced themselves from during the social crises of the '60s and '70s. Most would learn from those experiences, start again and build successful careers and happy lives.

Others never did find an ethical framework. From that generation came the catastrophic financial frauds of the first decade of the twenty-first century. Their narcissism and greed would ultimately contribute to worldwide economic disaster.

Ten years after the twelve of us first assembled around our dining table, we had gone off script. The players had changed. Some were missing and others had been added. Some of the children had become adults and new babies had been born. Maybe life wasn't playing out as I had once imagined, but then I suppose it never does.

Give me a song and a stage.

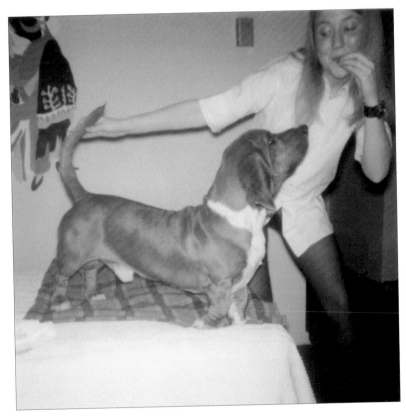

Mary Lil coaching Tex for the dog show.

Tex and Howie getting settled for their afternoon nap.

Ted and me in our matching Texas rose shirts.

BALLOON-RIDING AT THE ROZSA ROUNDUP.

GOLF IN THE FALL – NO DOUBT MARY LIL'S AT HOME BAKING HER OWN BIRTHDAY CAKE.

Mary Lil's Arctic trip.

Living off the land – and the water – throughout 1,100 miles across the Arctic.

Welcoming Mario Bernardi to the Calgary Philharmonic.

My golf girls celebrating the Alberta Golf Hall of Fame award.

OUR ROZSA PETROLEUM FAMILY.

CHAPTER TWENTY

Bricks and Mortar

By the time the '90s dawned, both of Ruth Ann's children were grown and she and her husband, Doug Rayner, were happily living on a country acreage west of town where they could keep their horses. Mary Lil came back from Mexico to introduce us to Patrick Henri Daniel Meunier-Coquet and announce that they were getting married, and a few years later they moved to Calgary. Patrick became the Mexican Consul General, their daughter Mary Cristina was born in 1992 and, once again, the dinner table was being reassembled. However, young Ted left Rozsa Petroleum at that time to go back to Texas to work with Landmark and then Halliburton and, in 1994, he and his third wife presented us with Charles, our youngest grandchild. Ted's three older children were all busy in university or launching their careers, so the players around the table were in constant motion, and frankly I'd given up trying to be the dramaturge. But I guess it was Karen, Ruth Ann's daughter, who finally opened my eyes to the fact that the times they were a'changin.'

Karen had been dating Jim Rice for about a year and of course he had been instantly enveloped in the Rozsa clan because he was truly a wonderful young man who obviously adored our granddaughter. He was a soldier with the Canadian Army at that time, and he came with her to all the family dinners and was introduced to all the visiting kin and none of us thought for a moment they wouldn't one day be married. I say all this up front because I most certainly can't excuse my behaviour when Karen and I met one afternoon at the shopping centre.

I had been over at Ted's office and dropped in at the shopping centre on my way home, where I unexpectedly – and delightedly – ran into Karen. She was holding a couple of magazines and we chatted about her day and, naturally, I asked her about Jim. She said he was just fine but that he was going to be stationed in Cyprus for a tour of duty. She said she was looking for a new apartment, and then showed me the Renter's Guide she had been holding. I took a long hard look at her and suddenly realized she wasn't telling me the whole story. "An apartment for you? Or for you and Jim?"

"For the two of us."

I still cringe when I remember my reaction. Without even thinking, I grabbed that Renter's Guide out of her hand and smacked her across the face with it. I had suddenly been transported back to those tiny judgmental congregations where I had been raised, where every out-of-bounds action had an equal and opposite response designed to keep the individual in line and the community intact.

I could tell from the look on her face that Karen was devastated by what I had done, and I was immediately and abjectly sorry. And then, following a very long pause, I was completely shamed by her calm and reasoned explanation. "Mammaw, I was on my way to Granddaddy's office to tell him that Jim and I are moving in together. I wanted to tell him first because I knew that neither of you would approve. I planned to come out to your house this afternoon to tell you, too. Jim and I are both adults, we love each other and one day we will be married. There's no reason for him to keep an apartment since he will be away on tours of duty much of the time, so we're renting this apartment together."

Five years later, Jim and Karen were indeed married, and are now the parents of two wonderful children. They're still living happily ever after, but I've never forgiven myself for the way I treated her that day, However, I'm grateful to say that Karen tosses it off with, "Oh Mammaw, don't worry about it. With all your other

grandchildren coming along and very likely getting ready to do the same thing, I just took one for the team."

Ted wanted to ensure that the grandchildren had access to university so he had set up an educational trust that would cover their tuitions and living costs. He had no desire to influence their career choices. His only objective was to provide them with the tools to get them there, so he designed the trust to pay their fees along with a monthly living allowance for ten years, giving them ample time and resources for graduate school if any of them should decide to take advantage of that opportunity, too. Of course, back in the '80s, neither of us anticipated the arrival of our second set of grandchildren, so I've been reshuffling the deck to include Mary Cristina and Charles in Ted's plan.

Howie, Ruth Ann's eldest, was the first to fly the nest. He majored in sports physiology at the University of British Columbia, where he also took up sky-diving. And I don't mean he just tried it on a dare. He took it up *big* time. Before we could even mount a decent argument against it, he was competing locally, then internationally, and then he became an instructor, even talking his mother into risking a dive with him. He did assure us, however, that sky-diving wasn't his life's calling. After graduation, he and his Swedish girlfriend, Hella, lived in Florida for a time deciding whether or not they were good enough to join the golf tour. But shortly after they married in 1995, he decided he would rather become an emergency medic, and now he lives his dream life as a ski patrol medic in the winter and a tour guide in Sweden in the summer.

Ted had fought so hard for his own education and truly believed that his scholarship had provided the key that opened all the doors to the success he had achieved. It had given direction to his ravenous appetite for learning that endured throughout his life, and I suspect his thinking was that an education in their chosen fields would unlock the same kinds of opportunities for the grandchildren as well as for the other young people we were able to help through university.

I wish I could say that all his soul-searching about providing a legacy of education was arising in the golden glow of retirement from Rozsa Petroleum, but Ted was still going strong at seventy-five. He had been awarded the Canadian Society of Exploration Geophysicists gold medal in recognition of his outstanding contributions to the petroleum industry in 1987, and three years later he received an Honorary Doctorate of Engineering from Michigan Tech, his alma mater, as well as an Honorary Doctorate of Laws from the University of Calgary. In 1991, he was made an Officer of the Order of Canada, his proudest moment, and then in 1994 the Rotary Club of Calgary game him their Integrity Award.

He had absolutely no inclination to rest on his laurels, but he *was* getting more and more impatient about having to wait for tee times during the few vacations I coerced him into taking. He finally declared that he'd just as soon give up the place in Maui if he had to spend eight hours on a plane to get there and another forty-eight hours just to get on a golf course. But always at the back of his mind was the idea that those of us who had been so richly rewarded for our life's work had a responsibility to pay those rewards forward to the generations coming along. The challenge was in finding the best way to do that. And as he played less golf, he got more and more interested in finding ways to maximize that impact. As these things often do, everything fell into place with a phone call.

Jim Palmer, the senior partner at the law firm that handled Ted's business, was one of the CPO directors who had helped to negotiate the Maestro's Endowment Fund and, by this time, he was Chancellor of the University of Calgary as well. Once again, he called and invited Ted to lunch. This time, I was asked to join them. Jim said he wanted us to meet Murray Fraser, who was the newly appointed president and vice-chancellor of the university. Ted would tell you that he was hardly so naïve as to think there wasn't an ulterior motive involved, but, since I would be along as a buffer, he figured it would probably turn out to be a social visit. So after a lovely lunch at the faculty club, we were invited on a field trip accompanied by two very interesting guides.

By this time, the university had matured, and it boasted excellent professional schools of law, business, medicine and engineering, thanks to the enormous generosity of community philanthropists, many of them successful professionals who were graduates of those faculties. But because the university had grown so quickly, the undergraduate programs, particularly those of the fine arts, were the poor stepchildren of the very powerful graduate schools. This didn't surprise either of us because we had spent a lifetime raising funds to support the Calgary Philharmonic, and we commiserated endlessly with others who had championed theatre or dance or the visual arts so we knew how they all struggled to stay afloat even at the best of times.

We all had our one-minute elevator speeches honed to crystal clarity about why the arts are important to humankind, but I think the best one I ever heard came from one of the young fellows who rescued the Calgary Stampeders football team during the financial crisis of the '80s. He was launching a season ticket sale to support the team, and when a TV reporter asked him why Calgarians should spend their hard-earned money on football tickets – especially during the tough times – he said, "Because a healthy community is built by people. All kinds of people who come together to celebrate, to get involved in the excitement of competitive sports, or make music together, or express themselves artistically. All these things tell us who were are as human beings and bring us together despite our differences. Hell, I'm pretty certain I'll *never* want to go to see a ballet, but I know for sure I don't want to live in a city *without* a ballet company. We need *all* of these things because that diversity is what makes Calgary a great city and attracts other people to build their businesses here. Bottom line? It's having all those choices that makes Calgary a great place to live and raise our families."

Our guides on our U of C field trip had heard all the elevator speeches too, but both Murray Fraser and John Roberts, dean of the

Faculty of Fine Arts, wanted us to know how they were hoping to support the development of that faculty. As we wandered through the building, I could hear the music of the horns and violins and cellos coming at us from different directions and assumed we were getting close to the studios, but finally I had to ask, "Where are the students practicing?" Dean Roberts said, "Follow me," and led us down the hall to the stairwell door, opened it and motioned me inside. From my spot on the landing I could see up one flight of stairs and down another. A student sat on each landing, perched atop his backpack, his instrument poised, pausing only for a brief look at the intruders.

When I stepped back into the hallway and the music started again, I said, "Are your studios full? Is that why they're practising in the stairwell?" It was John's answer that opened the door to what would eventually become the Rozsa Centre for the Performing Arts, both at the University of Calgary and, three years later, at Michigan Tech.

Through a much longer conversation that afternoon and many more of the same over the subsequent months, we started thinking about how we could ensure that those students could have a music facility at hand that would actually prepare them for a performance career. Without one, it seemed to me that all their music education would be pointless. It would be as if we expected our medical students to walk into an operating theatre to meet their first surgical patients having had lots of textbook learning but no hands-on hospital experience.

Once we all agreed that the music faculty desperately needed performance theatres as well as studio space for their music students, both John Roberts and Murray Fraser jumped to the challenge with infectious enthusiasm. The first order of business was to find matching funds, so of course they looked to the provincial government for assistance, reasoning that the new premier, a home-grown Calgarian by the name of Ralph Klein, would be eager to contribute on the province's behalf to the University of Calgary. Not so. We would have to make this happen using only private funds. Fortunately there were many other Calgarians who stepped up to help including Clarisse Evans, Martha and Harry Cohen, and Hy and Jenny Belzberg along with the Sophie Eckhardt-Gramatté Foundation and companies like Husky Oil, CIBC, and Scotia Bank.

Reflecting back on this process, I realized that many of the family contributors to civic projects we had been involved with over the years included relatively recent immigrants to Calgary, and I wondered why that was. Was it because many of us had grown up through financially difficult times, or was it simply that we had been raised with the expectation that we would contribute how and when and where we could? Harry Cohen was one of six sons of a very poor immigrant family in Winnipeg – so poor they had neither a furnace nor a bathtub. Martha, Harry's wife, was an only child who grew up during the Depression knowing that the only way her parents could keep their home was through the help of their relatives who pulled together to survive those hard times. Her parents adopted two girls orphaned in the Nazi concentration camps, and Martha forever after devoted her life to helping young people, both through her career in social work and in her passion for the arts. Both Harry and Martha gave of their time in addition to their treasure and, besides their contribution toward the Rozsa Centre, the beautiful Martha Cohen Theatre in the Centre for the Performing Arts was among their many, many gifts to Calgarians.

As the funding for the Rozsa Centre fell into place, we started looking for an architect and were thrilled when Fred Valentine was chosen to design the building. We had always admired the beautiful Nova Building in downtown Calgary that Fred had designed, and understood his passion for building in the context of the locality and its history. What we hadn't realized, though, was that Fred had also designed the perfect little composer's studio at the Banff School of Fine Arts. It was nestled nearby the school in the woods of Tunnel Mountain overlooking one of the most spectacular views in the Rockies. Music historians have said that Mozart only wrote down the notes that appeared as if by magic in his head – wrote them down without corrections or changes as they appeared to him. Seeing that little gem of a studio, you can imagine how the luxury of time in the peace and quiet of that sun-flooded space might inspire even greater works of genius in some yet-undiscovered twenty-first-century composer.

Fred had also contributed to the design of the 1988 Olympic Games structures and the TransAlta building, so we knew that each one of his creations was unique and perfectly designed for both its function and its place. The first thing he told us was that he envisioned a big barn-like building to reflect the prairie landscape all around us, and his initial drawings showed us how he could combine that vision with the functionality of a performance hall surrounded by 'stables' on each side. The stables would house practice studios for the students along with additional small meeting rooms. Even the corridors were designed to bow out to accommodate mini-rehearsals as the musicians awaited their turns on stage. With conference halls, reception spaces, theatres for recitals, lectures, and performances, we were confident this would be an arts centre that would never sit empty between concerts.

When the sod was turned, our only lingering concern was whether we could have perfect acoustics in the big concert hall because it truly was barn-like just as Fred had envisioned. We needn't have worried, however, because Fred chose the Danish acoustical engineer Niels Jordan who designed the Glenn Gould Studio in the Toronto CBC building. As construction progressed, Niels came to 'tune' the building. It was quite a media event and, as I remember, he came several times over the subsequent months to fine-tune it until, at its opening in March of 1997, it was declared the best performance space in the country. The acoustics are so perfect a microphone really isn't necessary for a speaker standing on the stage. In fact, the building is so sensitive you can hear the sound of the bow on the violin strings before you can hear the note played, and sound engineers have to wrestle with that issue when recordings are being made!

The grand hall was named in honour of Sophie Eckhardt-Gramatté, a prolific Canadian composer. I wish I had known her; she must have been a fabulous character. She was born in Moscow in 1899 to an aristocratic Russian mother and a reportedly 'mysterious' father. Her mother had been a pupil of both Anton and Nicholas Rubenstein and in her youth she taught piano and French to the children of Leo Tolstoy. Sophie was born after the collapse of her parents' marriage, and rumour had it that she was actually the daughter of her mother's lover, Xavier Friedman, who also happened to be her piano student.

For some reason, Sophie was sent as an infant to be raised by foster parents at an English commune modelled on Leo Tolstoy's principles of communism, but at the age of five she and her mother moved to Paris, where she began learning to play both piano and violin and started creating short musical pieces. At nine, she enrolled at the Paris Conservatoire de Musique, where she studied with Gabriel Fauré, and by eleven was giving her first concerts in Paris, Geneva, and Berlin. Unquestionably, she was a prodigy, but apparently Sophie was a difficult child to manage because what she really wanted to do was to compose, not perform. Making matters even more difficult, she and her mother had to eke out a living during the early years of the First World War in Berlin, where Sophie was reduced to playing in cafes and beer gardens to earn their rent money.

Eventually, she was discovered by the great violinist Joseph Joachim, who arranged for her to study with the Polish violinist Bronislaw Hubermann, and the teenaged Sophie began to circulate among the circle of influential European musicians and artists. She met and married the visual artist Walter Gramatté in 1920, who became her lifelong soul mate despite his early death and her subsequent marriage to Dr. Ferdinand Eckhardt, an art historian. Eckhardt encouraged her to give up her performance career altogether and to dedicate her life to composing. Unfortunately, though, they moved to Vienna in 1939 and were trapped there for the duration of World War II, so her compositions were ignored by the Nazi government, and it wasn't until 1950 that she won the Austrian State Prize for Composition.

In 1953, Sophie and Ferdinand moved to Winnipeg when he was appointed Director of the Winnipeg Art Gallery, and she became a very successful teacher and composer, writing more than 175 compositions including two symphonies, eight concertos, including a triple concerto for trumpet, clarinet, bassoon, strings and timpani, three string quartets and numerous other works for violin and piano. Sophie died in 1974. In her memory, a National Music Competition for the Performance of Canadian Music was founded and is held annually at Brandon University. I think she would have been pleased to know that the Canadian pianists Anton Kuerti and Marc-André Hamelin were invited to play the opening concerts in the magnificent hall named in her honour.

We had such fun working with Murray Fraser throughout the design and construction of the building. He arranged for the whole family to don hard hats and steel-toed boots to tramp through the building site to imagine the finishing touches, and when it came time to dedicate the centre, Murray presented me with a sign that flashed 'Lola's Place' in day-glow neon. Sadly though, three months before the Rozsa Centre opened in 1997, Murray Fraser died suddenly, and we didn't have the opportunity to properly thank him for his tireless commitment to this wonderful project. It could never have been realized without his exceptional talent for bringing people together around our shared vision for a world-class music facility at the university, and both Ted and I mourned his loss as we attended the first concert dedicated to this fine man.

Unfortunately, though, Ted's hearing had begun to fail, and he was never really able to enjoy music again. We had sold the place in Maui and had been talked into buying a condominium in Palm Springs on the promise he could get there in a couple of hours and would have his choice of dozens of golf courses to play at his leisure. It was perfect for Ted because, as much as he loved to play golf, he also loved his work, and California was accessible at a moment's notice when space opened up in his appointment calendar. We had many happy vacations there and were able to share the condominium with friends and family but, one afternoon as we were playing golf, Ted fell. I hadn't seen what had happened, and he insisted he'd just tripped over something. But I was concerned enough to take him into the local hospital. They checked him over and recommended that we go home right away for a thorough workup.

I knew Ted was dangerously dismissive of his own aches and pains. At one point, he'd been playing golf in Calgary and miss-hit a few shots he knew he shouldn't have, so at the end of eighteen he walked off the course and went directly to the hospital to be checked over. Sure enough he was right. He had had a heart attack.

So just as soon as we landed back in Calgary, we went into the Foothills Hospital and Terry Myles, a wonderful neurosurgeon who had treated Ted earlier for his hearing loss, determined that, despite the fact neither of us could recall any injury, Ted had had a bleed on his brain. That was what had caused his dizziness and his fall on the golf course. Terry operated on him successfully and stopped the bleed, but the hearing loss was progressive. The kids used to say, "Dad couldn't hear but he loved music, he couldn't maintain his balance but he loved to play golf. It's a good thing he wasn't a runner – he'd probably lose his feet!"

I know that losing his hearing was very difficult for Ted. Music had been such a big part of his life and just as he was able to contribute toward building the Rozsa Centres both at the University of Calgary and at Michigan Tech, he lost his ability to enjoy the performances of the generation of students who had received his gifts. But there's an old adage about philanthropy: "You must plant trees in whose shade you will never sit." I hope he knows how very many trees have blossomed because of his generosity, and how many more young students are sitting in their shade enjoying the fruits of his labour. I know in my heart that one day they, too, will have an opportunity to repay his kindness and will open doors for the generation that will follow them.

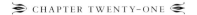

CHAPTER TWENTY-ONE

The Rozsa Foundation

As the twentieth century closed, Ted and I felt the great circle of life spinning us in its axis. Ruth Ann's husband had passed away in 1998 only a few weeks after being diagnosed with pancreatic cancer. But scarcely a year later Karen and Jim, her daughter and son-in-law who live in Calgary, presented us with our first great-grandchild. Little Tristan was truly a light in our lives and, when his sister Emma joined the family three years later, they would be very frequent and very welcome visitors as our own lives slowed down with advancing age. Ted would soon be eighty-five, and he was reluctantly winding up Rozsa Petroleum, so he was facing his retirement years believing that there was still much to be done if his health would permit.

On the first day of the new century, though, we looked back over the sixty years of our marriage and counted our blessings. I could hardly believe I was the same person who fifty years previously had so desperately resisted Ted's vision for our future in Calgary. It was as though my anxiety about staying in the safe and secure fold of my family blinded me to the infinite variety of choices we might make. I so vividly remember him saying, "C'mon. It's only a year, and it'll be an adventure we'll tell our grandchildren about!" Now, of course, I know how much smaller my life would have been had I married that cotton farmer back in north Texas. It was Ted's foresight and entrepreneurial genius that gave our family opportunities far, far beyond what I had ever imagined possible.

But, at the dawn of the twenty-first century, we were eager to see how our grandchildren would build their own lives. Young Ted's older children had struggled through their parents' break-up, but by this time all three were living in the States and were launching their careers. And, the year following Tristan's birth, Ted's first grandchild, Evan, was born in Texas, where his eldest son, Scott, and his family had located. With seven grandchildren and now two great-grandsons and a great-granddaughter, we felt we had most ably followed the biblical instruction to go forth and multiply. However, now that we were in the autumn of our own years, both of us wanted to leave something they could build upon – something that would not only enrich their own lives but also the lives of others. It was a discussion that would take almost two years, two years filled with a lot of soul-searching, because in September of 2001 we awoke one morning to the tragedy of 9/11.

For the first time since 1812, the United States was attacked on its own soil – not for reasons of territorial expansion or any declaration of war – but seemingly only to kill defenceless American civilians and to call attention to alleged American and Israeli crimes against Palestine. The fact that the attack was launched by terrorist thugs outside of any state-supported sponsorship made it so incomprehensible to most of us that the real body count of almost three thousand was utterly dwarfed by the hundreds of millions of Americans that would ultimately be victimized by it far into the future. It would take more than ten years to finally track down the madman who had financed the attack, and we are still recovering from senseless wars in Iraq and Afghanistan that have brought the United States to the brink of financial ruin. Conspiracy theories continue to ricochet around the Internet, we automatically remove our shoes going through airport security, and far too many American political candidates have discovered that the best way to whip up support is to inflame ignorant religious prejudices. A lot of this posturing has nothing to do with anything except political gamesmanship. It's certainly not statesmanship. Worse, the lingering fear of 'the other' continues to cripple Americans' understanding of the Islamic world.

Living here in Calgary, I think we have had an enormous advantage through this tragic time. Our diversity has woven us such a rich tapestry of visual arts, music, theatre and dance, and our great-grandchildren are growing up with schoolmates from every nationality, race, and faith. For them, there is no 'other' to fear. The children who share their classrooms, compete with them on their sports teams, and play with them in their school bands are their friends, no matter whether they wear toques, baseball caps, yarmulkes, turbans or hijabs.

The great-grandchildren see beyond the differences to the commonalities. To them, music is just music; people are just people. Not that I know anything about iPads and iPods and iPhones, but I do understand that every generation has its own ways to communicate. And I also know that the children of this generation are so connected to one another that the world has become a much more familiar place. I have complete confidence that the children who will inherit the complex international issues we adults haven't figured out will be able to cross the barriers we've erected over the years simply because they don't perceive those barriers. They know that our similarities are far more important than our differences, whether those differences are racial or cultural or national. We're all ordinary people and we have to count on one another more than ever before.

It was against the pervasive coverage of the 9/11 tragedy in the first years of the new century that Ted and I discussed how we might offer the family a way to stay involved in the arts initiatives that had brought us such joy throughout the years. Undoubtedly, all the news coverage caused a bubbling up of the realization that no matter what differences might divide us, the arts bring people together – all kinds of people from all cultures.

We had happily worked among so many who devoted their lives to the arts, and discovered that the not-for-profit world is largely peopled by those who have enormous passion for their particular causes. They work tirelessly to advance those initiatives in creative and engaging ways. Most exist on shoestring budgets, ploughing 90 per cent of their limited funding dollars back into running their programs rather than squandering them on additional staff that might lighten their workload. Ted would likely say that the corporate world is justly humbled by the non-profits' commitment to make life better, brighter, and more accessible to all of us. And *I'm* pretty sure that the boards of most publicly traded companies would love to find employees as wholeheartedly dedicated to increasing their share price as non-profit employees and their volunteers are to fulfilling their philanthropic missions. But I think both of us realized along the way, that as talented and committed as they are, almost all of them could profit by using the basic tools of business to help them run their day-to-day operations. Ted saw that rewriting the bylaws to comply with grant donors' requirements would open the door to new Alberta Performing Arts Stabilization Fund (APASF) funding, and he suggested that a good way for the CPO to stimulate earned revenue would be to simply have the Calgary Opera hire the orchestra as needed. To kick start it, he contributed the funds to the opera to do just that, confident that it would be a practice that would be sustainable.

We had both started as volunteers helping to organize galas and used book sales and talent shows to raise funding dollars. And eventually we both took our turns as directors on the boards of different arts organizations, so we were certainly aware of the strengths and talents of their leadership. However, as capable as they were, many had no business background at all. No human resources training, only basic bookkeeping at best, little understanding of governance principles and, as the technology became more and more sophisticated, most had very little familiarity with software programs that could lighten their load or the funds to invest in the hardware to run them.

When the time came that we could make a more substantial contribution to some of those organizations, Ted decided to build a foundation that could administer his endowment fund more efficiently. We hadn't given much serious thought as to how those funds might be distributed after the grandchildren had all been educated and we had completed the Rozsa Centres in Calgary and in Houghton, Michigan. Then coincidentally, Ted received the news that he was to be honoured in 2002 with the Edmund C. Bovey Award. We had no way of knowing it then, but this award was to pave the way for extending Ted's legacy to the community and our family's continuing support of the arts.

However, our most immediate plans were to go to Houghton for the opening ceremony of the Rozsa Center at Michigan Tech. Ted, even after his brain surgery, was still experiencing a lot of fatigue. He decided that, rather than play less-than-stellar golf, his career on the links was over. He still liked to go to the Country Club to join his golfing buddies for brunch on Saturday mornings so he could have his favourite Mulligatawny soup, and he'd invariably ask the waiter to "tell the chef to dig deep to get at all the goodies." Those weekend brunches kept him abreast of the oil patch news and very current with what was happening in the economy.

Ted was very much involved with building the second Rozsa Centre, but, in 2000, just as we were getting ready to go to Houghton to cut the ribbon for the opening, I was annoyed enough by what I assumed was a little sty on my eye that I made an appointment with my doctor to have it removed. When he came back to talk with me following the biopsy, I admit it was the only time in my life that I was genuinely frightened. I'm sure that anyone who hears the word malignant for the first time reacts in the same way. I froze. I could see that he was talking to me, but all I could think of was getting out of there. I don't think I heard another word he said. I simply didn't have time to deal with cancer.

I needed to go to Houghton with Ted because his hearing was failing so quickly and I didn't want him to miss a word of the celebration that was being planned in his honour. In hindsight, though, I think I did the right thing because that time away also gave me a chance to process the medical options in my own mind and to prepare myself to deal with the radiation treatments. It gave me time to realize that my fear of losing my sight was far, far greater than my fear of death. I had always been a voracious reader and, despite having progressive macular degeneration, I had thus far retained enough sight to read the newspaper every day along with large-print books.

So, on the way home from Houghton, I girded myself for the surgery and to be fitted for the mask that would pinpoint the targeted tumour site for the twenty follow-up radiation treatments. But in all honesty, the worst of the ordeal was only the fatigue caused by the radiation. The very happy outcome was that the doctor was able to remove the tumour in its entirety and that I'm still able, with the aid of a magnifying glass, to read my newspaper from cover to cover and keep up with my boys on the Calgary Flames. However, I must say that it didn't slow down the relentless pace of ageing, which, as they rightly say, ain't for sissies. But it does help to have a sense of humour.

One night, barely a year later, I got out of bed to go to the bathroom and fell. When I realized I couldn't get up, I was pretty sure I had broken my hip, so I called to Ted to help. However, since he was almost deaf I simply couldn't wake him, so I slithered over to the nearest corner of the bedroom where he had left his golf clubs. I pushed over the golf bag, grabbed the putter, and started banging on the wall to attract his attention. If I could have slithered any further toward the bed, maybe I'd have made a better club selection, but, let's face it, my options were somewhat constrained. If I hadn't been in quite so much pain, I'm sure I would have been laughing out loud because it was such a totally absurd scene.

And making matters even more ridiculous, as I lay there on the floor I worried about the fact that I was about to receive the YWCA's Woman of Distinction Award. I was overjoyed to have been selected and was so looking forward to the ceremony, but I wondered what they'd think if they could see me writhing about on the carpet flailing the putter at everything I could reach. Distinctly ludicrous maybe, but definitely not distinguished.

However once I got Ted's attention and we made it to the hospital, I was almost relieved when they agreed with my diagnosis. I had known lots of people who'd had hip replacements and they'd seemed to bounce back pretty quickly, so at that point my only concern was postponing a few dates in my calendar. It was only mid-April after all; the Women of Distinction event wasn't until mid-June. I'd be up-and-at-'em in plenty of time. However, when I surmised as much to the surgeon, he frowned and asked, "And how old are you now?" If I could have hrumphed, I would have. I was barely eighty. Okay, so I was eighty-one. But I had shaken off cancer, and frankly I didn't have a lot of time to waste on being immobile. I was busy; we were *all* busy!

Ruth Ann and her family lived a considerable distance out of town, and Karen had two-year-old Tristan to look after. Young Ted and his new family were still in Texas, and Mary Lil, who had been a very active member of two major civic committees, had just announced her candidacy for City Council in the municipal election of 2001. I was incredibly proud of her for stepping up and offering her service and would have given anything to see her elected. But, after Patrick decided to return to Mexico, Mary Lil was a single mother. She was raising Mary Cristina on her own and the challenge of scheduling her own calendar around her nine-year-old's was too much for her nannie, and occasionally they required the help of the whole family. Believe me, my hip surgery couldn't have come at a more inconvenient time.

And then it got worse.

What started out to be a pretty routine recovery ended up taking more than a month in the hospital, and while I was there Ted had to be admitted for a couple of days as well. I asked Mary Lil to withdraw from the election. We needed her help. To this day, I regret those circumstances. She would have been a very effective City Councillor, and I hope that one day she will consider public service again.

Thankfully, with the family's help, by the middle of June I had recovered enough to attend the Women of Distinction Awards. As early as 1979, the women of the YWCA had wanted to recognize women in Calgary for their professional achievements as well as for their dedication and contributions to the community. Each year thereafter, ten women were selected, and those who shared the podium with me in 2001 were from business, the professions, the sciences, the voluntary sector, education, health and wellness, and social services, all of them very accomplished in their work and so deserving of recognition. Over the years, the prestige of the award had grown and corporate Calgary had stepped up to help sponsor the annual event, so their sponsorships, combined with ticket sales to the ceremony, raised significant funds to support the Y's programs directed at family violence prevention.

It was an unexpected honour for me to be selected in the Arts and Culture category, and I was delighted to be able to attend, even though I was still wheelchair bound after my hip surgery. Following a reception at the Palliser, Ruth Ann and Ted and I went over to the Jack Singer Hall where 1,300 people had assembled to show their appreciation for those marvellous women. In her opening address, the chair of the Y's board said that for almost a hundred years, the YWCA had worked to build strength in the community through building strength in women. "Today," she said, "we can all see the capacity of the human spirit, the human ability to strive and make great gains.... We can see that one person can make a difference. The young women who are here today as guests are being introduced to ten extraordinary women – women who have made that difference." Ted wheeled me up to the podium to receive my award and, as thrilled as I was, I must say that Ted was even prouder. I treasure that beautiful moment to this day.

Then, in an embarrassment of riches, later that month I was also awarded an Honorary Doctor of Laws from the University of Calgary. I'm sure the university wanted us both to know how much the Rozsa Centre meant to the students who finally had a world-class music facility, but in all honesty we were grateful for the opportunity to reciprocate. Sixty years prior, when we started buying season tickets to the mostly amateur Calgary Symphony performances, the board realized how much their music meant to both of us, and they invited us to get involved in a more meaningful way. That opened doors neither of us could have expected. For me, it meant that the love of music nurtured by my parents, siblings, and church would continue to grow. For Ted, that open door led to a life-long passion for classical music. When we were ultimately able to contribute to the music faculty at the university, we were only passing along our appreciation for the gifts we had received. Our offering back to the community could never match the value of those rewards or the priceless gifts of friendship we have been offered across Calgary and the opportunities we have been afforded through their generosity.

The great circle of life was still spinning us in its axis, but when it was time for Ted to receive the Bovey Award, we were both finally up and around.

The Bovey Award is unique in Canada. It honours individuals from the business community for outstanding support of the arts by presenting them with a cheque for $20,000 to be distributed to the arts organizations of their choice. At the presentation ceremony, which was held at U of C's faculty club, Ted announced that he would match the award funds and challenge other businesses to contribute in order to create a new foundation that would support best business practices in performing arts companies. Instead of just making a donation to one arts company, our intention was to enable the Rozsa Foundation to recognize top arts managers in Alberta and provide their organizations with mentoring and financial support for their continuing administrative development. Very quickly, other businesses rose to his challenge and pledged matching funds. This idea, which was enthusiastically supported by the City of Calgary, the Calgary Centre for Non-Profit Management, the Alberta Performing Arts Stabilization Fund, and the Calgary Professional Arts Alliance, gained traction almost immediately. The presentation of the first annual Rozsa Award for Excellence in Arts Management was scheduled for May, 2003.

Ted decoupled the foundation from his company and source of funds, and asked Mary Lil to take over its management. Her first step was to conduct an environmental scan of current support of the arts in Calgary, and with that information we were able to focus on our mission and subsequently on our investment policy. Mary Lil determined that the work of many very successful arts managers was going unnoticed. But, on the other hand, the administrative weakness in others was giving the community a poor public perception of the arts. To make matters even more difficult, there had been severe budget cuts during the early '90s, which had resulted in the elimination of most middle management positions in arts organizations, and the demographics showed that senior managers were reaching retirement age with no apparent successors available to step into those roles. Those who remained typically had no specific arts management training since only one educational institution in the province offered anything related to arts management. Most were learning on the job from those ill-equipped to teach them the skills that were needed.

We had three broad strategic priorities. First, we wanted to help build administrative capacity in arts organizations by increasing management expertise, organizational stability, and stronger more diverse boards and by giving them access to up-to-date research and business models. Second, we hoped to offer funds that would encourage engaging and varied artistic experiences that educate the public and build loyal audiences. And finally, we wanted to positively influence public opinion and support for the arts.

So why offer an award for arts management? Why wouldn't we simply offer a business scholarship to someone entering the field of arts management? In all honesty, we believed it was important to hit the ground running. The timing, we felt, was critical. There needed to be a way to call attention to best practices as well as to offer financial and educational incentives to the organization that would encourage them to continue their business development. We needed another elevator speech: "The partners in the awards program believe that the arts are an integral and necessary component of a healthy community. All arts organizations must be effectively managed to achieve and maintain financial sustainability so they can serve their community well. When outstanding arts managers of today are recognized, the field becomes more attractive for future leaders, and a standard of excellence is established."

The award would be given after a competitive nomination process was completed, and we were excited by the immediate response of the arts community. That first year, we had to repeat the elevator speech quite a lot, but when our jury made their selection and decided that the first award would go to Bob McPhee, general director and CEO of the Calgary Opera, each piece of our planning fell into place.

Bob began his career as a performing artist, but over the last three decades he's been involved primarily in marketing, production, and senior management, working in the four disciplines of theatre, dance, orchestra, and opera. When he was president of the Edmonton Concert Hall Foundation, Bob raised $45 million toward the construction of the Winspear Centre for Music, and in 2003 he produced the incredibly successful world premiere of the John Estacio and John Murrell opera *Filumena*. To other arts organizations, we were able to say *this* is what successful management makes possible. In every way, Bob personified exactly what we hoped would become the model for aspiring arts managers from every discipline.

Three years after he was awarded the Rozsa Foundation's Award for Excellence, Bob produced Estacio and Murrell's succeeding opera, *Frobisher*. He continues to win awards for his leadership in the arts, he chaired the board of Opera.ca, and now he sits on the board of OPERA America.

Bob applied some of the prize toward enrolling Sherri Rau, his CFO at the Calgary Opera, in the University of Calgary's Haskayne School of Management's Essentials Program. After completing the program, her response was,: "For someone like me whose education has been focused totally on accounting, the Haskayne Management Essentials Program has been an excellent overview of management strategies in all areas. Some of the courses underscored things we're good at already, and some have highlighted where we can improve a little bit too."

We were thrilled by Bob's and Sherri's responses to this recognition and announced that the 2004 Rozsa Award competition was ready to receive nominations. The elevator speech was no longer required. The arts community got it and began clamouring for opportunities to nominate their CEOs. And those who recognized their own organizations weren't eligible for reasons of management inefficiencies took a good hard look at ways they could improve their performance.

As with any new initiative, we were going through our own growing pains and were having to impose a more formal administrative role to build the endowment fund as well as to oversee the competition. At the start, we had thought our family could manage both roles, and Ruth Ann and Ted and I served as directors from the beginning, but we very quickly learned we would need a full-time administrator as well as a small staff, plus additional people to serve on our board of directors. The family met and agreed that Mary Lil would be the foundation's first administrator, and we looked for board members inside the family as well as from the arts community. Naturally we wanted to keep the grandchildren closely involved; however, some are at that stage of life where they're so consumed by the demands of child-rearing and establishing their own careers that their contributions to the foundation's board will have to wait. Fortunately, though, we have recruited bright and creative board members from the community who are incredibly generous with their time and their ideas, and the foundation is thriving.

As the decade rolled along, however, it became clear that both Ted and I would have to retire from a hands-on role with the foundation. Mary Lil was doing a superb job as president of the foundation and Ruth Ann, along with her daughter, Karen Rice, represented the family on the board. However, Ted and I were having to learn to adapt to the realities of age. At the 2005 awards ceremony, the board presented us with a beautiful glass sculpture, which we gratefully accepted for our efforts, knowing that the foundation was well and truly launched.

His Order of Canada award was Ted's proudest moment.

At Mozart on the Mountain with thousands of CPO fans.

Breaking ground for the Rozsa Centre at the University of Calgary with Hy and Jenny Belzberg, Jim Palmer, Murray Fraser, Dean Roberts, and Ann McCaig.

Where Murray Fraser found this neon sign I can't imagine, but I'll treasure it forever!

Inside the "great barn" of the Rozsa Centre's performance hall.

The whole family came to celebrate Ted's and my honorary
doctorates from the University of Calgary.

MICHIGAN TECHNOLOGICAL UNIVERSITY'S ROZSA CENTER IN HOUGHTON, MICHIGAN. (PHOTO: MICHIGAN TECHNOLOGICAL UNIVERSITY PHOTO SERVICES.)

CHAPTER TWENTY-TWO

"Somethin' Might Be Gainin' on Ya."

Wheelchair bound or not, life carried on, but at this stage I'm afraid it's one step forward and more than a few back. At one point, when our great-granddaughter, Emma, was a toddler much attached to her favourite doll, Ted and I were both hobbling about in a health care facility. Her mother brought Emma for a visit and insisted that Ted and I needed a brisk walk down the corridor to the visitors' lounge. I couldn't understand why the other visitors in the hallway were giggling at us until I turned around in my wheelchair and saw that Ted was behind me dutifully limping along with his walker, followed by Emma pushing her doll's stroller. All we needed to make a parade was a marching band and a couple of Shriners in clown cars. Like I say, it ain't for sissies and you need a sense of humour.

But the fact was, Ted was getting increasingly unsteady on his feet. It was harder for him to get around on his own, so we hired a driver to get us back and forth around the city because my eyesight was pretty poor by that time too. Paul Budgen became like a member of the family, always on deck to take Ted to the golf course, or pick up Mary Cristina from school, or deliver me to church on Sunday mornings. I hope he knows how very much he has sustained our quality of life for so many years.

However, when I fell and injured my back in the winter of 2004, the kids insisted that Ted move into an assisted-living accommodation while I was in the hospital recovering. I was assured that the staff doted on him, but I was also pretty sure he was missing access to his office. He had just completed the sale of Rozsa Petroleum, and I knew he'd want to be attending to the final details. Then, about a month later when I was released, the doctors advised the kids that we should both stay in the residence because, until I was more mobile, I would need some help. It wasn't a happy time for either of us, I'm afraid. Despite the excellent care and the lovely accommodations, we both missed our home and within a couple of weeks I asked our caregiver whether she would consider moving with us back to our home on Lake Bonaventure. She readily agreed, and Ted and I both heaved a sigh of relief the moment we drove up to the front door.

Others, I'm sure, thought we were crazy for leaving what was truly a lovely spot. But I'm afraid we both had too many irons in the fire to retire. The Philharmonic had created a spot on the board for the Rozsa family and the children were taking their turns as director, but Ted and I were continuing to stay closely involved in other ways. And since the Rozsa Foundation was actively encouraging strategic alliances between arts organizations, we were eager to see how the Philharmonic might work with other initiatives like the Calgary Opera and the Honens Piano Competition.

Since its inception in 1991, Ted had contributed quietly to the Esther Honens Competition, and we were inspired by its almost immediate international esteem. We of course had been familiar with the Van Cliburn International Piano Competition in Fort Worth, Texas, but so much of its reputation rests on the considerable talent of its very charismatic founder. We were concerned for that very reason that it might not be sustainable, so we watched with considerable interest as the Esther Honens competition developed.

Although born in Pittsburgh, Esther was raised in Calgary and she became a very good amateur pianist with a huge passion for music. In due course, she married and went to work as the office manager for Birks Jewellers, where she stayed for twenty-five years. And happily, her husband, John Hillier, was a partner in a very successful plumbing and supply company, so she was able to invest much of her salary in real estate. After his death, she married Harold Honens, and together they assembled extensive real estate holdings and were able to help support both the Calgary Philharmonic and the Kiwanis Music Festival.

As she aged, though, Esther wanted to leave Calgary a legacy that would ensure its position at the centre of the world's musical stage. She wrote: "My vision is to identify the finest of today's pianists, to bring them to Calgary for a competition that will be held in the highest international esteem, and to create a legacy of musical excellence that can be enjoyed by Canadians for countless generations." In 1991, she pledged $5 million toward launching the competition. Her vision immediately resonated with the people who could help her make it happen and, in 1992, five days before she died, she attended the first Honens International Piano Competition.

The competition is held every three years and attracts the very best young pianists from around the world. By 2012, fifty quarter-finalists were announced. The competition finals launch the concert careers of its three top winners through an artistic and career development program that is unmatched worldwide.

Esther should be proud. She was able to support her passion at all levels of the arts in Calgary, from the children's Kiwanis Music Festival to the professionals of the CPO. The competition named for her has brought our city and its music to the attention of international culture as aspiring concert pianists now recognize that opportunity resides in Calgary. They're flocking here in hope of gaining the recognition that will jump-start their careers. But this priceless gift has been offered not only to the generations of pianists who will benefit, it's also a gift of love to Calgary. To my mind, this is the kind of legacy we should all aspire to leave.

So, by the time Ted and I moved back home, we were both very interested in the jury selection for the 2004 Rozsa Foundation

Award. The second year, we received even more nominations, and Bob McPhee joined the selection jury. We saw his role on the jury as critical to the selection process, and we decided to ask that past award winners be available to serve in this role and to attend the presentation ceremonies in subsequent years. Their participation as past recipients of the award has added an element to the process that has resulted in further refining the award criteria.

In 2004, Anne Green, the founding director of WordFest, was awarded the second annual Rozsa Foundation Award for Excellence. Born in 1996, WordFest had been the brainchild of the collaborative efforts of the Banff Centre, the Calgary Public Library, Mount Royal University, and the Writers Guild of Alberta, all of whom were determined to create a Banff-Calgary International Writers Festival. It started with an A-List of fifty Canadian writers, including Margaret Atwood, Roch Carrier, Wayson Choy, Tomson Highway, Paul Quarrington and Sheri-D Wilson, and it continues as the premier literary event of the year. By 2004, WordFest was attracting world-renowned writers and had incorporated the Summit Salon, an exclusive writers' retreat hosted by the Banff Centre, which is scheduled to immediately follow WordFest.

When Anne received the Rozsa Award, she was able to access both the Centre for Non-Profit Management and the Haskayne School of Business. She wrote, "I have been working with the Centre for Non-Profit Management on refining an organizational design. This is a process that is a luxury, and we are finding it to be valuable in and of itself. It has already been very beneficial for my staff.... The expertise of the Centre is a unique contribution in that it does not duplicate any expertise in that area within our Board or staff.... With regards to the Haskayne Case Study, a marketing study is a perfect use of this element of the Award in that it is both a practical project with immediate useful information and one that has not diverted too much energy away from the essential aspects of running the organization."

Anne continued to build WordFest's reputation across Canada and over the years it has grown to attract more than 14,000 people to a six-day annual festival that features upwards of seventy writers. And like other award recipients, Anne built strategic alliances between the festival and other community initiatives like First Calgary Financial's youth education program, Book Rapport. Don't you *love* that name?

After sixteen years at its helm, Anne retired from WordFest. It is a tribute to her excellent leadership that it continues to thrive and that it is still regarded as a world-class and ground-breaking festival of the literary arts.

The foundation was off to an excellent start under Mary Lil's capable direction, but I could see that Ted needed help to wind up his business affairs, so I was relieved when young Ted announced that he and his family had decided to move back to Calgary. He had worked with his father and I was hopeful that, with his help, Ted could finally put Rozsa Petroleum to bed. They came back early in 2005 and we were delighted to be able to get to know eleven-year-old Charles. Mary Cristina, his thirteen-year-old cousin, was also a frequent visitor, and she often brought her flute along to play for her grandfather. I think the fact that he had been so busy when the older children were living at the lake made Ted appreciate this second crop of grandchildren even more. He finally had the time to enjoy them.

Ted was about to have his ninetieth birthday, and the family planned a big party at the Country Club. We invited everyone Ted had known over the years: our extended families, all the guys on his geophysical crews, his business colleagues, his golfing buddies, including those who'd helped organize the Doodlebug tournaments, people he had volunteered with in the arts organizations and at the Glenbow, those from the universities who'd made the Rozsa Centres a reality, the students who had received his scholarships, and the many, many friends with whom we had travelled this long journey. It's times like these when you realize how very rich your life has been and how blessed you are by the friendships you have been offered. I think he was surprised by the flood of well-wishers because he knew he liked his solitude and he never saw himself as an extravert, so he tended to minimize his effect on the people he knew. He was annoyed that he was so unstable on his feet that he needed to be in a wheelchair for the occasion, but it certainly didn't get in the way of his enjoyment of the evening, and he managed to visit with everyone there. People knew that his hearing was failing, so they made a special effort to talk with him one-on-one, which made their visits even more meaningful to Ted. He said it was the best birthday he'd ever celebrated.

As we were all leaving, however, Terry and Anne Myles stopped to visit a moment with Ruth Ann, and Terry asked why her father was in the wheelchair. When she told them that Ted was stumbling quite frequently, Terry suggested bringing him in for a quick neurological checkup. We put that appointment on our to-do list, and promptly went back to all the excitement planned for the 2005 Rozsa Award.

More nominations than ever before came in over the transom that year, and the jury's task was getting more difficult because so many more organizations were being challenged to address their business practices. Finally, though, the jury's unanimous decision awarded the prize to Kathi Sundstrom, the general manager of Decidedly Jazz Danceworks. They agreed that her exceptional management skills had enabled DJD to become one of Canada's most innovative and successful dance companies. Kathi had proven herself as one of Alberta's most adept arts managers, taking DJD from a struggling founder-driven company ten years before, through a period of tremendous growth to become a mature and sustainable company.

Kathi had achieved operating surpluses and increased the company's operating budget by 237 per cent in ten years to $2.6 million. By implementing effective marketing strategies, DJD had doubled paid attendance at their annual performances. Their audience was loyal and growing and building incredible community connections through its dance school.

Following the award ceremony, Kathi wrote, "Decidedly Jazz used the Rozsa Award funds toward our Customer Relations Management program. We were successful in refining our strategic marketing plan, making considerable and valuable investment in developing and building the capacity and core competency of our Marketing/Development staff, and gained immense insight through the research we conducted. On the consulting side, the expert legal opinion rendered has enabled us to deal with the changes to the Revenue Canada Act which directly affected our HR practices. I thank you personally and on behalf of Decidedly Jazz for what the Award has helped us to achieve."

Since the award, DJD has toured extensively from coast to coast and continues to create ground-breaking work in Calgary, which is still its home base. And like other award winners, DJD has also collaborated with other community arts organizations. In 2009, *Skyscraper* premiered as part of One Yellow Rabbit's High Performance Rodeo. It was a new site-specific work that took audiences on an interactive exploration through Calgary's historic Grain Exchange building.

In only three years, the Rozsa Award had reached three widely varied arts organizations: The Calgary Opera, WordFest, and Decidedly Jazz Danceworks. They challenged Ted and me to step out of our usual comfort zone where we had spent so many volunteer hours, and we were learning how the issues regarding funding affected all of those winning organizations – plus those that weren't so well managed – in very similar ways. There was no question that these three award recipients were exceptionally talented business managers and that they had built healthy and loyal audiences. But they had also put away funds for the inevitable rainy days when the economy would hit a downturn. There were too many enormously talented and creative people who failed simply because they couldn't ride out the lean years. But to our frustration, too many of them rejected the challenge to incorporate good business planning because they believed it was diametrically opposed to the artistic mind. "Artists shouldn't have to plan for profitability and positive cash flow," they said. "They should do their art."

I suppose that, in a sense, artists are entrepreneurs much like Ted was. They have faith in their creativity and the courage to act on it, confident that what they dream can come to fruition. Artists are willing to risk everything to ask the difficult questions, to make us think in new ways, to make us see what has never been visible before, to make us imagine what might be possible. "But in return," they say, "the public should be willing to invest in our creativity because it's creativity that advances the culture. Think of public investment in the arts as what research and development funding is to the sciences. Neither is expendable," they say, "because without taking creative leaps of faith – through art or through science – society can't progress."

My only response is to agree but to suggest that no scientific researcher ever gets public *or* private funding without a solid business plan in place. Perhaps what artists have to consider is a creative team that involves both disciplines. Kathi Sundstrom, the business manager of Decidedly Jazz, very carefully built that team ensuring that the dancers who brought such creativity to their performances also invested their talent in the DJD Dance School. It was the student fees that increased their revenues and provided them a healthy surplus. It was their student dancers who then brought their friends and families that grew their loyal audience. And that surplus allowed them to take the risks that advanced their art.

The conversation with all of the nominees was so interesting and we were challenged by all of them to think differently about many things. I think Ted would agree that the foundation had given us an amazing opportunity to look at all the arts in new and creative ways and that at this stage of our lives it was a truly mind-expanding experience. But more than anything else, for me anyway, I loved hearing their stories. How had they discovered that passion to create? How did their families help to nurture their talent? Who were the teachers who recognized those talents and opened doors for them?

We were thoroughly enjoying ourselves and, aside from Ted's shaky footing, we felt pretty lucky.

That spring, little Evan announced that we had a new great-grandson. He had a new baby brother named Satchel. Ted and I both laughed, and delightedly agreed that his namesake, the baseball player, should be even more famous for his wisdom than he was for his fastball. At this stage of life, we certainly understood what Satchel Paige meant when he said, *"Never look back; somethin' might be gainin' on ya!"*

A few months later, we made an appointment with Terry Myles, as promised, and as he was examining Ted, it became pretty clear that he was concerned, not only about his falls, but also about a dropped foot and his slurred speech. He called in Dr. Zechondy to consult with him, and they arranged for Ted to have some further tests.

I remember thinking how fortunate we were to know Terry. He had been so kind to both of us through Ted's earlier surgery and seemed to have limitless time to explain what was happening, and indeed he was being equally thorough with us this time. So when he called a few weeks later, I wasn't at all alarmed that he asked us to come back in. However, when he sat us down to explain his diagnosis, I was dumbfounded. I had missed seeing the obvious.

Ted had Amyotrophic Lateral Sclerosis.

CHAPTER TWENTY-THREE

Hail and Farewell

On the fourth of July, 1939, Lou Gehrig announced his retirement from baseball. I remember because Ted and I had only met a few weeks before, and it was a holiday so we were both at Ann and Ed's house in Olney, Texas. The sports reporters had been covering the story for weeks and everyone knew this powerful Yankee hitter was in a serious slump. He'd played more than two thousand consecutive games – hitting four home runs in one of them. However he was going through a rough patch; it seemed like he'd lost all his strength. He was still hitting the ball every time; it just wasn't going anywhere, but when he benched himself it was a terrible shock. We heard the hail and farewell speeches on the radio that fourth of July afternoon. The Yankees' manager described Lou Gehrig as "the finest example of a ballplayer, sportsman and citizen that baseball has ever known." And then the team retired his uniform number.

Sitting there in Terry Myles' office at the Foothills Hospital that sunny September afternoon in 2005, I remember thinking, that was sixty-six years ago. Ted and I have been married sixty-six years. Amyotrophic Lateral Sclerosis. I couldn't even pronounce the words, but I knew immediately what they meant. Lou Gehrig's Disease.

It wasn't my finest moment. I had gotten used to Ted getting old. We were *both* getting *old*, for heaven's sake, so stumbling and falling and dropping things was just what we did. Thankfully both of us seemed to have kept most of our marbles, and if we could keep our sense of humour too, then it wasn't so bad. I was sure Terry had made a mistake. But there were all these other people in the room with us. Terry introduced them as our coordinated, multi-specialist team, and he started talking about known patterns and treatment protocols, but their names and titles escaped me and I found myself looking for the exit. This was not what I was prepared to hear.

But Ted seemed to be relieved now that it had a name. He finally knew what was going on and he could prepare himself. I suppose it was the scientist in him but, as soon as he knew there were people on hand who could supply him with the information he needed, he visibly relaxed. Terry told us that the ALS Society would be of enormous practical help. They would have equipment we could use that would make Ted more comfortable as time passed, and we went home armed with resource pamphlets and phone numbers and assurances that we could call any of them at any time.

I still hadn't accepted Terry's diagnosis, but by the time I walked into the house I knew I'd have to stop the revolving door of caregivers we'd had since we checked out of the assisted-living residence. Neither of us really had the patience to deal with any of them, and I guess I'd fooled myself into thinking we could get back to managing on our own, but right then I didn't have the strength to figure out what had to be done. Those first few weeks I seemed to be on an endless rollercoaster, circling between the highs of outright denial and raging at the injustice of it all, and then plunging into depths of fear and grief.

Ted, on the other hand, went into research mode. He read that ALS is a form of motor neuron disease caused by the degeneration of upper and lower neurons located in the spinal cord and brain. It's characterized by rapidly progressive weakness, muscle atrophy, and respiratory compromise. Motor neurons, among the largest of all nerve cells, reach from the brain to the spinal cord and from the spinal cord to the muscles throughout the body with connections to the brain. When they die, the ability of the brain to start and control muscle movement dies with them. With all voluntary muscle action affected, patients in the later stages are totally paralyzed. But the disease doesn't affect the five senses of taste, touch, sight, hearing, and smell. Nor does it affect cognitive function. Over time, he would simply be imprisoned by his own body. There is no cure.

What *I* read came from Eleanor, Lou Gehrig's wife: "The cause of this cruel disease is unknown. The motor function of the central nervous system is destroyed but the mind remains fully aware to the end." What all of that meant, we would be forced to learn together. Ted never once complained. Ever.

It took me fully a month to get to a place where I could think straight, and thankfully it was Jane Rivest who both literally and figuratively took me by the hand to show me the way. Terry had said that Jane would be calling us to set up an appointment to meet the family and to help us discover how our treatment goals could be met with the assistance of the ALS Society. Jane's dearest friend, Betty Norman, had been diagnosed when she was only fifty-eight and, despite the fact that she had no experience as a caregiver, she looked after Betty for the duration of her eleven-month struggle. Since then, Jane has been a tireless advocate for those living with this terrible disease *and* their families. Quite simply, her primary goal is to make a positive difference – to make each day the best possible for all of us.

On the day we all assembled in our living room to meet Jane, I was still adamantly resisting Terry's diagnosis. But very slowly and thoroughly she answered all the kids' questions, and then laid out what services and equipment the ALS Society could provide, making it very clear that help was a phone call away. She immediately picked up on the fact that Ted had the marvellous ability to retreat into his head and that as long as his brain allowed him to keep imagining new ideas, he could stay fully engaged in his life. "Right now," she told Ted, "you might want us to arrange to have a chair lift installed so you can continue to work in your office downstairs. And if the time comes when you need a computer that is voice-activated, we can supply that as well."

The months that followed seemed to race by as Ted's physical limitations became more and more apparent. By that time, I was relieved that the round-the-clock care nurses from the Focus on Caring Agency were on site, and I grew to both appreciate and admire how capable they were as they took care of Ted. They became a critical part of our family. I realized that, had we not had their help, Ted would have had to move into the hospital. And as far as I was concerned, that was never going to happen.

But the disease was relentless. Ted was having muscle spasms and could no longer negotiate around the house with his walker. He had to move into a wheelchair. We arranged to have two hospital beds moved into our bedroom so he could be in a sitting position during the night to make his breathing a little easier, and then he required oxygen twenty-four hours a day. However, because I have COPD, I'm also tethered to an oxygen tank. Fortunately, though, we could still laugh every day as we tried to untangle ourselves from our respective air hoses while we wandered about in our respective wheelchairs. We were like a couple of double-dutch skippers snarled in our ropes.

Then, as the muscles around Ted's face and throat weakened and his tongue lost its strength, chewing and swallowing became more difficult. It took more time and energy to finish eating his meals and he started losing weight quite quickly. We were advised that it's important to correct this problem in its early stages, so we turned three hearty meals a day into six little appetizer-size mini-meals. Then we put the blender into overdrive and whipped up thick creamy vegetable soups and fruit smoothies of all kinds. But oddly, it was even harder for him to swallow thin liquids like water, so we had to add a thickening agent to it to make sure he could stay sufficiently hydrated.

As Ted moved through his illness, I realized he was teaching us what he valued most. He was still dreaming up new drilling techniques, and he took to reading articles in endless copies of the *National Geographic*, which he liked to tell us about, whether we expressed any interest or not. His speech was slurred, but he had infinite patience with us and we figured out what he was trying to say most of the time. And then I happened to read something in the ALS manual that Jane had given us: "Hope, faith, love, and a strong will to live offer no promises of immortality, only proof of our uniqueness as human beings, and the chance to experience full growth, even under the grimmest of circumstances. The clock provides only a technical measure of how long we live. Far more real than the ticking of time is the way we open up the minutes and invest them with meaning." Ted may not have written those words, but he had lived them every day of his life and he continued to live them to the end.

Through the Christmas season, we had lots of visitors. Karen and her little ones, and Mary Lil's Cristina, I think, were his favourites. Mary Cristina would bring her flute and play for him while he tapped out her timing. I think it meant a lot to him because he could enjoy her and the music and he didn't have to try to talk. But young Ted wasn't coming by, and I couldn't understand why he was staying away. I tried to contact him, but with no success, and, each time I tried, I alternated between worry and downright anger. But when I finally found out what he was having to deal with, I realized how we each have lessons to learn as we pass through our lives. As someone far more insightful than I has said, "If you learn from your suffering, and really come to understand the lesson you were taught, you might be able to help someone else who's now in the phase you may have just completed." Maybe that's what it's all about after all. At the time though, I was too filled with my own grief and so overcome by my own helplessness in the face of Ted's illness that I didn't realize I hadn't had the opportunity to follow Nannie's first rule of compassion: "When you are faced with something you can't understand in someone you love, you have to take the time to really listen. Put yourself in his skin and see it through his eyes." Although I wouldn't understand what had happened and why until much later, young Ted finally let me know that he hoped that the decision he'd had to make at that dreadful time in both our lives honoured the values his father and I had modelled for him.

Maybe that's what it's all about after all.

2006 arrived without much celebration that New Year's Eve because I had stumbled into a door and broken my right shoulder, and Mary Lil had fallen on the ski hill and did the same to her left shoulder a week or so later. Although I wasn't convinced I was *totally* decrepit, I realized that if my children were falling apart too, it was a bad sign. So, when she called to suggest we see the new year in together, I thought I'd better pull myself together just to prove I still could.

She brought along a bottle of chilled champagne so we could raise our glasses in a toast following dinner, and set it – along with a couple of champagne flutes – on the table in front of us. As the big moment arrived, both of us leaned forward to pour the champagne and realized that since she was sitting to my right, next to my broken shoulder, neither of us could reach the bottle. We were a pitiful pair. Even when we changed places, neither of us could get the cork out anyway. If you could have heard us giggling, you would have thought it was time to close the bar.

We were both so exhausted and emotionally drained by that time, I think Ted was relieved to hear us laughing for a change. He was entering the final stage of his illness and had weakened considerably so that talking was getting more and more difficult for him. Much of the time we spent just holding hands while I told him about conversations with people who had called to ask about him.

We also tried to keep him informed by telling him about all the nominees for the Rozsa Foundation Excellence Award, and I think he was rooting for Stephen Schroeder. As executive director, Stephen had been involved with One Yellow Rabbit Performance Theatre for fourteen years and, under his tenure, the budget grew to $1.5 million, the donor base expanded, and audience numbers increased substantially. It was a remarkable accomplishment, given the prolific activity of the company and the experimental nature of their work.

In February, Mary took me out for a birthday gathering and Ruth Ann stayed with Ted to watch the opening ceremonies of the Winter Olympic Games in Turin, Italy. She reported that he was dozing on and off, but at one point woke up suddenly asking, "Where is Mother?" Ruth Ann, thinking he was asking about me, explained that I was out for the evening with Mary. But Ted was confused and mumbled, "Well tell her to open the damn door!" He seemed to be talking with someone in his dream. Several years later, I would remember that experience when I had one of my own.

At this point we were all feeding him baby food whenever we could talk him into taking just a bite, but he never lost his dignity and he never uttered a word of complaint. By the end of February, Ted was no longer trying to talk, and Jane let us know his struggle wouldn't last much longer, so Ruth Ann, Karen, Mary Lil, and Cristina moved into the house to help care for him. The last night he was lucid, he seemed to be very agitated, and Jane came and arranged for a doctor to give him a shot of morphine, which calmed him down enough for us to have one last conversation. He talked about drilling, and then he looked at me for a long moment and said, "Well Hon, I love you. It's time for you to take my place." He closed his eyes and lost consciousness.

Two days later, I was sitting beside Ted on the bed holding his hand when he slipped away. Jane and the girls had all stayed with us throughout the long hours of our last vigil, and I know that if their love could have saved him he would be with us today. Bob Pynn arrived about ten minutes later saying that he had an overpowering feeling that he should be with us that morning, so he came right over.

Ted and Bob had both championed the CPO over the years and as archdeacon and dean of the Anglican Cathedral, Bob was a founding member of the Faithful City Team, a small group of dedicated people who view spirituality as critical to the social good. I thought to myself how strange are the works of God – to bring my dear husband, a mostly un-churched agnostic, to a mutually respectful friendship with a deeply spiritual man of faith. I was so grateful for that friendship, particularly on that morning as I said goodbye to the man I had loved for sixty-six years.

Ted's funeral service was held at Grace Presbyterian Church. Bob Pynn led the service and members of the CPO played one last concert for him. In my heart of hearts, I know he was listening and that he was thankful for being able to help the orchestra grow to become one of the finest in Canada. He was a good and kind man. He left the world a better place.

Sixty-six years before, after Babe Ruth gave his remarks on the occasion of Lou Gehrig's retirement at Yankee Stadium, Gehrig stood as 62,000 fans thundered their hail and farewell. Ted and I heard him say, "Today I consider myself the luckiest man on the face of the earth. I have been in ballparks for seventeen years and have never received anything but kindness and encouragement from you fans. Look at these grand men. Which of you wouldn't consider it the highlight of his career just to associate with them for even one day? When you have a father and mother who worked all their lives so that you can have an education and build your body – it's a blessing. When you have a wife who has been a tower of strength and shown more courage than you dreamed existed – that's the finest I know."

Had he had the opportunity, Ted's thanks would have echoed those sentiments almost word for word. He also considered himself the luckiest man on the face of the earth.

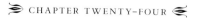

CHAPTER TWENTY-FOUR

Keepin' On

I came home from Ted's funeral to an empty house.

Oh, I suppose there may have been other people there, but, for me, the house was empty and I was alone. The chatter going on around me couldn't penetrate the fog of grief that lay over me, and the thought of spending the rest of my life without Ted was physically painful. For a very long time, I felt like my life had ended too; I couldn't imagine how I could continue to live without the half of my heart that had ceased to beat. We had lived together for sixty-six very full and very happy years, and there aren't many in this world to whom that gift has been given. I was eighty-six years old – old enough to have comforted too many widows as they grieved their own losses – so I knew how lucky I was to have had Ted by my side for so many years. Yet, even knowing that to be true, rational thinking was powerless against my grief, and many, many weeks went by before I could put my feet on the floor.

One morning, after Sally, my caregiver, had wheeled me into the kitchen insisting that I eat something, I noticed she had left the door to the pantry ajar. I turned back to the table to see that she had poured cereal into a bowl for me, and suddenly I was flooded with memories of all the children and all the visiting relatives gathered in the kitchen, lined up so that Ted could record their heights on the pantry door. I could hear them all laughing as Ted grabbed a cereal box to balance on the tops of their heads in order to draw a straight

271

line "to record accurate data." I turned back toward the pantry door and there were dozens of perfect horizontal pencil lines measuring the growth of each of the grandchildren, the great-grandchildren, the in-laws, the Estes kin, and more than a few totally innocent bystanders who had been caught up in the whole process.

It was so Ted. It never mattered why we were all gathered or what we may have been celebrating, Ted liked to collect the data. I started smiling, and of course I shed more tears, but, for the first time in a very long time, they were tears of happy memories.

We were such an odd couple. Ted liked to be up and at 'em before dawn; I was a night owl and could barely form words before noon. He was so intelligent and so creative, but, living inside his head the way he did made him feel a little awkward with people, so he counted on me to steer him through the social occasions, and together we made a pretty good team. We really never even argued with one another. The kids say, "No, but the two of you had some pretty spirited debates even though Dad would usually admit defeat before you did." I suspect he just decided, whatever the issue might have been, it wasn't worth the time he expended defending it.

By Easter, I was at least sitting up and taking nourishment, and the kids insisted we all go to the Country Club, as usual, for the children's celebration. There would be a bunny and an Easter egg hunt and candy-filled baskets and entertainment for the little ones. How could I refuse? Karen and her family had just returned from their trip to Disneyland, and Tristan and Emma wanted to present me with my very own Minnie Mouse ears and tell me all about their adventures. Fuelled by all that Easter candy, they were having a wonderful time, and Tristan was totally captivated by the clown making balloon animals. He could make anything on demand, no two of his creations were alike, and finally Tristan begged him for some of his stock so he could try to make his own.

Try as he might though, Tristan simply could not blow up any of his balloons ... nor could his parents ... or his grandparents, for that matter. When I couldn't bear to look at that disappointed little face any longer, I said, "Here Tristan, give it to me. I'll blow it up for you." Now, as you can undoubtedly appreciate, I'm a veteran of countless birthday parties and have blown up a great many more balloons than I care to remember. I was absolutely confident that even while attached to my oxygen tank I could blow up a child's balloon, for heaven's sake.

I stretched it horizontally and vertically once or twice, held it to my lips, gave a mighty blow and blew the balloon – and my teeth – clear to the opposite end of the table. Both Emma and Tristan shrieked in terror and ran to hide their heads in Karen's lap while all *my* children collapsed in hysterics. I adjusted my Minnie Mouse ears, signalled the waiter to retrieve the errant dentures, and glared at my children in that universal mother glare that says they'd better settle down and behave – or else! They didn't; it just made the whole fiasco even funnier. I think it was the first time any of us had had a good laugh in a very long time.

So, party tricks aside, life around me went on as usual. As Ted had hoped, Stephen Schroeder from One Yellow Rabbit Theatre received the foundation's Award for Excellence that spring. He wrote, "One Yellow Rabbit found good value in the Haskayne Business School marketing audit. The students who participated were organized, well informed in advance, and did a lot during the process to enhance their understanding of our company (including attending a couple of performances). They also showed good insight, and asked excellent questions. Although some of them were not as knowledgeable about the not-for-profit sector at the beginning of the project, they quickly adapted their thinking appropriately. Interestingly, the students' conclusions tended to support the direction of OYR's own internal strategic planning which is currently underway. It is very useful to have an objective analysis conducted by a third party in conjunction with internally-driven strategic planning."

A year later, Stephen was honoured by the Lieutenant Governor of Alberta's Distinguished Artist Award, and additionally recognized as one of Calgary's Top 40 Under 40 in *Calgary Magazine*'s prestigious survey of the talented young entrepreneurs who work to promote the city and make it more competitive and vibrant. In their article about him, they noted that Stephen continues to mentor managers of smaller arts organizations and still finds time to produce some shows and choreograph short dance works. Clearly, he has been able to successfully marry the disciplines of business and art to his company's enormous benefit.

However, I think the board was coming to the realization that, without the creative drive toward innovation, the arts organizations would be risking the very thing that artists know is crucial to growth. It's a delicate balancing act to ensure that both exemplary management and creative innovation grow side by side, so the board agreed they needed a way to indicate that fact to developing organizations. Those that may not be mature enough to be considered for the Award for Excellence in Management should be encouraged to submit their nominations for an Innovation Award. The conversations about how best to develop criteria for such an award continued for several months until it was finally decided that it would be presented for extraordinary innovation in *one* area of arts management: financial, human resources, governance and business systems, partnership development, or community engagement, along with sound business practices in all areas of company endeavour.

I'm afraid I was peripheral to many of those discussions that spring simply because I was so mired in my own misery that I could barely follow the conversations. The kids were wonderful and visited often, and Ted came by frequently to watch the golf tournaments on TV with me. But Ruth Ann and Mary Lil became alarmed enough about my lingering despair that they decided I'd have to be physically wrenched out of it. They said I needed the healing balm of tropical breezes. They were right, of course. Some of our happiest times were in Maui with our family and friends, so they were pretty sure if they could get me back to Hawaii, I'd start realizing there was still much to enjoy and more to look forward to. In retrospect, though, I think both my daughters would agree that it would have been easier to launch a payload to the moon.

I should preface this story by saying that there were sufficient physical limitations to make any airline very, very nervous about taking me anywhere, and both Mary Lil and Ruth Ann knew that, too. I was riddled with osteoporosis, and every time I tripped over my feet or stumbled against a wall, I broke something or other. So I was confined to a wheelchair, plus I was tethered to an oxygen tank. And, lest we forget, Hawaii is eight hours away. But, like their parents, I'm afraid, my daughters refuse to acknowledge that *any*thing might present an impossible barrier. These may have been annoying little speed bumps on the way to our destination but, as they said to every harried airline official unfortunate enough to answer their phone calls, "Not to worry, we can take care of that."

My guess is that the two of them eventually worked their way up the corporate ladder to the airline's CEO who finally gave up when they said they had found a way to pack along enough oxygen in a tank that was guaranteed to pass the very rigorous standards demanded by the airline safety regulations. (Not that I'm suggesting that NASA is missing anything, but perhaps an audit of their inventory might be in order.) The night before our departure, they both came to pack everything I could conceivably need. I was glad that Mary Cristina was coming along for many reasons, not the least of which was that I could see we were going to need an extra Sherpa to transport all the equipment. But I was trying very hard *not* to say what I was thinking.

When we arrived at the airport the next day, the girls unloaded everything, transferred me to an airline-sized wheelchair, folded up my chair and added it to the mountain of luggage, and we all offered up a fervent prayer that somehow it would all be there when we arrived on the Big Island. By the time we finally made our way to the departures lounge, the three of them were sweating, and I had started giggling at the absurdity of the whole exercise.

When the flight was called, I needed to sit near the front of the plane because I couldn't walk down the length of it to get to the bathrooms. But even a short stroll on a bumpy flight was a challenge, and it took the three of them to hold me upright and steer me down the aisle. We had to clear U.S. customs in Vancouver, made a crazy transfer to ground oxygen, and, eventually, even though the flight attendants kept eyeing my enormous oxygen tank with quite a lot of apprehension, eight hours passed without any real disaster and the pilot announced we'd be landing in Kona within a few minutes. By this time, I was having great fun and could hardly wait to see what would happen next. As we started our descent, the plane banked far enough to the left that I could see out the window to the landing strip, and that's when I realized we had forgotten one teensy problem.

The little Kona Airport had no gangways; the only way off the plane was down a steep and very narrow flight of steel steps. The attendants suggested we wait to deplane until everyone else was off the flight. I thought that was a very good idea because I knew it was going to take at least that long for somebody to figure out how in the world they could get me, the wheelchair, and the monster oxygen tank down those stairs – together. As soon as they opened the door, however, the soft evening breeze wafted in carrying the scent of the tropical flowers and the sounds of the birds cooing in the nearby palms. Mary Lil and Ruth Ann were right. All I needed was the healing balm of that breeze. I could feel it go to work the minute it hit my lungs.

Hmm, I thought, I've forgotten how quickly the sun sets in Hawaii. Our fellow passengers were scurrying to the terminal to claim their baggage. No doubt they were in a hurry to get where they were going because, as I remembered it, the only road around the island was cut through miles of black lava and, at night, visibility was really an issue. Thank goodness the girls had the foresight to reserve a car, I was thinking. If we hurry we can get to the Mauna Lani before it gets too dark.

We watched as the last of the passengers disappeared and then the pilots deplaned, and, just before she slipped out the door, the final flight attendant said that if we could wait until the cleaning crew finished tidying and restocking, they would take us down on the hydraulic lift at the back of the plane that was used to empty the garbage. With a cheery wave she was gone.

Okay then. That sounded like a plan.

We continued to watch the terminal as slowly the lights blinked off one by one, and the gate closed. I desperately wanted to ask whether anyone thought our luggage might still be accessible, but I knew if I opened my mouth I'd start laughing and I'd never be able to stop. Pretty soon, sure enough, the garbage truck pulled up beside the plane and, as promised, the crew gathered the debris and prepared the plane for its next departure. When they were finished, they helped the girls wrestle me into the wheelchair and down the aisle and out the rear door to the hydraulic lift. They pushed a button and the garbage and I slowly descended to the truck waiting below. At least it descended to the *top* of the garbage truck which was – oh I'd guess – maybe ten feet off the ground? The plan evidently was to dump me and the garbage from that height because that was as close to the tarmac as the hydraulic life could go.

It was a head-scratcher.

By this time, the girls and I were *all* hysterical. None of us had the least bit of composure. We were laughing so hard we could bare-ly catch our breath and Mary Cristina collapsed, tears streaming. Finally, Mary Lil choked out, "Now what?" We were getting dan-gerously demented and the poor service crew was desperate to get rid of us. Somehow they were going to have to figure out how to pluck me off that lift.

Necessity, with a generous dollop of desperation, was the moth-er of invention on that very late night because, within a few minutes, a fork lift appeared from somewhere out of the dark. It came at me with its fork waving menacingly close to any number of vital organs, but eventually it settled itself and very neatly picked me and the chair off the hydraulic lift and deposited us both on the ground.

A quick but heartfelt thank you had to suffice because we knew we had to hurry to get to the rental car office to claim our transportation. But, of course, that office had closed too. The minute the last passenger left the terminal, despite the fact our mountain of luggage was still strewn on the carousel, everyone in the place headed home.

Mary Lil took off across the lava toward the highway to flag down a passing car and, as luck would have it, the first one to stop for her was a taxi driven by a singing cowboy, a paniolo from the Parker Ranch up the mountain in Waimea. By the time they got back to pick up the rest of us, they were both in full voice and our Tex Ritter let us know that Loretta Lynn was a resident of the Big Island and he assured us she'd love for us drop by to say howdy. He loaded us and our gear into his cab and, singing all the country and western songs that fifty-six years at the Calgary Stampede had ever taught us, we barrelled on down the highway to the Mauna Lani.

It was the most fun I ever had with my boots on! And from that moment, I knew I could keep on keepin' on.

Our trip back to Calgary was comparatively uneventful, unless of course you're counting the transfer through the Los Angeles airport at five a.m. By that time I was laid out on a stretcher – accompanied by Ruth Ann, Mary Lil, and Cristina plus a retinue of paramedics – not to mention the same mountain of luggage. I figured I'd better make the most of the opportunity, so I donned my sunglasses, wrapped my hair in a very chic silk scarf, gave a royal wave to all the curious onlookers, and nodded encouragingly to the lady I heard telling her friend, "That must be Elizabeth Taylor."

We got back to Calgary in time to announce that the Rozsa Foundation Award for Innovation in One Area of Arts Management would be open for nominations in the coming year and we eagerly looked forward to awarding two prizes in 2007. By this time, the Excellence Award's value had grown substantially, and it included both cash and educational benefits.

We had decided to open the field of nominees to arts organizations throughout the province and, much to my delight, Tony Luppino from the Art Gallery of Alberta in Edmonton received the award that year. Like other entrepreneurial winners, Tony was a master at engaging the art-going public by offering classes for school children as well as adults. He challenged people to think beyond their comfort zones to consider expressing their own creativity in novel ways, and naturally this process reinforced the public's interest in repeated visits.

He later wrote to thank the Foundation and said: "The Rozsa Award for Excellence in Arts Management has had an immediate and lasting positive effect on the Art Gallery of Alberta and on my own approach to leadership within that organization. Donna Finley of Framework was able to join the Board retreat and bring not only a business strategy building expertise but the so-important 'outsider' perspective to the review. Her questions and insights from other non-profit Arts organizations undergoing high risk transformations were valuable. The most successful element in the Award benefits package was without a doubt the marketing audit by the Haskayne School MBA class."

That same year we awarded the Rozsa Innovation Award for the first time. It went to Xstine Cook, the founding director of the Calgary Animated Objects Society. I was so interested in reading about Xstine. Her organization's mandate is to engage emerging and established artists, creating a community of artists learning from one another and experimenting with their ideas. She wrote: "Spawned in the shadow, or shall we say stench, of a chicken factory in 2003, the Calgary Animated Objects Society, a.k.a. CAOS, burst onto the Art scene with a mandate to develop and promote the Arts of puppetry, mask, and animated objects. Bringing the world's best manipulators to Calgary is our primary obsession. The International Festival of Animated Objects (IFAO) is a biennial celebration of the Arts of mask, puppetry and all things animated."

With each Rozsa Award, I felt that I was learning more about the arts community in Calgary, and now throughout the province, than I ever had imagined existed. Ted and I had been so involved with the music community that we hadn't really had the luxury of expanding our horizons, but these annual celebrations introduced me to some of the most fascinating young artists I had ever met, and my learning curve was steep indeed. Fortunately, they were all kind enough to humour what I'm sure were my pretty elementary questions about their work, and they were very generous with their time with me. Each age has its rewards and, for me, this was absolutely the best part of my tenth decade.

Unfortunately, however, every age also has its downside and on my way through the last half of that decade, I discovered the road downhill is pretty rocky. The spirit is willing but the flesh is hopeless, I'm afraid. It seemed every time I turned around my blood pressure would rocket up or bottom out for no particular reason, or I'd break something or other, and Amy and Sally, the wonderful caregivers who looked after me, were hyper-alert to any change at all. That meant I spent far too much time in ambulances and emergency rooms – so much so that I was on a first-name basis with the EMS folks as well as the nurses in the Rockyview Hospital's Emergency Room. It got to the point that we'd instantly recognize one another and I'd insist on catching up on the continuing sagas of their lives, which were, after all, much more interesting than *my* litany of aches and pains.

I decided that if I was to cope with this ageing process, I would have to force mind over matter. If it didn't hurt too much, going forward I'd ignore whatever I broke next. However, practically before I made the announcement to anyone mildly interested in hearing it, sure enough, I fell again. This time I landed on my side and could tell I was developing a bruise, but I made up my mind there was no way I was going anywhere. I could heal at home just as easily as at the hospital. And that's that!

Well, a day or two went by and every time I took a deep breath it felt like a rhinoceros was sitting on my chest and, since I had trouble getting enough oxygen anyway, I realized maybe this wasn't going to be one of those times I could heal at home. Very grudgingly – but in agony by this time – I allowed the girls to take me to the Rockyview Hospital. Apparently I had broken a couple of ribs in my fall, and the nurses in Emergency loaded me up on morphine to ease the pain before they transported me to a room. And then they topped up the morphine with more morphine.

What happened later I honestly don't remember, but apparently the girls felt that I was sedated enough to get a night's rest so they left to go home. Mary Lil said she went to her house to get fifteen-year-old Mary Cristina settled for the night, but before she went to bed, decided she'd better go back up to the hospital to check on me. When she got to my room, she could see that my breathing was laboured and that my eyes had glazed over, and she was frightened enough to call the nurse, who came in and listened to my heart and lungs. She told Mary Lil to get the family back as quickly as possible.

Ruth Ann and Karen came immediately, and Mary Lil asked Ted to pick up Mary Cristina and come to the hospital, saying that I was sinking fast. When they arrived, I was apparently flailing about and calling out Ted's name as well as the names of all my family, and then I guess I fell back on the bed and stopped breathing altogether. Mary Lil said she assumed that I had died because for several minutes I didn't draw a breath. They were sitting next to me on the bed and, a few minutes later, I took a shallow breath and opened my eyes for just a moment. The nurse told them my pulse had returned and that it appeared that I was going to be okay, so eventually they left to go home for the night.

The next morning, Mary Lil came back to the hospital and found me sitting bolt upright in my bed despite my broken ribs. The nurse had braided my hair, and Mary Lil said I looked like a young girl – smooth skin, bright eyes – she said I was glowing like a new bride. Even though I knew I couldn't make what I had to tell her make sense, I could hardly wait to try.

I told her I remembered her brother coming in and kissing my cheek, but then when I looked up I could see a big oak table high on a brilliant white alabaster mountain, and sitting around that table were my mother and father and my siblings – and then I saw Ted. I was so happy I was there, and I called and tried to climb up the hill to get to them. I called out their names but they wouldn't help me. They were all there; I tried and tried to climb up to them. I could see them perfectly clearly, and I knew they could see me too, but they wouldn't help me. So I came back.

It was truly the most beautiful experience I've ever had. However, for obvious reasons I was pretty reluctant to repeat that story to anyone I didn't know well because I knew how crazy it sounded. A day or so later though, Jack Stewart, the minister from Grace Presbyterian Church, came in to visit me and I asked him what he thought. "It's perfectly obvious Lola," he said, "they didn't help you because you're not ready yet. They were telling you to go back and finish what you need to do."

What did I need to finish? What else did I have to do? I decided I'd better find out what that was.

CHAPTER TWENTY-FIVE

What's It All About?

Oh yes, I've heard all the scientific theories about why so many people have similar near-death visions despite their cultural differences, their religious beliefs, and their life experiences. Biologists say the dying brain isn't having a spiritual experience; it isn't travelling toward the afterlife. It's simply that its neurotransmitters are shutting down and that this happens the same way for every human being.

Okay. But my question still remains. Why? And that's the question Jean Ritchie, who wrote about this phenomenon, also asks. "If everything, including the soul and personality, is going to dust and ashes, why does the brain lay on this last wonderful floor show for people who are near death, or facing actual death, who relax into peacefulness and describe their wonderful visions? Why would the brain bother?" I can't answer that question nor, I would imagine, can anyone else. But I will say emphatically that this experience was a gift. And, as a result of that gift, I know with absolute confidence that when my own time comes I will make that passage anticipating the joy that awaits me when my family welcomes me back at that heavenly table.

The fact remained, though, they didn't want me yet. I wasn't finished with my job here. What in the world was I supposed to do? And then I had another birthday and along with it came another gift.

Mary Lil arranged with the Philharmonic for me to sponsor an annual children's concert that would be scheduled on a Sunday

afternoon each year to coincide with my birthday, so we can celebrate with balloons and streamers and a concert arranged especially
for little people. It was a complete surprise. The CPO now insists
that I welcome everyone from the stage – which is a good thing
because there's nothing I enjoy more than an audience of children.
I always tell them to make their parents behave and sit up straight,
and to have fun applauding whenever they hear something they especially like. And, if they have time after the concert, to come find
me and tell me what they liked best.

The first year, the CPO decided they'd start with a crowd-pleas-
er and presented *The Magical Forces of Nature*. It's full of wildly evoc-
ative music that paints sound pictures of the wind rustling through
the trees, the songs of birds, and splashes in puddles – the sounds
that children hear as they play outdoors. But the work also booms
and crackles and roars with the stormy sounds that might sometimes
frighten them. The children were absolutely transfixed. And sure
enough, many of them made a beeline to me after the concert. I'm so
accessible because, in my wheelchair, I'm at their level. Believe me,
that's audience feedback at its best.

In subsequent years, the CPO commissioned a work for the children's concert called *Paint Brush for Piccolo*, which was great fun, and
added *The Listener, How the Gimquat Found Her Song, Peter and the
Wolf*, and *The Little Prince* to the repertoire. And recently, they have
been very clever about hosting prior-to-the-concert casual Sunday
brunches for the parents called 'Toast and Trumpets,' so the grown-
ups will stay out of the way while their children have their faces
painted and go to the petting zoo with the instruments.

How painfully I remember trying to introduce my own children to classical music. Each one of them could tell you stories about
being forced into scratchy uncomfortable dress-up clothes only to
be confined for two solid hours of unfamiliar music behind some
big guy in the row in front of them blocking their view of the stage.
It was torture. And it was equal torture for their parents because
even we knew it was too much, too early. They all loved music

but they loved the music of their peers and, in those days, the CPO didn't have the wherewithal in their budget to offer music directed primarily to children. The amazing thing was that those early experiences didn't turn them off classical music altogether. Mary Lil undoubtedly remembered those horrible evenings during her own childhood and knew there had to be a better way. Along with me, today's children – and their parents – are the lucky recipients of her gift. I can't imagine a better way to celebrate my birthday and I look forward to it every year.

My world has definitely grown smaller as I've aged. I don't mean that I feel isolated or unconnected because, most assuredly, I'm neither. My weekly telephone calls to each member of the younger Estes clan continue, and we keep processing the news of the family through my nieces and nephews. My own children have finally accepted the fact that if they're within a hundred yards of those phone calls they, too, will be conscripted to talk on the various extension phones scattered about the house. As a result, all of us stay very well connected, and even my widely scattered grandchildren remember to call whenever they have news to report. Absolutely nothing makes me happier than to hear, "Hey Mammaw! Sup?"

My vision wasn't getting any better in 2008, but fortunately my hearing was perfect, so I spent lots of time on the phone discussing the merits of the Rozsa Awards' nominees. That was the year we initiated the Human Resources Award because we could see that this area of arts management was frequently a stumbling block, so we now had three awards to present. That year, Murray Kilgour from the School of the Alberta Ballet received the first Rozsa Human Resources Award, Bob Davis from the Rosebud Theatre received the Rozsa Innovation Award, and Les Siemieniuk from the Calgary Folk Music Festival received the Rozsa Award for Excellence in Arts Management.

The Folk Music Festival choice was a popular favourite with Calgarians, largely because of Les Siemieniuk's encyclopedic knowledge of folk music and his passion for nurturing the up-and-coming young artists. Every year the event has attracted the very best of the genre, and the multi-generational audience that camps out on Prince's Island on blankets and lawn chairs for the duration of the four-day festival do so rain or shine. It's simply *the* place to be once Stampede is over in late July. In a review of last year's festival, Stephen Hunt wrote: "It's your one shot at a little old-time acoustic bliss in a twenty-first-century life engulfed by buttons. For one long weekend a year, our city gets to pull on its tri-coloured knit caps, lock arms with the oilsands exec sitting next to you, and river dance under the moonlight for a few hours."

I guess my world was getting smaller because I realized that so much of my enjoyment of the award recipients was based on hearing their stories at the Rozsa Foundation celebrations. As much as I would have loved to buy seasons tickets to every organization that had won the awards over the years, I knew I would have to rely on the reviews supplied by others – except in the case of my beloved Calgary Flames, of course.

I confess, even now when all they're bringing me is despair, I remain a diehard hockey fan schooled since the early '50s by the old Calgary Stampeders who played in a league comprised of eight teams housed across the western states and provinces. They played in the old Stampede Corral building where we could barely see the ice because of the hoarfrost expelled by every breathing body in the arena. If I remember correctly, it must have been real ice, not the artificial stuff, because the temperature in the Corral always seemed to be well below freezing. The only thing that building protected us against was blizzards, so we went to every game layered in long johns and loaded with blankets.

Those were the days when Gerry Couture and Sid Finney and Archie Scott and Max Quackenbush and Gus Kyle played along with Fred and Sandy Hucul. We all had seasons tickets to those games – all the ex-pats – all of us cheering for the Stampeders who were teaching us a game none of us, other than Michigan-born Ted, had ever seen played before.

After the Flames came to Calgary in 1980, and the '88 Olympics brought us the Saddledome, the-good-ol'-hockey-game got all citified and sophisticated and seasons tickets were hard to get. When they won the Stanley Cup in 1989, the delirious Flames fans went crazy – as did I! I take full credit for that Cup because I could tell Ken King was going to have a hard time keeping that bald head warm through all the playoff games, so I presented him with my old red wool hat to wear during those final agonizing weeks and obviously it worked its magic.

Since then, I've suffered through all their slumps and cheered them through nail-biting playoffs, but I've never given up on them, and anyone who chooses to visit me on game night had better like to watch it on TV because that's what I'll be doing. Mary Lil always loved to go to the Flames games, too, and she often went with friends who had two young sons who were big fans. One night, for some reason, none of them had tickets to the game, so Mary Lil suggested they come by my house and watch the game on TV since she knew I'd like the company. We had a great time and argued over the character flaws in the opposition, and the little boys grew mighty impressed by my encyclopedic grasp of hockey stats. So the following week their father called me and asked, "If we bring the beer and pizza, the boys want to know if we can come over and watch the game with you again?" On game night we were all in full-throated cheer when the front door opened and in walked Mary Lil. I think she was mad at me for stealing her friends, but she was a sport about it. Those little boys are all grown up now, but they still like to come by to watch an occasional game.

So it's not that my world is getting smaller; the world now is coming to me. Until this stage of life, I guess I'd met it head on. Thanks to Amy and Sally, who spoil me with their kindnesses and take care of all the household responsibilities these days, my visitors are always welcome. And, if there's a party going on, they'll get me there! But, as my home became the centre of my universe, I realized to my chagrin that I'd managed to collect an awful lot of stuff over the years. Maybe, I thought, that's what I still need to do. Maybe the universe was telling me to start weeding it all out and getting my house in order.

Years ago, I'd started collecting Royal Doulton figurines and realized to my annoyance that I had absolutely no further interest in them, despite the fact that many collectors evidently keep up a brisk business buying and trading them. My nieces back in Texas had often admired them, so I decided to divide them up between the girls. However, even though I'd packed all of them in bubble wrap and Styrofoam, I realized it would still be a miracle if any of them survived the U.S. Mail, so I called Ruth Ann and Mary Lil and told them we needed to sweet-talk another airline into taking me to Texas. This time it went pretty smoothly, at least until we got to Customs. Obviously the agent was quite interested in the bulging carry-on bags and evidently thought we were international smugglers trafficking in priceless art pieces. The girls were gazing off into the distance trying to disassociate themselves from the whole confrontation, as if to say, "Who *is* this crazy old woman and why doesn't *some*body have control over her?" However, the poor man finally had to admit defeat and we proceeded. A fork lift wasn't required to complete the transaction.

But what the trip back to Texas brought to the front of my mind was how quickly I was losing my family of siblings. I was the youngest of seven, so unfortunately I've had to say goodbye to my oldest brother and my sisters over the last ten years. My brother Charlie and I were the last of Nannie's and Preacher's family. I was desperate to have one last reunion where all the children and grandchildren could gather to hear the stories that had been told around Nannie's old oak table. When I got back home, I rummaged through my keepsakes and once again found her book. She had written her memoir, *Manners of the Manse*, in 1959, and, once I read it again, I started assembling all the photo albums that Karen had created over the years along with sixty-odd years of eclectic memorabilia.

The pile of papers strewn across my dining room table grew every day as I remembered where I'd packed away almost-forgotten keepsakes. One day, Mary Cristina came to visit, and, of course, I sent her on the mission too, until finally she stopped me and said, "Mammaw, what are you going to *do* with all this stuff?" I hesitated to tell her for fear I'd see that look teenagers give you when they think the plaques and tangles have taken over and tipped you into full-blown senility. But all she said was, "That's a good idea Mammaw. I love going to visit the old people in Texas – it'll be fun to take all this stuff along." Aha! If I could talk Mary Cristina into another trip, surely I could figure out how to talk someone into taking us. I targeted November, 2009. I would take the Canadian cousins to celebrate American Thanksgiving in north Texas with all the extended Estes family clan.

As much as I wanted to plan the logistics of the trip, we really had more immediate concerns because we were getting ready to celebrate another season of Rozsa Awards. That was the year that Tom McFall, the executive director and curator of the Alberta Craft Council received the honour. In only ten years, he had taken the organization from a position of looming deficit, which a succession of directors had been unable to find the way out of, to one of spectacular success. Under his leadership and strategic planning, he was able to implement great change almost upon his arrival, re-engaging member artists, eliminating the debt, and moving the operations to a more profitable and accessible venue in downtown Edmonton.

As he says, "Crafts are an integral and unique part of cultural heritage that are to be encouraged, developed and preserved for the cultural, social, educational and economic well-being of the people of Alberta." The Craft Council's artists include potters, glass sculptors, jewellery designers, fibre artists, and furniture makers. Tom's goal has been to gain recognition for fine crafts as a serious, relevant, and professional art form, and toward that intention the Craft Council presented an exhibition at the Smithsonian in 2007. Alberta fine crafters continue to exhibit internationally and the Alberta Council is now among the largest and most successful in Canada.

After all the Awards excitement died down that spring and Mary Cristina was on her school vacation, I put her to work rifling through what she calls the largest filing cabinet on earth. I have a lovely yellow guest-room-come-office that's hardly ever used, so through the years I filled it with all the records and documents I knew I'd eventually have to deal with. By this time, there were piles of paper stacked on all the furniture as well as carpeting the floor and, since I was no longer able to bushwhack through it all, I'd send her on missions to find stuff I wanted to take along to Texas. She would tell you that as that summer wore on I became obsessed with this project, and that she lived in terror of misplacing anything I'd found, so maybe I was a little single-minded.

But it wasn't until I cornered my dear children that I realized I must have looked like some kind of deranged dervish. I told them we absolutely had to take the family back to Texas for Thanksgiving. They'd have to charter us a plane and, "Yes, I know I'm soon to be ninety, but that only means there's no time to waste, so get on it!" They knew this was no time to try to be reasonable. "I'm going to see my brother Charlie one more time and you're coming with me and that's that!" They scattered in three directions.

Practically before the day was out they found us a plane. All that remained was to find a medic who would not only declare me healthy enough to fly but would also volunteer to accompany me. Fortunately, I knew his phone number by heart. When he heard my request, he said, "Of course I'll go with you Mammaw. It will be my pleasure." Howie promised to meet me at the airport.

Oxygen was going to be a problem again, but my nephew had arranged for his doctor in Texas to give me a prescription so that I could have oxygen at the hotel where we'd be staying. Plus, we had a prescription for more portable tanks from my doctor in Calgary, and so that we could buy Department of Transport travelling tanks for the plane. We were awash in oxygen. Had anyone struck a match, that plane would have launched like a rocket.

Mary Cristina, Mary Lil, and I went to the airport and boarded the plane with Howie to wait for the others to arrive. Unfortunately, he had brought his medical paraphernalia along and he insisted on taking my blood pressure. Not a good idea. He raised one eyebrow in the direction of Mary Lil and said, "Mammaw's not going anywhere unless her pressure comes down." I'm sure all *that* did was elevate Mary Lil's blood pressure, but they started to negotiate.

"What will it take to give her clearance to fly?" asked Mary Lil. It sounded to me like she was offering a bribe. I was willing to top it up if it would help.

"It's 190. She could stroke out. She's not going anywhere."

"So you're saying that if it's below 190, she can go." Mary Lil's good at this sort of thing. I was sort of enjoying watching the two of them battle it out when I saw Ruth Ann and her friend Mike arriving. They boarded the plane and immediately realized there was a battle of wills going on, so they were wise enough to stay out of the fray.

For the next hour or so, there was stony silence while we sat on the runway with the engines idling. I concentrated on thinking pleasant thoughts and Howie took my pressure every few minutes until finally he said, "It's 189. Let's go."

We took off and headed for Casper, where the customs agent and I remembered one another from the flight three years before. When he discovered Nannie's book was in my carry-on, I told him my hope was to use it to jump-start the old stories we'd grown up with so that Charlie and I could transmit all that family lore to our grandchildren as well as to the grand-nieces and nephews. Finally, once he finished rummaging through my bags looking for contraband, we had quite a nice visit.

There's nothing like celebrating Thanksgiving in north Texas. For one thing, it's the best time of the year. The heat and humidity are over but the winter rain hasn't started, so it's the best of all times to gather the clan to celebrate. Some would say it's better even than Christmas because it's also the season of back-to-back football games. Not that the games get in the way; the multigenerational stories weave through the plays and no one even drops a beat when the occasional contentious call on the field interrupts.

Charlie and his wife Mildred had assembled every cousin, niece and nephew, grandchild, great-grandchild, and childhood friend within the state of Texas to give thanks for their son's remission from cancer, so their house was brimming with love. My nieces and nephews had all come, along with my grandson Scott and his wife Paige plus their boys Evan and Satchel. On our first evening, we all sat in a circle and told one another about the most significant thing that had happened to us in the past few months. We were family; we didn't need small talk. We knew what a luxury it was to share our stories with the people who care about us.

The next day was Thanksgiving. There were far too many of us to fit around their table, and neither Charlie nor I could remember what had happened to Nannie's oak table that had room for thirty of us, so he made reservations for dinner at the Golden Corral, the only place in town large enough. But of course we had to vacate the restaurant by two o'clock in the afternoon because that's when the entire state of Texas closed for the kick-off.

We all trailed back for more stories, and Louise Tobin, my childhood friend from Denton, regaled us with her checkered past. She had run away from home at sixteen to go to New York to be a singer, joined Benny Goodman's band, married Harry James – the famous big band leader and trumpeter – lost Harry to Betty Grable, the movie star – and then married Peanuts Hucko, the great jazz clarinettist. That was at the height of the swing/jazz era during the war years, so she certainly had the most exciting stories to tell, but everyone had his turn in the spotlight and we chattered on through the late night, full of turkey and trimmin's and old Texas tales.

As the "Remember Whens?" ebbed and flowed in and around the football games and the laughter began even before the storytellers came to their punch lines, I suddenly realized that what I had so desperately wanted for my children wasn't just a connection to my family of seven siblings. The connection I wanted for them was both vertical *and* horizontal. It isn't a single lifeline; it's a densely woven and widely cast web. In the best of times, it's a hammock where you can rest and reflect on your good fortune with all the people who are happy for you. And, in the worst of times, it's a parachute supported by those same people who keep you from crashing.

It's the gathering that counts. It's the people around the table who love you, despite it all: your siblings, their spouses, their extended families, the children, their children, their friends, old friends, new friends.

Southerners will always ask, "And who are your people?" They don't mean to be nosey; what they want to know is how *your* extended web of family and friends relates to theirs. Inevitably, if you have any Southern connection at all, they will discover you're within three degrees of separation, and thus you're kissin' kin. You know their stories, or at least parts of them, and they know yours. They know you understand how the tragic history of the South, even four generations past, has shaped their character in ways no one from the North could possibly comprehend. Southern storytellers sprinkle their tales like seed pods across the South and, when they discover you're kin – no matter how distant – those stories will become part of yours so you will cast them even beyond. And when it's time for you to leave, they'll say, "Now y'all hurry back." And mean it.

But as we boarded the plane to come back to Calgary, I think I finally realized that I was going home; *truly* going home. Home, where we had raised our children and where they had raised theirs, was where I wanted to be as my own life was drawing to a close. Maybe for the very first time I truly understood that home isn't a geographic location. It's where your heart lives. I knew Charlie and I wouldn't likely see one another again – at least until we join our family at that heavenly table on the alabaster mountain. But if we have told those stories just right, they'll find their way to our great-grandchildren's progeny, no matter where they might be.

And then I had an epiphany. I knew what I had to do.

It was time for me to tell *our* story. I would try to show how Ted and I had had the privilege of a charmed life. How we found one another in the depth of the Depression, and how we started with nothing except the values gifted to us by generations of honest, hardworking, and loving people. How they taught us that it's not what a man has, or even what he does, that expresses his worth. It's whether he has a kind and generous soul and is willing to work to leave this world a little better than he found it. How we built a life for our children and lived long enough to welcome *their* grandchildren. I would tell how along the way we were blessed with countless gifts of friendship and had a wonderful adventure. I'll say that we have had an extraordinary lifetime that has added new threads to the rich and multicoloured tapestry passed to us by our forebears. I'll try to show our great-grandchildren how each of us weaves our own stories textured by our own experiences, and then passes the loom along to their children. I hope they will understand that no matter what distance may separate us, what really matters are the threads between us that enrich our lives, and that the stories we pass along reinforce those ties with each telling.

I'll start by describing the taste of summer strawberries still warm from the rich black earth....

Ted recording the data on T.J.

Celebrating my birthday at the CPO Children's Concert.

MAYOR BRONCONNIER CONGRATULATING BOB MCPHEE, WINNER OF THE FIRST ROZSA FOUNDATION AWARD FOR EXCELLENCE IN ARTS MANAGEMENT.

Just a Bunch of Flames Fans! Bill, Quinn, and Nick Todd.

The Kwongs and the Belzbergs have been wonderful supporters of the Rozsa Foundation Awards throughout the years.

This is me…. just before I offered to blow up Tristan's balloon.
(I wasn't quite so happy a moment later.)

Celebrating the 2012 Rozsa Award with Stephen McHolm from the
Honens Competition.

WHAT A WONDERFUL ADVENTURE WE'VE HAD; WHAT RICH BLESSINGS WE HAVE
RECEIVED.

Acknowledgments

Undoubtedly, it was my mother's hand that led me back to *Manners of the Manse*, the memoir she had written about her life as the Preacher's wife in small town Cumberland Presbyterian congregations so many years ago. As I re-read those stories from the perspective of my tenth decade, I at last understood how all of us are so profoundly shaped by those who come before us. She still guides my journey, reminding me that none of us travels alone. So it is with many, many thanks to the countless people who have enriched our lives more than any of them will ever know that I express my gratitude, especially those who have helped me remember some of our mutual experiences in Calgary's oil patch and community endeavours.

It wouldn't surprise me either if Mama had a hand in bringing Susie Sparks back into my life to help me write this book! Susie had been one of the little girls who stepped off the plane from New Orleans into the brutal cold of November, 1949. She and her family moved into one of the Shell houses close to ours, and they shared those early getting-acquainted-with-Calgary experiences with Ted and me and our children. Susie and I spent many happy afternoons together reminiscing and unfolding my memories like tattered old letters, worn by age but treasured enough to store away to look at again in the fullness of time.

Both Dick Baillie and Sandy McDonald regaled me again with their stories of those early days when Frontier Geophysical was in its infancy and, thanks to the Petroleum Oral History Collection housed at the Glenbow Museum, I was able to recall the other pioneers of the Alberta oil industry too.

Tim Rawlings sorted out the CPO archival memories I'd stored over the years, helping me put them in chronological order, and our dear friends, Hy and Jenny Belzberg reminded me about the old days when we were all learning how to be effective community volunteers. They have been enormously generous in their development work with the Calgary Philharmonic Orchestra through the years, and equally generous with the Rozsa Centre at the university.

Nomi Whalen and I had both been aspiring actresses when the MAC 14 theatre group was very active, but while I was cast as the matriarch, my glamorous friend Nomi was usually the femme fatale! She reminded me of those times as well as the days when we were both trying to organize the first Women's Auxiliary of Theatre Calgary, and what fun we had.

My thanks as well to Jack Stewart and Victor Kim, Ministers at Grace Presbyterian Church, who have offered me their friendship along with a generous helping of encouragement as this project took on a life of its own. They never wavered in their conviction that I could complete it.

But it has been Amy Praxides and Sally Jeslava who have quite literally kept me going! They've attended to my health, they've kept the household running, welcomed my visitors, made sure I could get to every social event, and over the years have become so much more than my caregivers. They have become my truly cherished friends.

It was my children and grandchildren, however, who kept me humble. They proofed the first drafts of this book and, thanks to Google, were able to catch some of my most glaring errors in dates and details. They know how much I love them, but I know I can't possibly thank them enough for their care and their never-ceasing kindnesses toward me. They have made this project possible.

So Ruth Ann, Ted, and Mary, for your unflagging support, for sharing your own memories, for the countless trips into the yellow room to bushwhack through the boxes of photos and stacks of memorabilia, thank you. To Karen and Mary Cristina, my Calgary-based granddaughters, thank you for your memories, your wonderful creativity, and especially for sharing your technological expertise. To Howie, Scott, T.J., Stacey, and Charles, thank you for keeping me current with all of your news as you build your careers and families. You will never know how much I enjoy our visits and appreciate your very frequent phone calls to keep me updated and in the loop.

And finally, to my great-grandchildren Tristan, Emma, Evan, and Satchel, I send my love. One day, I hope you might share this story with *your* great-grandchildren.

What a privilege it has been to walk through this life with all of you.

Index

B

Babbs Christian Endeavor Society (youth group), 13
Bach, Johann Sebastian
  Christ Lay in Death's Dark Prison, 177
  Christmas Oratorio, 176
  St. John's Passion, 177
Baillie, Dick, 115–18, 148
Baillie, Gerrie, 80
Baillie, Wilf, 80, 115, 118, 125
Baker Lake, 190, 192
balloon animals, 272
Banff, 101
Banff-Calgary International Writers Festival, 256
Banff Centre, 256
Banff School of Fine Arts, 202, 227
Banff Springs Hotel, 127
bankruptcies, 200
Bartlesville, 47
Basset Oil, 185, 200
  invitation to young Ted and Reed to join, 194
Baton Rouge, Louisiana, 84
Bay City, Michigan, 76, 79
Bay of Pigs, 169
bear attacks on Shell company cars, 102–3
Becker's Bungalows on Tunnel Mountain, 101
beer parlours, 118
Belgium, 68
Bell, Max, 178
Belzberg, Hy and Jenny, 227
  generosity toward the Philharmonic, 202
Belzberg, Jenny
  development of new community leaders, 202
Bennet family, 3
Benny the Bookworm Sale, 138–40, 180
  funds to Board of the Philharmonic, 139
  learning experience for Lola, 141
  music of Philharmonic at, 140
  papier mâché worm, 140
Berlin Wall, 169
Bernardi, Mario, 201
Birks Jewellers, 255
Birmingham, Alabama 16th Street Church bombing, 167
Bishop, Jack, 70
black-eyed peas, 109
Blake, Nadine, 138
blizzards, 62
bobbed hair, 12, 21–22, 29
Boogie Woogie Bugle Boy, 181
book discussion groups, 120

Book Rapport, 257
boom and bust cycles, 90, 112, 194, 197, 200
  bust of the '80s caught many of children's generation at vulnerable time, 206, 208
  downturn (1988), 206
  oil industry slump, 148–51
bootleggers, 17
Borgia, Lucrezia, 3
Boston Pops Orchestra, 179
Boston Pops Party featuring Arthur Fiedler, 180
Bowness Lagoon, 106
Bowness Park, 93
Brandon University, 230
bread man, 100
Brennan's (restaurant in French Quarter, New Orleans), 83
bridge parties, 43–44, 120
Brinkerhoff, Gerry, 123
Bristow, Oklahoma, 65
British class hierarchy, 131
British Columbia, 113
British Dominions Land Settlement Company, 124
Broadway show tunes, 125
Brown v. the Board of Education Supreme Court ruling, 165
Budgen, Paul, 253
buffalo (Charles William Estes), 30
Buick car, 87
building legislation (resulting from Babbs Switch fire), 14
bust. *See* boom and bust cycles
butterfly effect, 27–28

C

Cajun cooking, 82–83
Calgary, 199, 241
  acclimating to, 99–110
  Americans in (*See* Americans in Calgary)
  autumn in, 103
  big-city status, 120
  business people dressed to the nines, 91
  children walked home for lunch, no matter the weather, 105
  cow town image, 90, 120, 135
  diversity, 235
  downtown, 91
  generosity of Calgarians, 141
  house building, 103, 120–21, 147
  housing shortage, 199
  no social barriers, 141
  October in, 104